The Law Professor's Handbook

The Law Professor's Handbook

A Practical Guide to Teaching Law

Madeleine Schachter

Carolina Academic Press
Durham, North Carolina

Library of Congress Cataloging-in-Publication Data

Schachter, Madeleine.
The law professor's handbook: a practical guide to teaching law / by Madeleine Schachter.
p. cm.
Includes bibliographical references and index.
ISBN 0-89089-550-3
1. Law—Study and teaching—United States. 2. Law teachers—United States—Handbooks, manuals, etc. I. Title.

KF272.S29 2003
340'.071'173—dc22

2003065395

Carolina Academic Press
700 Kent Street
Durham, NC 27701
Telephone (919) 489-7486
Fax (919) 493-5668
www.cap-press.com

Printed in the United States of America

for David Stagliano,
Mark and Emily

Table of Contents

The Law Professor's Handbook

Introduction

What makes a professor a *teacher*? To teach is to educate, to impart knowledge, and, most importantly, to inspire. The thesaurus lists several interesting and arguably provocative words under "teach," including "advise," "brainwash," "catechize," "cram," "demonstrate," "direct," "discipline," "drill," "lecture," and "tutor."[1] More apt descriptions to which you might aspire include "coach," "communicate," "explain," "edify," "interpret," "imbue," "nurture," and, perhaps most significantly, "prepare."[2]

"Good" teaching has been conceptualized as "a complex process that begins and ends with students. It takes into account who they are, what they already know, what interests they may already have, and what they will need to know."[3] Ultimately, your task transcends the mere transfer of the substantive knowledge you've acquired to your pupils. "In a sense, the real difference between being an expert in something and being an expert who teaches is showing your students how you got—and how they can get—the rabbit out of the hat."[4] The critical task is not to teach students to *know*, but rather to teach them to *think*, to *analyze*, to *conceptualize*. A teacher is an enabler, a catalyst for students' self-discovery.

The Law Professor's Handbook is designed to assist you as you transition from practitioner to professor. Simply because you've mastered a high level of substantive expertise, refined your advocacy and negotiation skills, and have extensive experience in analytical thinking, writing, and other scholarly pursuits, doesn't necessarily mean that you're prepared to educate others. Brian MacNamara of the John Jay College of Criminal Justice points out that "[d]octors are taught how to diagnose, lawyers are taught how to argue, and actors

1. *Roget's Interactive Thesaurus* (Lexico Publishing Group, LLC 1st ed. 2003), *at* <http://thesaurus.reference.com/search?q=teach>.

2. *Id.*

3. Diane M. Enerson, Director, Center for Excellence in Learning and Teaching, *What is Good Teaching?* Penn State University (1997), *at* <http://www.psu.edu/celt/PST/intro.html>.

4. *Id.*

are taught how to perform.... [But t]he new law professor is expected to know how to teach either by divine guidance or by virtue of having spent many years on the other side of the lectern."[5] Another professor notes that "[t]here is no class that one takes to learn how to teach. Sure, one can gain some degree of comfort, even mastery, over the substance of a particular area of law outside of the classroom. But it is a considerable challenge to figure out how best to convey that information and understanding to one's students. Succeeding at teaching is much more art than science...."[6] One university teacher candidly confessed that "teaching was exactly like sex for me—something you weren't supposed to talk about or focus on in any way but that you were supposed to be able to do properly when the time came."[7]

If you're not currently embarking on a teaching career but have been engaged in the profession for some time, this *Handbook* may assist you as you reflect on your teaching techniques. Technology increasingly is playing a pivotal role in education; how might you incorporate digital media into your course? Some have concluded that "[l]ess emphasis will be placed on lecturing and greater emphasis on facilitating the education process, for example, by providing learning assistance in time patterns and modes tailored to the needs of individual students."[8] What fresh approaches might you consider working into your lesson plans to involve all of the members of a large class? If you've been teaching the same courses semester after semester, how might you vary your lessons a bit in order to stimulate yourself as well as your students?

This book also is designed to assist those who are joining the adjunct faculty of a law school. Synonyms for "adjunct" include "accessory," "addendum," "appendage," and "auxiliary;"[9] by definition, an adjunct is something that attaches as a supplementary part. As an adjunct professor, one inevitably is on the periphery of the faculty. While the pedagogical expectations are compa-

---

5. Brian MacNamara, *Teaching Law Teaching,* Institute for Law School Teaching, The Law Teacher (Fall 2002), *at* <http://law.gonzaga.edu/ilst/Newsletters/Fall02/macnama.htm>.

6. Robert B. Porter, *A Seneca Indian in King Arthur's Law School: Observations Along the Journey,* 7 Mich. J. Race & L. 529, 535 (2002), *at* <http://students.law.umich.edu/mjrl/>.

7. *See* Diane M. Enerson, R. Neill Johnson, Susannah Milner, Kathryn M. Plank, *The Penn State Teacher II: Learning to Teach, Teaching to Learn,* Penn State University (quoting Jane Tompkins), *at* <http://www.psu.edu/celt/PST/intro.html>.

8. James J. Duderstadt, Daniel E. Atkins, Douglas Van Houweling, "The Development of Institutional Strategies," *Higher Education in the Digital Age: Technology Issues and Strategies for American Colleges and Universities* (The Oryx Press 2002).

9. *Roget's Interactive Thesaurus* (Lexico Publishing Group LLC 1st ed. 2003), *at* <http://thesaurus.reference.com/search?q=adjunct>.

rable to those imposed on the full-time teaching staff, the capacity to integrate oneself into the school's environment and transition to the task of teaching can be far more challenging. Peer support is more remote and tenuous, an on-campus presence is less frequent, and communication with administrative personnel may be merely fortuitous or the result only of more concerted effort on the part of the adjunct.

How does this *Handbook* fit in with your role as a teacher? You might consider analogizing to the task of preparing and serving a meal. The chef has already read a number of cookbooks, he's eaten at a range of restaurants and sampled several types of cuisine, and he's browsed markets and stores selling cooking equipment. He'll begin by carefully planning the meal, taking into account the utensils he'll need and the ingredients he must purchase. He'll analyze the timing so that the vegetables finish cooking before the dessert is to be served. And he'll deliberate about the guest list, the seating configuration, and ways to stimulate an interesting and lively dialogue.

In the context of teaching a law school course, you'll likewise already have acquired significant substantive expertise; you'll have read applicable statutes, caselaw, and commentary and you'll have interacted with others who practice and write in your field. Now you'll need to develop a syllabus, select a text or other materials, and possibly integrate visual or electronic media into your presentation. You'll orchestrate the timing so that the course is broken down into the appropriate number of class sessions and the pacing of each class suitably comports with the overall time-frame you've been allotted. And you'll reflect about the use of seating charts, how best to interact with and involve your students, and ways to stimulate an informative and dynamic discussion.

This *Handbook* is the *amuse bouche.* It's the morsel that a fellow (albeit part-time) chef has laid before you to entice you to prepare for the meal. It's not, to borrow a related metaphor, the meat and potatoes. It doesn't offer substantive course outlines or PowerPoint bullet points for your lectures. The *Handbook* is the prelude. It prepares you, whets your appetite, and contextualizes your teaching experience.

The *Handbook* offers information about the application process and factors to take into account in choosing amongst offers of faculty appointment. There's information about designing a course, crafting a syllabus, and choosing textual materials. If you've decided to create course materials, such as a tutorial or a Web-based book, what intellectual property laws should you consider? Before the semester even begins, it's important to reflect on the course's requirements and your grading standards so that you've established a fair and impartial system and can timely apprise students of the criteria. Might collaborative teaching approaches be appropriate for your course? Do you want to incorporate in-class lecture enhancements or perhaps utilize asynchronous or synchronous electronic methods? In addition to the Socratic method, what other pedagogical techniques might you use to stimulate student participation and manage class discussion?

If you have discretion as to the methods by which you'll evaluate students, should you use absolute or norm-referenced grading standards? How might you handle a suspected case of plagiarism? As you assume the role of a professor, how might you react sensitively to a student who is academically challenged, inattentive, experiencing personal difficulties, or seeking career advice? Where can you locate resources to help you along the way?[10]

In an effort to facilitate review of matters of particular interest, headings, a table of contents, and a detailed index have been included in the *Handbook*. Cross-references also have been incorporated to enable additional textual review. For instance, if you're teaching a required course and the school has mandated use of a particular evaluative technique, such as a final exam, you may decide to skip the discussion about options for course requirements. If you're in a position to select the components of class grades, however, perhaps it will help to refer to the *Handbook* for the formula for standard deviation or to review approaches for appraisal of active, but inadequately trenchant, comments from a pupil.

One of the most challenging aspects of working on this book was crafting a title. I felt quite presumptuous denoting this work a "guide" for law professors. There simply is no correct or proper way to teach; nor should there be. The diversity of teaching styles is part of what enhances education, broadens perspectives, and reminds us that there is not necessarily a clear, definitive answer to every problem and an exclusive means to acquire it.

Nor does the task of teaching law import a simple, methodological approach readily transferable from one inculcator to another. Even were educational endeavors susceptible to precise and orderly formulation, conformity would be defeated by the variations in courses' substantive material and the divergent emphases on legal methods and analytical and advocacy skills in dif-

10. References to sources in footnotes and lists of selected resources are included in the book for further investigation, but of course it would be futile even to aspire to comprehensively list all available useful sources. As this *Handbook* goes to press in late 2003, the number of informative books, web-sites, articles, and other tools continues to proliferate exponentially. Resources are not endorsed and of course no adverse inference should be drawn from omission of reference to any resource. Citational information has been included for further research purposes, but note that as to electronic resources in particular, the sponsorship, operation, and authorship of web-sites may change and content may be added, deleted, or modified.

ferent courses. Even when the same course is offered at the same academic institution, individual professors' approaches are not consistent. There are different teaching methods, emphases on disparate nuances of the material, and use of various techniques for stimulating thoughtful reflection by students and provoking class discussion. Significantly, too, professors span a range of disparate ideological, educational, professional, cultural, and social backgrounds. It is to the students' good fortune that they are exposed to such diversity. One must endeavor to impart one's own knowledge and share one's skill in a way that inspires and excites others to do so in their own way. The welcome diversity of students and its synergistic effect on the overall dynamics of a composite class would thwart any aspiration of uniform guidance. In sum, the heterogeneity is to be encouraged, rather than repressed.

As well, the policies and regulations of individual law schools vary. This *Handbook* offers general guidelines, likely distorted by the limited experiences of the author at law school (at New York University) and as an adjunct professor (at Fordham University School of Law).[11] It's therefore important that you become familiar with your school's procedures.

This *Handbook* is designed merely to offer some thoughts about teaching law students, with occasional illustrations of techniques I've used in a Law of Internet Speech course or an Informational and Decisional Privacy in the Internet Era course. The *Handbook* basically is comprised of commonsensical notions and selected resources about ways to prepare for and conduct class, approaches to teaching, and methods for the fair evaluation of students. It's more or less what would occur to you if you had the time to observe a few classes taught by your colleagues, browse some helpful web-sites, and network with other faculty.

---

11. The author is an in-house attorney at Time Warner Book Group, which is part of Time Warner Inc., and an Adjunct Professor at Fordham University School of Law. The materials included in this book are intended to provoke thought, present divergent viewpoints, and offer pedagogical options. To the extent views are expressed or inferred, nothing herein should be construed as necessarily expressing the views of anyone other than the author or as constituting legal advice.

CHAPTER 1

THE DECISION TO TEACH

Motivations for Teaching

Teaching is a noble task. Russian-born violinist Jascha Heifetz was asked why he had accepted an appointment as Professor of Music at the University of California. "'Violin-playing is a perishable art. It must be passed on as a personal skill; otherwise it is lost,'" he stated. Smiling a bit, he continued, "'I remember my old violin professor in Russia. He said that someday I would be good enough to teach.'"[1] John Sexton, the President of New York University and the former Dean of New York University School of Law, vividly contextualized the long-lasting impact of educational institutions:

> Consider this reality: there are only 85 human institutions that have been in continuous operation for more than 500 years. Two you could get with a little thought: the Catholic Church and the British Parliament. If I tell you there are eight cantons in Switzerland, you're up to ten.
>
> But the striking point is that of the remaining 75 institutions that have been in continuous operation for more than five centuries, 70 of them are universities, beginning with Al-Azhar University in Egypt. That universities endure in this way testifies powerfully to the ideal that knowledge and learning deserve a special house of their own, and all of us—faculty, students and everyone associated with our university—are privileged to be the inhabitants of that house.[2]

People teach for a variety of reasons. Sophie Sparrow of Franklin Pierce Law Center, for instance, teaches because she is "awed and fascinated by the

---

1. Jascha Heifetz (quoted in Clifton Fadiman and André Bernard, eds., *Bartlett's Book of Anecdotes,* 262(4) (Little, Brown and Company 2000 ed.)).

2. John Sexton (quoted in Sam Dillon, *Commencement Speeches: Reflections on War, Peace, and How to Live Vitally and Act Globally,* N.Y. Times, June 1, 2003, at 41).

power in learning."[3] The act of imparting knowledge and cultivating a discipline of reasoned thinking in others is an inspiring and worthy endeavor. Henry Brooks Adams notably commented, "A teacher affects eternity; he can never tell where his influence stops."[4] It is extremely rewarding for a professor to dispatch a class of better informed, fair-minded, analytical thinkers. The service that lawyers perform within society, protecting the rights of others, obviously is enhanced when the lawyers have been rigorously trained and are substantively knowledgeable and committed to engaging in ethical conduct. Tony Arnold of the Chapman University School of Law teaches because, amongst other reasons, he "care[s] very much about what a student will do with his or her education."[5] As a law professor, you render a meaningful public service. You labor at the behest of the student body, committed to furthering the education of your students and contributing to the professionalism and integrity of the legal community.

Teaching law provides an opportunity and a context to instill in others a respect for the law. The rigors of intellectualism serve as the quoin of an understanding about the system of justice in a democratic society. Abraham Lincoln asked:

> What constitutes the bulwark of our own liberty and independence? It is not our frowning battlements, our bristling sea coasts, the guns of our war steamers, or the strength of our gallant and disciplined army. These are not our reliance against a resumption of tyranny in our fair land. All of them may be turned against our liberties, without making us stronger or weaker for the struggle. Our reliance is in *the love of liberty* which God has planted in our bosoms. Our defense is in the preservation of the spirit which prizes liberty as the heritage of all men, in all lands, everywhere. Destroy this spirit, and you have planted the seeds of despotism around your own doors. Familiarize yourselves with the chains of bondage, and you are preparing your own limbs to wear them. Accustomed to trample on the rights of those around you, you have lost the genius of your own

---

3. Sophie Sparrow, *Why I Teach*, Institute for Law School Teaching, The Law Teacher (Spring 2003), *at* <http://law.gonzaga.edu/ilst/Newsletters/Spring03/Spring03Newsletter.pdf>.

4. Henry Brooks Adams (quoted in Justin Kaplan, ed., *Bartlett's Book of Quotations*, 535:26 (Little, Brown and Company 16th ed. 1992)).

5. Tony Arnold, *Why I Teach*, Institute for Law School Teaching, The Law Teacher (Fall 2001), *at* <http://law.gonzaga.edu/ilst/Newsletters/Fall01/arnold.htm>.

independence, and become the fit subjects of the first cunning tyrant who rises.[6]

Fraught with imperfections and inequities, the American legal system nonetheless is deservedly imbued with respect and admiration for its strident commitment to justice. As a professor, you open the window for your students' view into the legal system. You can inspire both respect and a commitment to redress inequities.

St. John's University School of Law Assistant Dean for Externships and Assistant Professor for Clinical Education Keri Gould describes the best part of teaching as "getting students to love what they're doing."[7] Teaching enables one to share a special bond with students, to be a "part of the academic enterprise[,]...grappling with ideas just like they are."[8] The professor perpetually toils in the posture of a student, learning through teaching and embarking on a common quest for knowledge and understanding. Teaching is a formidable but inspiring task, affording opportunities to glimpse a student's moment of epiphany as he grasps what had been an elusive concept, thereby providing fertile foundation for a special and enduring memory.

Teaching also makes possible unique bonds with academic colleagues, facilitating scholarly exchanges. Where the practitioner labors in the pragmatic realm of implementing a plan or redressing a perceived wrong, the scholar can muse virtually indefinitely about abstract notions. These may relate to such fundamental notions as conceptualizations about ourselves and the ways in which our government and our society should be ordered. The professor not only has only the luxury of engaging in intellectual thought, but is even expected to ponder and debate such fundamental legal theories as whether justice is a perceived transcendent value. The Declaration of Independence declares our right to life, liberty, and happiness. How does the law work to determine the scope and nature of these profound rights? How do the rights inter-relate with one another, pragmatically and hierarchically? One journalist opined, "With all due respect to life and liberty, it is this third battleground—characterized not as a fixed goal but a constant chase—that both

---

6. Abraham Lincoln, *Speech at Edwardsville, Illinois* (Sept. 11, 1858), *reprinted in* Roy P. Basler, ed., *Lincoln: His Speeches and Writings*, 473 (Da Capo Press 2d ed. 2001).

7. Telephone Interview with Keri K. Gould, Assistant Dean for Externships and Assistant Professor for Clinical Education, St. John's University School of Law (June 17, 2003).

8. Jeffrey A. Brauch, *Why I Must Teach*, 34 U. Toledo L. Rev. (2002), *at* <http://www.utlaw.edu/lawreview/publication_archives/Volume%2034%20no_1_%20f02/brauch.html>.

animates Americans' daily lives and ties them into knots."[9] It's the law professor who toils most conspicuously to sort through these issues.

Teaching law school confers numerous other benefits. The professor is positioned to reflect on the doctrinal underpinnings of particular legal subjects. A practitioner may reflexively repeat clauses previously drafted, reiterate arguments advanced in prior cases, or routinely recite similar advice to clients. By contrast, the teacher effectively is required to deliberate about the rationales underlying jurisprudential principles, as well as the continued viability of legal theories in light of changed circumstances, new technologies, and developing law. There's enormous opportunity to become immersed in legal research, investigating legal issues and engaging in intellectual meanderings simply to satisfy one's curiosity. And as you endeavor to presciently observe an emerging trend in the law, you're positioned to galvanize intellectualism and reason for a principled response.

In addition to considering the efficacy and elasticity of legal doctrines, teaching courses in law inevitably demands that the professor stay abreast of current legal developments. That "pile" of cases, statutory updates, and new regulations that typically seems to breed of its own accord on a corner of the practitioner's desk must be read and integrated into concepts about overall trends and normative perceptions of legal doctrine and policy. There's a huge difference between reading a newspaper account of a key decision by a court and reading the decision itself, the hearing transcript, the prior proceedings, the parties' briefings, and scholarly commentary about the parties' respective positions. Not only is your knowledge of the issues involved in the case significantly greater in the latter situation, but you gain a broader perspective about the parties' views. The result is a fuller understanding of the plaintiff's plaint and the defendant's rebuttal, as well as refined comprehension about the legal arguments that support each side.

Teaching is humbling. Like the hiker who sees a "false horizon" only to realize that arrival at the next bend reveals even more ahead, so, too, does mastery of a nuanced aspect of a set of legal principles reveal even more yet to be explored. Teaching also exposes the expert to theories and hypotheses posited by novices, whose nascent training remains unencumbered by thought entrenched through convention.

Another benefit of teaching is that in addition to serving the student body, in some sense, the professor's ultimate client is scholarship. The academic free-

---

9. John Leland, *Pursuing Happiness, Jefferson to J. Lo*, N.Y. Times, June 29, 2003, § 4, at 1.

dom attendant to intellectual enterprise renders the professor toiling at the behest of justice, of scholarship, of a commitment to a legal and moral approach to the resolution of problems and disputes. The teacher is not beholden to an individual or corporate client for whom the law must be zealously interpreted to advance a specified set of interests.

This is one reason that scholarly enterprise is considered by judges and legislators as they fashion legal doctrine. Journal articles are consulted in search of guidance for reasoning and deliberation. The argument you posit may have profound influence on the way in which the law ultimately is shaped.

Teaching is fun. It offers significant and meaningful opportunities, day after day, to share both one's knowledge and one's inquisitiveness with students. While educational methodologies are not without extensive criticism, the discipline of legal thinking "inculcates a group of intellectual attitudes or skills that appear to be important to conventional legal practices[, including]...the attitudes and skills of *analysis*, that is the skill of dividing legal materials into useful relevant parts, of *precision* in handling complex legal details, of *skepticism* about the meanings of words, intentions or 'facts,' and of *confidence* in treating and resolving complex or controverted legal issues."[10] The committed legal educator has the enviable task of helping to train others to approach complex problems through a prism of reasoned analysis, tempered by compassion, imbued with a commitment to ethical conduct.

The Learning Process

The Law School Experience

Extensive analyses have been undertaken with respect to the neuropsychological methodology of the learning process. There are numerous theories and studies relating to how people learn, assessing cognitive function, the role of memory, and understandings about intelligence. Cognitive learning, the impact of cultural and socio-political differences on education, and short-term and long-term memory functioning are but a few of the factors that impact education. Schema of knowledge and development learning theory also have been explored.[11] Indeed, legal scholarship has been analyzed even through

10. Philip C. Kissam, *The Discipline of Law Schools: The Making of Modern Lawyers*, 229 (Carolina Academic Press 2003).

11. *See, e.g.*, Steven I. Friedland, *How We Teach: A Survey of Teaching Techniques in American Law Schools*, 20 Seattle Univ. L.R. 1 (1996).

positron emission tornography ("PET") and functional magnetic resonance imaging ("fMRI") scans as a means of considering brain functioning of cognitive tasks.[12]

It's helpful to remind yourself from time to time that your students, even as upper-classmen, are still transitioning to law school and absorbing the discipline of legal thinking. This experience demands an approach that's quite different from their undergraduate experience. Legal education is rigorous, competitive, and admirably in zealous pursuit of scholarly analysis. Ethics specialist Stephen Gillers of New York University School of Law regards "[t]he law school classroom, traditional or clinical, [as] a place of ideas, properly so, a place that celebrates the life of the mind and rewards intellectual achievement."[13]

As a general matter, educational objectives encompass the transmittal of knowledge with ensuing comprehension, the application of legal principle to factual situation, analysis of conclusions into component parts, the synthesis of elements to form a logical conclusion, and the evaluation or formation of judgment about the relevance of data and the utility of applying particular principles to the instant facts. Professor Benjamin Bloom classified these in a taxonomy of educational objectives, consisting of knowledge, comprehension, application, analysis, synthesis, and evaluation.[14] The categorization "can provide a framework for discussion and development of many aspects of legal education."[15] The student's knowledge positions him to effectually identify an issue and grasp its implications, even extrapolating to understand potential ramifications. Legal principles are applied through an analytical process, requiring the student to "break down" the query and rule into components. Amongst the most challenging aspects of the discipline of the study of law is this process of analysis, the ability to recognize and disregard irrelevant information, to distinguish fact from supposition, to reason as to whether a posited conclusion is supportable by an extant rule, and to ferret out implicit but erroneous assumptions. A critical corollary skill is the ability to synthesize, to integrate multiple court decisions (possibly derived from or with a

---

12. *See* Oliver R. Goodenough, *Mapping Cortical Areas Associated With Legal Reasoning and Moral Intuition*, 41 Jurimetrics J. 429 (2001) (abstract *available at* <http://www.law.asu.edu/Programs/Jurimetrics/vol41/abstracts.aspx#Goodenough>).

13. Stephen Gillers, ed., *Looking at Law School: A Student Guide from the Society of American Law School Teachers*, 7 (Meridian Books 3d ed. 1990).

14. Benjamin S. Bloom, ed., *Taxonomy of Educational Objectives: Handbook I: Cognitive Domain*, 62–200 (Addison-Wesley Pub. Co. 1984).

15. *See* Paul S. Ferber, *Bloom's Taxonomy: Teachers' Framework*, Institute for Law School Teaching, The Law Teacher (Spring 1997), *at* <http://law.gonzaga.edu/ilst/Newsletters/Spring97/ferber.htm>.

gloss of statutory pronouncement) in order to infer an emerging legal doctrine. Finally, the student must assess the viability of his tentative conclusions, perhaps tempered by extra-judicial factors and social policy.

Certain pedagogical methods are relatively unique to the law school experience. Most conspicuously associated with legal education is the Socratic method (*see infra* at 154), in which the professor elicits responses from a student through a series of questions designed to test underlying assumptions and induce the application of salient facts. The professor obviously plays a critical role in this learning process. Gillers noted:

> The law teacher proposes to question the legal rule—the statute, constitutional construction, court decision—to test its implications and examine whether it follows from the reasons advanced. Drawing from work in philosophy, economics, the social and natural sciences, history, public policy, even literary criticism, attendant always to reason and disdainful of sloppy thinking, law teachers and law students discuss, sometimes heatedly, how through law and legal institutions society ought to resolve important questions of freedom, commerce, and civic responsibility. Academic insularity affords law students and law faculty the space to engage in free-roaming criticism.[16]

Ultimately, the law professor eschews the mere act of imparting information in favor of guiding students to develop the skills necessary to embark on their own journey of self-discovery. Students must take responsibility for diligently and conscientiously completing assignments, being attentive, and endeavoring to contribute meaningfully to the class dialogue; "[m]otivation is the fulcrum that moves student learning."[17] But a teacher can transmute inquisitiveness into epiphany by making pupils understand that they can succeed and by instilling a sense that the teacher is cheering them on and rooting for their success.

Objectives for the Professor

As a law school faculty member, you play an important role in the legal education of the student body, bringing substantive expertise, enthusiasm, and a strident commitment to scholarship. The school's adjunct professors simi-

---

16. Stephen Gillers, ed., *Looking at Law School: A Student Guide from the Society of American Law School Teachers,* at 7.

17. James B. Levy, *Motivating Students to Learn,* Institute for Law School Teaching, The Law Teacher (Spring 2002), *at* <http://law.gonzaga.edu/ilst/Newsletters/Spring02/levy.htm>.

larly serve an important role and help enrich the breadth of courses the school can offer its students and enhance the diversity of perspectives to the academic curricula and community.

To reiterate a theme raised earlier, what makes a teacher a *good* teacher? As you reflect on the professors with whom you particularly enjoyed learning, certain hackneyed themes emerge. The teachers you most enjoyed taking classes with undoubtedly were substantively knowledgeable, thoroughly informed about their fields, and aware of recent developments and trends. They were routinely prepared for class and well-organized, equipped with a plan for each session. They were good communicators, able to convey their knowledge in a clear and cogent manner. They spoke audibly, wrote eloquently, explained articulately. They were enthusiastic and perhaps even witty. They treated you and your classmates with respect, encouraging participation without resort to ridicule or intimidation.

It also may be helpful to pause and reflect on other situations in which you've heard presentations, such as when you've attended continuing legal education seminars. The presenters and panelists who kept your attention and left you better informed had many of the same qualities as the professors from whom you learned the most.

If your law school experience was decades ago, the qualities that made a professor's class especially enjoyable may seem more like a blur of platitudes. And your appreciation of the experience may have been at least to some degree a function of your interest in the subject matter. It's been helpful for me to reflect on my last several years in the role of a student, even though the lessons I take are far afield from the study of law. I study classical ballet with a tutor, Martha Chapman, who has performed with the Anglo American Ballet Company. As a professional dancer, Martha has a thorough grasp of ballet movement and terminology, just as you would expect any teacher to have a comprehensive working knowledge of his field. But Martha also is an excellent *teacher* of ballet, a phenomenon I attribute to several characteristics readily transferable to the teaching of any subject.

First, Martha has an intuitive recollection of what it's like to have been a student and how even as a professional, one must continue to strive to improve. She's frequently able to anticipate how I might move improperly and guide me by exaggerating the misstep to show why it would be problematic.

And Martha is empathetic, recalling the struggle to learn and the effort required. She understands that after an hour of pointe work, it's likely I'll whine a bit about the next set of pirouettes, lamenting that the (pretend) audience could just as easily get up and circle around me for a change. She also knows that mistakes are inevitable, commenting occasionally that "learning is messy."

If you've practiced law for a number of years, you probably typically review polished work product that's undergone multiple drafts before it's even been submitted to you. If you're coming from a clerkship, you may have been exposed to some very impressive and articulate advocacy. This was produced after completion of law school, possibly years of legal training, and maybe even by collaborative effort. Your students haven't had the benefit of such experience; that's why they're students.

Further, despite Martha's inevitable burden to correct my numerous mistakes, she's very encouraging. She generously praises my alignment when it's correct and my efforts to master a sequence of steps. Martha also has a broad perspective, contrasting my efforts over the course of a few months as opposed to critiquing every aspect of my progress within each lesson. She recently remarked approvingly, "You don't suck quite as much as you used to," rendering me flush with a sense of accomplishment.

Martha also is the consummate professional. Studio arrangements are made and confirmed in advance, she arrives on time, and she doesn't rush off after a lesson in case I've got a question. She's thought about the barre work we'll do before the lesson begins but she's willing to digress briefly if I express an interest in working on another step.

One of the reasons that my lessons with Martha are so comfortable (other than in the physical sense, of course, in light of all that pointe work!) is that she graces me with the presumption that I'm trying to do better and the hope that I will improve. Martha wants me to succeed, which itself serves to inspire.

As you reflect on your personal objectives as a teacher, remember that teaching styles vary. One of your goals should be to adhere to the style that's most comfortable for you, continually striving, naturally, to refine and improve it. If it would be disconcerting for you to incorporate humor into your lectures, don't contrive to do so. It will seem unnatural and awkward. You can experiment with new technologies (*see infra* at 102) to try to enhance your lectures or to extend your class' dialogue beyond the temporal and spatial confines of the classroom. But if figuring out how to operate a laptop with an LCD projector causes angst, you may want to forgo a PowerPoint presentation, at least initially. There are numerous options set out for you in this *Handbook*, but remember that you're in the best position to determine which ones comport with your personal style and approach and are most suitable for the courses you'll be teaching.

Note, too, that students learn in different ways and thus it may be helpful from time to time to utilize different techniques in the classroom, in interactive on-line settings, or in one-on-one meetings with a student. Dennis Honabach points out, "A teaching technique that works well for some individuals may work poorly for others. What may be 'good teaching' in some situations with some students may be grossly ineffective teaching in other situations with other students."[18] The diversity of available pedagogical techniques offers ample means for experimentation and the integration of multiple methods.

The Application Process

Information About Law Schools

As of August 2003, the American Bar Association approved 188 institutions, 187 of which confer the Juris Doctor degree, and the U.S. Army Judge Advocate General's School, which offers an officer's resident graduate course (a specialized program beyond the J.D. degree). At that time, six of the 187 law schools, the Appalachian School of Law, Ave Maria School of Law, Barry University School of Law, the University of the District of Columbia School of Law, St. Thomas School of Law, and Western State University College of Law, had been provisionally approved.[19]

In January 2003, the ABA stated that student enrollment in ABA-approved law schools increased to 132,901 students in the Fall of 2002 from 127,601 students the prior year.[20] Notwithstanding the statistical increase, it's becoming increasingly competitive to gain acceptance to law school. It's also quite competitive to secure a faculty position. There are several ways you can find out about openings and fellowships (*see infra* at 21, 36–37).

The ABA does not rate schools other than to indicate their accreditation status. Schools vary in reputational stature, however. Several guides offer a sense of the hierarchical tier in which schools have been placed by various indicia. *U.S. News* is one such rating system that relies on a number of factors relating to ABA-approved law schools. These factors include quality assessment by deans and faculty members; median Law School Admission Test ("LSAT") scores; median undergraduate grade point averages ("GPAs"); the proportion of applicants accepted; employment rates at various temporal

---

18. Dennis R. Honabach, *Precision Teaching in Law School: An Essay in Support [of] Student-Centered Teaching and Assessment,* 34 U. Toledo L. Rev. (2002), *at* <http://www.utlaw.edu/lawreview/publication_archives/Volume%2034%20no_1_%20f02/honabach.html>.

19. *See* ABA-Approved Law Schools, ABA Network, *available at* <http://www.abanet.org/legaled/approved/lawschool/approved.html>.

20. Memorandum from David Rosenlieb, Data Specialist, Section of Legal Education and Admissions to the Bar, to Deans of ABA-Approved Law Schools, "Fall 2002 Enrollment Statistics" (January 30, 2003).

markers; bar passage rates; expenditures per student for instruction, library, and supporting services; student-teacher ratios; average per-student spending (including on financial aid); and the total number of volumes and titles in the library.[21] The statistical indicators used by *U.S. News* include "inputs," consisting of "measures of the qualities that students and faculty bring to the educational experience," and "outputs," consisting of "measures of graduates' achievements that can be credited to their educational experience."[22]

While these studies offer a means for comparison, even their sponsors concede that "[e]ducational excellence is difficult to define, much less measure directly;" the indicators are offered as "proxies for quality, much as blood pressure and cholesterol levels are indicators of health."[23] The publication's editors expressly caution that "[t]he rankings can inform your thinking—but they won't hand you an easy answer."[24]

The comprehensiveness and validity of these rankings have been subject to criticism nevertheless. The Association of American Law Schools ("AALS"), joined by other groups, issued a statement in 1990 which it subsequently endorsed, eschewing ranking and rating of law schools based on the *U.S. News* data as "meaningless or grossly misleading."[25] A report commissioned by the AALS noted, amongst other concerns, that "conspicuous by its absence is any *student* assessment of school quality."[26] Remember that the quality of education assuredly is commendable regardless of a school's placement within the ratings. As a general matter, your students will be dedicated and of high intellectual caliber regardless of the particular academic institution with which you're affiliated.

Nevertheless, the profession of education, like virtually every other career, has a hierarchy of prestige. Law schools generally are relegated to one of only a

---

21. *America's Best Graduate Schools 2004,* USNews.com, *at* <http://www.usnews.com/usnews/edu/grad/rankings/about/04law_meth_brief.php>.

22. *America's Best Graduate Schools (2004): The Ranking Methodology,* USNews.com, *at* <http://www.usnews.com/usnews/edu/grad/rankings/about/04law_meth_brief.php>; *see also America's Best Graduate Schools (2004): Law Methodology,* USNews.com, *at* <http://www.usnews.com/usnews/edu/grad/rankings/about/04law_meth_brief.php>.

23. Gayle Garrett, Robert J. Morse, Samuel Flanigan, *Making Sense of All Those Numbers,* U.S. News & World Rpt., Apr. 9, 2001, at 65.

24. *America's Best Graduate Schools (2004): Mine the Data—How to Use Our Lists Wisely,* USNews.com, *at* <http://www.usnews.com/usnews/edu/grad/rankings/about/04rank.b_brief.php>.

25. Association of American Law Schools, *Statement Regarding Law School Rankings, available at* <http://www.aals.org/rank.html>.

26. Stephen P. Klein and Laura Hamilton, *The Validity of the U.S. News and World Report Ranking of ABA Law Schools* (Feb. 18, 1998), *at* <http://www.aals.org/validity.html>.

few "tiers" and there's often a tacit presumption that the prestige of one's faculty appointment is correlated to the prestige of the school. If you're fortunate enough to be choosing amongst more than one offer of employment, the schools' relative rating is a relevant factor. But certainly it shouldn't be the sole factor. Is one of the schools you're considering looking to develop or broaden a curriculum in your area of specialty? Are there disparities in opportunities for scholarly writing and participation in colloquia with others in your field? Which school is located where any family accompanying you would be better situated, in a city or town in which you prefer to live and work, with a more appealing climate, greater proximity to sports or cultural events in which you'd like to partake? Is there opportunity for tenure or other advancement if you so aspire?

Particularly significant is the impression you've formed of your prospective colleagues. I've always believed that there's a fundamental analytical distinction between an offer of employment and an offer of chocolate. In the former case, it's wise to pause and reflect, no matter how lucrative the proposed remuneration and putative prestige of the position, as to whether you'll enjoy going to work everyday, whether you anticipate that there's a great deal you can learn from your co-workers, and whether the enterprise has overall meaning for you. An offer of chocolate, by contrast, merits no follow-up questions as far as I'm concerned.

Becoming a Candidate for a Faculty Position

Law schools generally seek scholarly applicants who are enthusiastic about teaching, have published scholarly works, and have manifested an intention to continue writing analytical legal commentary. There are some fairly traditional approaches to applying for a faculty position with a law school. Many full-time professors have a background rooted in exceptional academic performance in law school and a judicial clerkship, possibly including government service such as a stint as an Assistant U.S. Attorney. Some faculty also secured a graduate law degree or pursued graduate studies in fields other than law, earning a masters or doctorate degree in political science, history, or philosophy, for instance. The credentials typically are quite impressive; the law school experience may have included membership in or even a leadership role on the law review, the clerkship may have been for an appellate court or even for a U.S. Supreme Court justice, the government service may have been as a high-ranking official or advisor in a presidential administration. Publication of scholarly works, especially in notable law reviews, is deemed highly significant. The backgrounds of applicants for adjunct positions may be a bit more varied. Many have been or currently are practitioners, engaged in government service, or working as in-house counsel at companies, industry associations, or advocacy groups. Ultimately, a demonstrable capacity for legal scholarship is an indispensable criterion for any faculty appointment.

Thus the intellectualism promoted by the law school environment places a premium on the qualifications that suggest legal scholarship. As a result, law schools generally tend to hire those who have demonstrated some mastery of the study of law and an interest in pursuing scholarship. Indeed, many have question whether law schools better prepare one to engage in the *study* of law than in the *practice* of law. Scott Turow, author of a book about his experience as a first-year student at Harvard Law School, lamented several years after he graduated that "[t]he words 'practice' and 'practice skills' have long been taken by the law faculties as implying a roving anti-intellectualism that seeks to soak anything theoretical from legal education and turn law school into a high-powered trade school."[27] Law schools recently have moved towards incorporating some experiential learning into the curricula (*see infra* at 174), but generally continue to emphasize theory more than practice. While questions legitimately may be raised about the utility of such an approach for preparing one to practice in the profession, the intellectual stimulation and immersion in the broad doctrinal sweep and evolution of legal principles has a venerated tradition and unique value.

There are several resources you can consult for general background information about individual schools and job openings for faculty, clinical positions, and fellowship openings. The Association of American Law Schools Directory has extensive information about schools.[28] The AALS offers various services for those interested in employment as a law teacher. First, it acts as a conduit, transmitting information about candidates to schools through the Faculty Appointments Register, and passing on information about openings to candidates for positions at schools via the *Placement Bulletin*.[29] Many prospective applicants attend the Faculty Recruitment Conference sponsored by the AALS, which usually is held in Washington, DC each Fall and is designed to facilitate interviews of applicants. The process sometimes is referred to by applicants as "the meat market," a time when law school administrative personnel schedule a compressed slate of interviews with applicants over the course of a few days. The Faculty Appointments Register, a compilation of data about applicants, is

---

27. Scott Turow, *One L: The Turbulent True Story of a First Year at Harvard Law School,* 282 (Warner Books 1997 ed.).

28. A description of the AALS Faculty Recruitment Services is *available at* <http://www.aals.org/frs/top.html>; *see also* <http://www.aals.org/frs/index.html>.

29. AALS Faculty Recruitment Services, *Placement Bulletin, available at* <www.aals.org/frs/pb/index.html>.

reviewed by deans and others engaged in recruiting in preparation for the Faculty Recruitment Conference. Candidates may submit their qualifications by completing a form on-line and registering for a fee with AALS.

AALS recently estimated that during the past five years, 10.5 percent of candidates who sought law teaching positions through the AALS process were successful.[30] The process is particularly suited to the applicant who wishes to consider a number of schools and is open to re-locating because it enables him to efficiently and expeditiously meet with a number of administrative personnel from law schools located in a variety of locations.

Another helpful source is the University of Pittsburgh Law School's Jurist Legal Intelligence site, which includes extensive listings of open positions.[31] The Society of American Law Teachers includes a section on job announcements and teaching conferences,[32] as well as information pertaining to recent salary surveys.[33] TeachLaw offers a section on "Resources for Lawyers Who Want to Be Law Professors."[34] Several general publications relating to law schools are available in print formats, and notwithstanding that they're primarily directed to prospective law students, they have extensive information relevant to your search. The *ABA LSAC Official Guide to ABA-Approved Law Schools 2004*[35] and *The Penguin Guide to American Law Schools*[36] are but mere examples of publications that offer extensive information about law schools. Those interested in a position with a law school's clinical faculty could consult the Clinical Legal Education Association,[37] which publishes a comprehensive listing of openings.

Information also is available as to the demographic composition of the faculty and the applicant pool. The Council on Legal Education Opportunity is a non-profit project of the American Bar Association Fund for Justice and Ed-

---

30. *See* Richard A. White, *Association of American Law Schools Statistical Report on Law School Faculty and Candidates for Law Faculty Positions (2000–2001), at* <http://www.aals.org/statistics/index.html>.

31. *See* Jurist Legal Intelligence, Law Teaching, *at* <http://jurist.law.pitt.edu/position.htm>.

32. *See* The Society of American Law Teachers, *at* <http://www.saltlaw.org>.

33. *The SALT Equalizer*, vol. 2003, issue 1 (Feb. 2003), *available at* <http://www.saltlaw.org/EQ-Feb2003.pdf>; *see also AAUP Faculty Salary Survey*, American Association of University Professors, The Chronicle of Higher Education, *available at* <http://chronicle.com/stats/aaup/2003/> (discussing matters pertaining to salaries of university educators).

34. *See* <http://teachlaw.law.uc.edu/>.

35. American Bar Association Law School Admission Council (2004).

36. Penguin USA 1999.

37. *See* <http://www.law.cuny.edu/clea.html>.

ucation, dedicated to diversifying the legal profession by expanding legal education opportunities for members of under-represented groups.[38] The AALS published a statistical comparison of women and minority faculty over a six-year period and analyzed the gender and ethnic/racial composition of candidates for law faculty positions.[39] The ABA has analyzed total minority enrollment from 1971 through 2002.[40]

There are some points to bear in mind as you prepare for the process. You'll want to be familiar with the schools to which you're applying and have a sense of the professional and academic backgrounds of those with whom you'll be meeting. You can begin by browsing the school's web-site. Look for an icon that refers to faculty or adjunct faculty, depending on your preference for a position, and scan the biographical information about the school's professors. Consider the general nature of their qualifications, their prior work experience, whether they have held previous teaching positions at other schools, and their educational backgrounds. Also peruse the lists you'll likely find of their writings, reviewing in particular the nature of the publications. Are they predominantly published in law journals? Do they reference works in progress? Do they appear to have published extensively before they assumed faculty positions?

If you're open to the possibility of more than one school or even more than one geographical location, you might target a search of the sites of professors who are teaching in the field you would like to pursue. Consider the same types of issues and qualifications you would if your search were narrowed to a single school.

Also scrutinize the schools' curricula. This may provide insight, at least to some degree, of the schools' likely hiring needs. Does it seem that the school to which you'd like to apply has several professors who have teaching experience and have previously published works relating to, say, Corporate Law? Is there a prominent professor teaching a course in Mergers and Acquisitions, seminar offerings in Project Finance, a clinic in Securities Law, and several faculty members who have professional backgrounds in general Corporate Law and Corporate Finance? This may suggest that the school has adequate staffing

38. *See What is CLEO,* American Bar Association, ABA Network, *available at* <http://www.abanet.org/cleo/whatis.html>.

39. Richard A. White, *Association of American Law Schools Statistical Report on Law School Faculty and Candidates for Law Faculty Positions (2000–2001), at* <http://www.aals.org/statistics/#women>.

40. Minority Enrollment 1971–2002, American Bar Association Network, *available at* <http://www.abanet.org/legaled/statistics/minstats.html>.

for Corporate Law course needs. Perhaps, though, there's some variation on a seminar that the school would like to add. Are courses currently offered on related subject matter such as E-Commerce or Technology Transactions?

Often newly-hired professors are expected to teach one or more basic courses. It's possible that the subject matter with which you feel most comfortable and about which you're most enthused doesn't fit with the school's current curriculum needs. It may simply be a question of deferring your interest for a few semesters until the curriculum can accommodate a particular course. Or there may be a way to integrate aspects of the subjects you'd especially like to teach into another course. While you were hoping, for example, to teach an advanced course in Technology Transactions, you might be asked to teach a course in basic Copyright Law. You nonetheless may find opportunities as you devise your syllabus (*see infra* at 43) to include material and stimulate a discussion about the valuation of electronic intellectual property assets, the transfer of on-line literary rights, or the scope of contributory and vicarious infringement claims as they relate to file sharing.

It's also helpful to speak with someone who is closely affiliated with the school. Have you worked with a current faculty member? Did you serve on a bar association committee with a member of the school's administration? Is it possible that you know someone who might facilitate an introduction?

Consider other ways to get acquainted with the academic institution itself. This can serve not only as a means of networking, but also can help you assess whether you feel comfortable at the school and can begin to visualize yourself working there. Law schools often seek volunteers to judge moot court competitions, for example. You might contact the school's Moot Court Board and offer to become involved. As you look at a school's web-site, check out the upcoming symposia and conferences. Is there one of special interest you might want to attend?

It's also a good idea to review or develop your portfolio of published articles and other works. Professor Tanya Hernández noted that "scholarship has become a critical feature of entering and thriving in an academic career."[41] There are several guides to the submission of articles for publication in law journals. The On-Line Directory of Law Reviews and Scholarly Legal Publications[42] sets forth information about law journals, indicating their fields of

---

41. Tanya K. Hernández, *Placing the Cart Before the Horse: Publishing Scholarship Before Entering the Legal Academy,* 7 Mich. J. Race & L. 517, 517 (2002), *at* <http://students.law.umich.edu/mjrl/>.

42. *See* <www.andersonpublishing.com/lawschool/directory>.

specialty, policies on simultaneous submission, and citation style requirements. The Directory for Successful Publishing in Legal Periodicals[43] includes such information as the substantive focus of journals, their manuscript styles, their acceptance rates, and the journals' respective submission and review processes. Numerous legal journals and newsletters maintain web-sites with similar information. In addition, compilations with links to on-line journals are available from Hieros Gamos[44] and the WWW Virtual Law Library.[45] You might also access ExpressO, a service of The Berkeley Electronic Press.[46] The service is an electronic manuscript delivery device through which an author can simultaneously submit articles to journals he selects by uploading one electronic file to the site.

Some recommend graduate legal education as an effective path to an academic career. Amongst other benefits, participation in an L.L.M. program offers an opportunity to collaborate on written work with faculty support and comprises an additional credential.[47]

You could also read impressions about teaching written by other professors. Professor Gabriel J. Chin of the University of Cincinnati College of Law and Professor Denise Morgan of New York Law School edited a guide entitled *Breaking Into the Academy: The 2002–2004 Michigan Journal of Race & Law Guide for Aspiring Law Professors.*[48] Other professors have helpfully posted "tips" for potential applicants. Brian Leiter of the University of Texas School of Law, for example, published "Information and Advice for Persons Interested in Teaching Law."[49] Professor Dan Burk summarized his tips under the heading "Stuff I Wish Someone Had Told Me Before the Meat Market...."[50] The Jurist Legal Intelligence site also includes posted commentary about the hiring process from the perspective of a recruiter.[51]

---

43. *See* <http://www.law.harvard.edu/library/research_guides/publishing_in_law_reviews.htm>.

44. *See The Comprehensive Legal and Government Portal, at* <http//www.hg.org>.

45. *See* <http://www.law.indiana.edu/v-lib/>.

46. ExpressO, The Berkeley Electronic Press, *at* <http://law.bepress.com/expresso/>.

47. *See, e.g.,* Gabriel J. Chin, *Graduate Degree Programs,* 7 Mich. J. Race & L. 481, 481–82 (2002), *at* <http://students.law.umich.edu/mjrl/>.

48. 7 Mich. J. Race & Law 457 (2002), *at* <http://students.law.umich.edu/mjrl/>.

49. Brian Leiter, *Information and Advice for Persons Interested in Teaching Law* (November 2002), *at* <http://www.utexas.edu/law/faculty/bleiter/GUIDE.HTM>.

50. Dan L. Burke, *Stuff I Wish Someone Had Told Me Before the Meat Market...., at* <http://www.law.miami.edu/~froomkin/wannabe.htm>.

51. Commentary, Jurist Legal Intelligence, Jurist Forum, *at* <http://jurist.law.pitt.edu/hiring.htm>.

If you're thinking about teaching but haven't yet decided that you want to pursue an academic career, you may want to try to volunteer as a guest lecturer. This may be helpful as well if you're considering becoming an adjunct faculty member but want to be sure that you have adequate time to make the necessary commitment. Guest lecturing offers a great deal of insight into the amount of time and effort you'll need to invest to conduct a single class session. Note, however, that adjunct professors are not necessarily on a conventional path to transition to a full-time or tenured faculty position. Although teaching experience is relevant to an academic career, full-time academicians are often drawn from other pools.

Once you've progressed through the AALS Recruitment Conference if that's the route you've pursued, the next step is to be contacted by interested institutions for further meetings. In addition to submitting to on-campus interviews, some schools may ask that you engage in a "job talk," in which you'll choose a subject and present it to faculty members, engage in a roundtable discussion to review recent scholarship, or deliver a lecture on a topic chosen by the law school. As with any presentation, you'll want to be thoroughly prepared so that you can knowledgeably articulate your thoughts without undue reliance on your notes. Consider in advance what questions might be asked and how you might respond. Be prepared to explain why the subject matter interests you. As you prepare for the recruitment interviews, take a moment to review your written work so that it's fresh in your mind to discuss.

Accepting a Position

The Full-Time Position

If you're fortunate to have received multiple offers, you'll be in the enviable position of having to choose amongst them. Even if you received a single offer (perhaps because you applied only to one school), you'll want to take a moment to reflect before making the decision to accept.

Consider visiting the campus again to get a feel for the law school. Perhaps ask to be admitted to the school's library. If you know other faculty members, you may want to get their thoughts about their experience at the school. If you don't know other professors, consider asking the dean or someone else with whom you met during the application process to facilitate an introduction to a few faculty members. You may want to arrange to meet for coffee or lunch to chat with them. You also can access the school's web-site or other resources, such as the Jurist Legal Intelligence site,[52] to peruse faculty profiles and individual faculty Web pages.

It's helpful to try to visualize yourself at the institution where you're accepting an appointment. Your role and daily routine will vary considerably from prior employment as a judicial clerk or a practicing attorney. Mark Dubois wryly described his transition from the private sector to the University of Connecticut School of Law, including the reduction in his income and the diminution in the size of his office. "It's not that I can't adapt to having my cheese moved," he remarked. "I have no cheese."[53]

You may have a number of questions that have been lurking in the back of your mind. Perhaps you decided not to raise them during the interview process, lest they appear to be of disproportionate significance or disrupt a discussion about your qualifications when time was limited. Now is a good time to raise these matters.

Some of the questions may simply be of logistical significance. How does one arrange for e-mail access or other IT support? How can you find out if the school's administration cancels classes because of inclement weather? What arrangements will be made for parking facilities? Where is your faculty mailbox located?

Other questions may relate to matters of professional etiquette. Do professors generally address students by their first names? Does the faculty exchange holiday cards? Even if you don't have specific matters you'd like to discuss, it can be quite comforting to see a few familiar faces when you arrive on campus and to begin to develop a rapport with your prospective colleagues.

You'll also want to ask about what's expected of faculty. Clarify the number of classes you're required to teach each semester or over the course of the year. What are the expectations regarding your presence on campus when classes are not in session? Are there express or tacit understandings about the volume of articles and other writings you'll be expected to author each year? Are there publications other than conventional law journals that the school regards as particularly worthy of scholarly contribution?

Your school may anticipate that you'll make certain contributions to the academic community in addition to your teaching duties. These may be explicitly quantified or simply tacitly understood by the faculty. Will you be expected to be a faculty advisor to a law journal? To serve on one or more faculty com-

52. *See* <http://jurist.law.pitt.edu/home_pgs.htm>.

53. Mark Dubois, *Why I Teach*, Institute for Law School Teaching, The Law Teacher (Spring 2002), *at* <http://law.gonzaga.edu/ilst/Newsletters/Spring02/dubois.htm>.

mittees? To design and organize a symposium or conference or participate in such endeavors? Will you have discretion to accept or decline requests to supervise independent study?

How much input will you have into the substantive assignment of your courses? To what degree will your scheduling preferences be taken into account? As a new hire, is it more likely you'll be assigned less popular 9:00 a.m. class sessions and those meeting late Friday afternoons?

You can sit down with a member of the administration to ask these questions. It also may be prudent to informally canvass some faculty members. Perhaps you're acquainted with someone who had been teaching at the school and retired. Professors may be able to give you some insight as to disparities they perceive amongst formal requirements imposed by the school, tacit understandings by the administration about ways that professors can contribute to the school community and promote its institutional reputation, and conventional practices that simply have evolved amongst the faculty. You'll gain some understanding as to whether you have the flexibility to decline a task the administration has requested that you undertake and whether the extent of your activities are relatively commensurate with those of other faculty.

Professor Danielle Conway-Jones of the University of Hawaii suggests that prospective candidates also probe the circumstances surrounding employment offers. "If, through delicate inquiry, you find that your appointment was controversial, you may want to consider whether that will make it more difficult for you to get promoted or tenured in the future."[54]

It's especially important to probe the source of any dissatisfaction amongst faculty. You frequently can elicit significant insights by prefacing your question with a statement acknowledging the positive comments you've heard and then focusing on any problems that presumably exist. "It sounds like you've been very happy here at New State University Law School," you might say. "Of course, no job anywhere is perfect. What *don't* you like about teaching here?" Or you could phrase your query as "If you could change one thing here, what would it be?" Asking the question of multiple faculty can elicit a consensus about a problem. It may reveal an issue that's of little moment to you. But it may alert you to a matter of concern that you can be better prepared to evaluate as you compare multiple offers of employment or that you can more ef-

---

54. Danielle Conway-Jones, *A Recruit's Guide to the On-Campus Interview Process and the Job Talk,* 7 Mich. J. Race & L. 523, 528 (2002), *at* <http://students.law.umich.edu/mjrl/>.

fectively address if you do accept the offer. And the inquiry can help divert the discussion from platitudes made routinely in the context of recruiting and stimulate explication of areas of challenge.

The Adjunct Position

Of course, much of what's been said about accepting a full-time position applies to the decision to accept an offer to join the school's adjunct faculty. If you live in a large metropolitan city, you may be in a position to consider more than one institution because of the presence and proximity of multiple schools. Or you may be looking for an adjunct position to enable you to continue your intellectual pursuits or because you are engaged in some other activity that is fairly portable, such as a professional writing endeavor. In those cases, you may be able to consider multiple geographical locations and thus several schools because you're willing to re-locate. Evaluating the schools and getting a sense of the job satisfaction and routines of other faculty members, including other adjuncts, is a useful investment of your time. Visiting the schools, consulting with others associated with the faculty, and questioning the administrative staff is as productive for the adjunct applicant as it is for one considering a full-time position.

You also may want to reflect on your motivations for teaching as an adjunct faculty member. If you're inclined to explore an adjunct role as a means of getting a taste of teaching as a law professor, it's useful to ascertain whether the school might be amenable to helping you transition to a tenured-track position. Because such a transition is less common, it's worth exploring whether the school is open to the possibility.

Consider as well your expectations about the position. Are you looking for an opportunity not only to conduct a class and engage with students, but also to participate in symposia or other scholarly activities with the university at large? Consult with other adjunct faculty to try to assess whether those with similar interests and aspirations were able to assimilate on some level. Perhaps also speak with those who currently are engaged in such activities. Do they need additional support?

Note that adjunct professors generally are not well compensated, especially when one considers the considerable expenditure of time necessary to perform effectively. In an impassioned journal article, Professor John Duncan of Texas Wesleyan University School of Law opines that

> the academic equivalent of the indentured servant is the adjunct faculty member in higher education. Adjuncts cannot say or do much about their plight. If they try to seek redress, they will simply not be

> rehired.... There is little collective bargaining; there is very little union power; adjuncts often are not included in bargaining units. A contract may exist but purely at the discretion of the university.... The full-time professors, and often the students, view the adjunct faculty as second-class teachers. The adjuncts lack benefits and the pay is nominal.[55]

Duncan concludes that if academic institutions do not commit to more equitable treatment of adjunct faculty members, "[t]he dilemma of adjunct faculty leads to what should be considered a violation of due process rights" and "the law should provide the appropriate protection."[56]

Understand that teaching, whether as a full-time or a part-time faculty member, requires a considerable commitment of time and energy. Your status will be largely irrelevant to students, even were they to focus on whether you are a full-time or adjunct faculty member, in terms of their expectations about the substance and quality of the course. Nor should it impact on the pedagogical commitment demanded by your students. As William Martin Sloane, a part-time faculty member, observed, "three credits is three credits, whether by sunshine or moonshine."[57]

Notwithstanding the considerable time commitment and minimal remuneration, adjunct professors derive great benefits from the experience. In addition to enjoying the same joys of teaching available to full-time professors, adjuncts are able to devote themselves to the law in a fashion not readily encompassed within the daily routine of a practitioner. There's vast opportunity to deliberate about the evolution of legal principles, their historical context, and the development of new trends.

One relatively less consequential but potential tangible benefit is that adjunct professors may be eligible to receive continuing legal education ("CLE") credit in certain states, including additional credit for the time spent preparing for each class hour. Standards for awards of CLE credit vary from state to state. Your school's registrar office likely will be able to advise you and furnish the appropriate certificate at the conclusion of the course if you're eligible to receive credit.

---

55. John C. Duncan, Jr., *The Indentured Servants of Academia: The Adjunct Faculty Dilemma and Their Limited Legal Remedies,* 74 Ind. L.J. 513, 515 (1999).

56. *Id.* at 515, 586.

57. William Martin Sloane, *How Adjuncts Can Do Something Useful While Everyone Else is at a Faculty Meeting,* Jurist Legal Intelligence, Lessons from the Web (2000), *at* <http://jurist.law.pitt.edu/lessons/lesapr00.htm>.

Preparation to Assume the Position

Familiarizing Yourself with the School

It's helpful to have some sense of the law school where you'll be teaching, particularly if you're not an alumnus. The school almost assuredly will have a website that will offer information about its history, the school's colors, and the school's motto, for example. Bookmark the school's site on your computer. Learn the names of the dean of the law school, the dean of academic affairs, the dean of student affairs, and the registrar; these are the administration personnel with whom you'll likely have the most contact. Faculty support personnel also are extremely knowledgeable about administrative and logistical matters and are able to direct you to the appropriate person if further consultation is necessary.

One of your most important tasks is to review the school's policies regarding admission, grading, disciplinary measures, and the like. You'll be charged with knowing these policies and complying with them. You'll need to understand the school's position if a student requests an extension on the deadline to submit a paper, is suspected of plagiarism, or is regularly absent from class. You needn't commit all of these to memory; it's the rare situation where you can't first check a policy if you're contemplating disciplining a student or setting the standards for the papers you'll be requiring. Even when a student has an inquiry, more than likely you'll be able to indicate that you need to check the school's policies before you respond.

It might also be appropriate to condition your response on compliance with the school's procedures, even placing the burden of confirming them on the student. A student might ask you whether his friend can audit three of the upcoming class sessions, but perhaps you can't recall the school's position on requests to audit or you're not sure whether the school has a policy. Or the request may not neatly fit within the school's policy; perhaps the administration has stated that requests to audit a course for the entire semester must be approved by the dean, but individual professors have discretion to grant such requests for a single class. This request from the student's friend falls in between. You might decide to refer the student to the appropriate administrator to ascertain the school's position, indicating that you don't have an objection provided the school approves.

Your basic task, therefore, is to review the school's policies and guidelines to get a sense as to which matters are addressed. It may not have occurred to you that scheduling the date on which a final exam would be administered is subject to the school's approval. Familiarizing yourself with the policies will sensitize you in a general way as to the matters on which the school has taken a position.

Of course, you'll want to take a moment to read through the school's security policies and protocols. It's important to know how to summon security personnel or report a fire in the event of an emergency.

Getting a sense of the school's physical setting will help you navigate around campus. You also can get some idea of the size and scope of the law school's library and computer facilities. In addition, it's helpful to know whether there's a cafeteria and where neighborhood restaurants are located.

You may want to get a sense of the enrollment of the school, in terms of quantity and diversity of students. The school's web-site will have information as to whether the school has an evening program as well as a day division, which can provide insight into the likely professional background and commuting experiences of the students enrolled in your classes.

It's also useful to get a sense of the school's faculty, especially with respect to the substantive areas in which they teach. This may facilitate interesting dialogues when you have an opportunity (or create an opportunity) to meet with other faculty. A review of the faculty's specialties and the school's course offerings can help you as you design your courses, suggesting topics addressed in the curriculum that you could integrate into your courses.

In addition, review of the curriculum will provide insight into the requirements for candidates for a Doctor of Law (J.D.) degree and whether they meet or exceed the requirements of the state in which the school is located, the American Bar Association, and the AALS. A fairly typical required courseload for first-year students might include Civil Procedure, Contracts, Criminal Law, Legal Methods and Writing, Property, Torts, and possibly Constitutional Law, although some schools may require or allow students to take one or more of these courses after their first year. Upper-class students typically are required to take Professional Responsibility and to fulfill a writing requirement. If you're not teaching a basic first-year course, information about course requirements can help you determine the substantive background students will have when they take your courses so that you can gauge the level accordingly.

In addition to the course curricula, law schools frequently host a number of centers and institutes, which organize conferences and host programs. Some of these may include an alumni network, industry or business leaders, or academicians from other schools. These activities, which often are categorized substantively, afford a multi-dimensional approach to the legal training of law students and enhance their preparation for professional careers. One or more of these may be related thematically to a course you're teaching and thus of special interest to you and your students.

The school also may have clinical and externship programs (*see infra* at 174), which help bridge students' academic and professional experiences. Clinics afford opportunities for students to integrate legal analysis with lawyering theory and skills. By assuming the role of a practitioner in problem-solving settings, students in clinics and externships begin the process of experiential and reflective learning. Like centers and institutes, clinics typically have a substantive theme, devoted to such issues as Criminal Defense, Housing Rights, Immigration Rights, or Domestic Violence. Externship programs are designed to integrate students into the practitioner community through the placement of students at governmental agencies, judicial clerkships, community-based entities, and other organizations.

Significant learning and experience are gained outside the classroom in other ways. If, for instance, you're an adjunct professor who is involved in a symposium or bar association or continuing legal education program that you feel may benefit the law school community, you can contact the school's administration to coordinate arrangements to electronically post information or distribute brochures.

Law schools generally also have several student publications that enrich students' academic experience and help students continue to master legal writing techniques. The school's law review is generally considered to be the most prestigious of these because selection for participation is especially competitive. Other publications may have particular substantive themes, such as journals devoted to issues relating to International Rights, Intellectual Property, or Environmental Law.

It's also common for schools to help students master advocacy skills through a Moot Court program. Typically, first-year students are introduced to skills relating to the drafting of appellate briefs and oral arguments as part of a Legal Writing or Legal Methods course. Thereafter, students may choose to continue to develop these skills by participating in an advanced Moot Court program that includes competitive matches against other schools.

Students also engage in a number of other activities, which may be under the exclusive auspices of a law school or integrated within the university community. Some law students join bar association groups, form groups related to particular religious or political affiliations, participate in public interest programs, or work on a school yearbook. Law school and university groups may sponsor intramural softball, tennis, or basketball games or other athletic activities.

Keeping Up With Legal Developments

As you prepare for the upcoming semester, you'll want to ensure that you're aware of current legal developments. There's the most obvious concern: an appellate court might reverse a lower court's ruling that you were intending to incorporate in your syllabus or a new federal or state law might affect the common law approach courts had adopted. And there's your scholarly interest in monitoring legal developments to try to divine trends and understand their socio-legal significance in the context of the subject you're teaching. Technological developments and newsworthy events also affect the law and thus impact the continuing viability of the principles you'll be covering.

In today's electronic era, your students will be wired, virtually continuously receiving and searching for bits of information. As you're en route to your classroom, an enterprising pupil probably is looking at a new posting on a legal news web-site, formulating a question for you upon your arrival. You can be confident that if you've been assigned a Law and Accounting class, your students will have questions about what they read in that morning's newspaper about whatever company is under federal investigation at the time. But they'll also be aware of updates about the investigation because they'll have been on-line moments before the class commences and may even be connected during the class session itself.

I felt this quite keenly because of the specific courses I've taught, but I think that it's pretty much a phenomenon with which all law professors are confronted to some degree. In my Law of Internet Speech course, for instance, I've always been fairly confident that the moment I step foot in the elevator en route to class, detached from my computer, is the moment the Ninth Circuit will issue, modify, or withdraw another decision. I've often said that in writing and teaching on this subject, I feel quite like a gerbil on an exercise wheel; I'm running really fast to keep up, but I don't necessarily seem to be getting anywhere.

This can be frustrating. I've assumed that it must be far more comfortable to work on a more discrete topic, one less susceptible to such dynamic developments. An analysis of medieval pension statutes, perhaps. But it's also very gratifying to try to expeditiously scrutinize new developments, integrate them into your understanding of extant legal doctrines, and stimulate your students to analyze emerging trends without resort to foundational scholarly commentary. You'll undoubtedly also benefit from hearing insightful and possibly novel musings from your students as they, too, grapple with the issues.

So how can you stay apprised of new developments? There are the obvious methods of course. You can regularly cite-check the cases to which you plan to allude. But it can be quite daunting to seemingly perpetually check citations for subsequent appellate history. Checking cites before each class session is akin to the directions on the back of the shampoo bottle, advising users to "Lather. Rinse. Repeat." Taken literally, we'd all still be in the shower, shampooing again. Other methods can help alert you to later proceedings and thus help alleviate repeated cite-checking or searches throughout the semester of at least more tangential cases or proposed legislation.

You can read a national daily newspaper and relevant legal periodicals, pursuing leads about more cursory references or summaries by reviewing the primary sources and the additional commentary surrounding them. You can attend symposia and conferences to hear what others in your field are focusing on. Subscribing to print and electronic periodicals published by relevant industry trade groups can help alert you of changes. You might want to develop a cluster of colleagues at your school and elsewhere with whom you can meet (remotely via conference call or e-mail if they're not geographically proximate) to exchange information and ideas. If you're using a print edition of a casebook, you'll be placed on a publisher's mailing list for information about supplements, but you can also contact the publisher to inquire as to whether one is forthcoming and to ask whether you might get an advance copy of a supplement that's in production.

Sites such as Jurist Legal Intelligence[58] include Web pages focused on updated legal news, and "an online peer-review guide to your specialty area."[59] The HierosGamos site includes legal news and references to law journal articles.[60] You also might want to subscribe to various on-line news and other sources to receive electronic "alerts" of developments. CNN.com,[61] for instance, sends subscribers "breaking news" advisories, briefly summarizing such news items as a plea in a high-profile criminal case or passage of a major piece of federal litigation.

One of the most effective ways to stay current is to subscribe to a law list. Such lists, sometimes referred to as a "listserv" or "lawprof" (*see infra* at 124), electronically distribute a wide range of information, including summaries of and commentary about legal developments. Not only do many of these lists afford timely notification, but they also are helpfully categorized. You can peruse brief descriptions of these lists and choose those that are the most relevant to your area of the law. If you're teaching Antitrust, for instance, you can confine your subscription to antitrust and trade regulation lists, without having to wade through a series of updates and postings about all other legal subjects. There's even a list, accessible through the ABA Network and hosted by the ABA's Section of Legal Education and Admissions to the Bar, for adjunct faculty members of ABA-approved law schools.[62]

---

58. *See* <http://jurist.law.pitt.edu>.

59. *See* <http://jurist.law.pitt.edu/intro.htm>.

60. HierosGamos Law and Legal Research Center, *at* <http://www.hg.org>.

61. *See* <www.cnn.com>.

62. *See* <http://mail.abanet.org/archives/leap-adjunct.html>.

Selected Resources

Becoming a Candidate for a Faculty Position:

American Bar Association Council on Legal Education Opportunity
web-site: <http://www.abanet.org/cleo/whatis.html>

Association of American Law Schools
1201 Connecticut Avenue, NW
Washington, DC 20036
tel.: 202–296–8851
fax: 202–296–8869
web-site: <www.aals.org>
AALS Directory of Law Teachers
web-site: <http://www.aals.org/about.html>

FindLaw Career Center
web-site: <http://careers.findlaw.com/cgi-bin/cruise10.pl>

HierosGamos Law and Legal Research Center
web-site: <http://www.hg.org>

Jurist Legal Intelligence, Law Teaching/Law Teaching Jobs
web-site: <http://jurist.law.pitt.edu/position.htm>

LexisNexis Career Materials At-A-Glance
web-site: <http://www.lexisnexis.com/lawschool/reference/>

Denise C. Morgan, *Advice for Law Professor Wannabes,* 7 Mich. J. Race & L. 458 (2002), *at* <http://students.law.umich.edu/mjrl/>

NALP Directory of Legal Employers
National Association for Law Placement
1025 Connecticut Avenue, NW
Washington, DC 20036–5413
tel.: 202–835–1001
fax: 202–835–1112
web-site: <http://www.nalp.org/ndle/index.htm>

National Bar Association
1225 Eleventh Street, NW
Washington, DC 20001
tel.: 202–842–3900
fax: 202–289–6170
web-site: <http://www.nationalbar.org/career/index.shtml>

Official Guide to ABA–Approved Law Schools
website: <http://officialguide.lsac.org/docs/cgi-bin/home.asp>

Clinical Programs: Clinical Legal Education Association
6020 South University Avenue
Chicago, IL 60637–2786
tel.: 773–702–9611
web-site: <http://www.law.cuny.edu/clea/clea.html>

Graduate Law Degrees: American Bar Association Overview of Post-JD Programs
web-site: <http://www.abanet.org/legaled/postjdprograms/postjd.html>

Information About Deanships: Symposium: Leadership in Legal Education, 34 U. Toledo L. Rev. (Fall 2002), *at* <http://www.law.utoledo.edu/lawreview/dean_essays_index.htm>

Teaching Fellowship Programs: See Michele Goodwin, *Intellectual Integration in the Legal Academy: Fellowships and Fantasies,* 7 Mich. J. Race & Law 470, 475 (2002), *at* <http://students.law.umich.edu/mjrl/>

Insights Into the Application Process: Don Zillman, Marina Angel, Jan Laitos, George Pring, Joseph Tomain, *Uncloaking Law School Hiring: A Recruit's Guide to the AALS Faculty Recruitment Conference, available at* <http://www.aals.org/frs/jle/intro.html>

Preparation of Scholarly Articles:

The Directory for Successful Publishing in Legal Periodicals, *at* <http://www.law.harvard.edu/library/research_guides/publishing_in_law_reviews.htm>

ExpressO, The Berkeley Electronic Press
web-site: <http://law.bepress.com/expresso/>

The On-Line Directory of Law Reviews and Scholarly Publications, *at* <www.andersonpublishing.com/lawschool/directory>

Richard A. Posner, *The Future of the Student-Edited Law Review,* 47 Stan. L. Rev. 1131 (1995)

Rebecca E. Zietlow, *Writing Scholarship While You Practice Law,* 7 Mich. J. Race & L. 511 (2002), *at* <http://students.law.umich.edu/mjrl/>

Information About Law Schools and the Nature of Law School Education:

American Bar Association Official Guide to ABA-Approved Law Schools web-site: <http://www.abanet.org/legaled/publications/officialguide.html>

American Bar Association, Law Schools Approved By the ABA web-site: <http://www.abanet.org/legaled/approvedlawschools/approved.html>

Carnegie Foundation for the Advancement of Teaching Legal Education Study web-site: <http://www.carnegiefoundation.org/PPP/legalstudy/index.htm>

FindLaw Lawyer Search
web-site: <http://www.findlaw.com/01topics/35tax/index.html>

Jurist Legal Intelligence, Law Professors/Teaching Law
web-site: <http://jurist.law.pitt.edu/home_pgs.htm>

Harry J. Haynsworth, *The Similarities and Differences Between Independent and University Affiliated Law Schools,* 34 U. Toledo L. Rev. (Fall 2002), *at* <http://www.law.utoledo.edu/lawreview/dean_essays_index.htm>

Peter A. Hook, *Creating an Online Tutorial and Pathfinder,* 94 Law Libr. J. 243 (2002) (Appendix: Bibliography—How People Learn)

Law School Admissions Council
tel.: 215–968–1001
fax: 215–968–1119
web-site: <http://www.lsac.org>

Mercer University Center for Teaching and Learning in Collaboration with the Instructional Technology Center
web-site: <http://www.mercer.edu/itc/>

Scott Turow, *One L: The Turbulent True Story of a First Year at Harvard Law School* (Warner Books 1997 ed.)

Teaching Resources:

FindLaw Faculty and Course Pages
web-site: <http://www.findlaw.com/courses/>

Institute for Law School Teaching
web-site: <http://law.gonzaga.edu/ilst.htm>

Vernellia R. Randall
The University of Dayton School of Law
300 College Park
Dayton, OH 45469–2779
web-site: <http://academic.udayton.edu/aep/>

Arturo López Torres and Mary Kay Lundwall, *Moving Beyond Langdell II: An Annotated Bibliography of Current Methods for Law Teaching,* 35 Gonz. L. Rev. 1 (2000) (includes sources categorized by course subject matter)

University of Western Australia, The Law School Teaching and Learning Committee
web-site: <http://www.csd.uwa.edu.au/tl/etq/LawSchool.html>

Westlaw, Faculty Professor Tools
web-site: <http://lawschool.westlaw.com/faculty/proftools.asp>

Updates on Legal Developments:

American Bar Association Network Adjunct Faculty Listserve Manager of Public Technology
tel.: 312–988–6751
web-site: <http://www.abanet.org/legaled/miscellaneous/adjunctlistserve.html>

Australian Legal Information Institute
web-site: <http://www.austlii.edu.au/>

The Avalon Project
The Lillian Goldman Law Library
127 Wall Street
New Haven, CT 06520
web-site: <http://www.yale.edu/lawweb/avalon/avalon.htm>

FindLaw, Legal Subjects
web-site: <http://www.findlaw.com/01topics/>

Informant
web-site: <http://informant.dartmouth.edu>

Law Lists
Lyonette Louis-Jacques
D'Angelo Law Library
1121 East 60 Street
Chicago, IL 60637
tel.: 773–702–9612
fax: 773–702–2889
web-sites: <http://www.lib.uchicago.edu/cgi-bin/law-lists>; <http://www.lib.uchicago.edu/~llou/lawlists/lawprof.txt>; *see also* Lyonette Louis-Jacques, *Legal Research Using the Internet* (2000), *at* <http://www.lib.uchicago.edu/~llou/mpoctalk.html>; <http://www.lectlaw.com/files/lws56.htm>

Oyez
web-site: <http://oyez.itcs.northwestern.edu/oyez/frontpage>

Teachlaw: Resources for Lawyers Who Want to Be Law Professors
web-site: <http://teachlaw.law.uc.edu>

Westlaw, Faculty Legal Scholarship Network
web-site: <http://lawschool.westlaw.com/faculty/mainpage.asp?mapinpage=3>

WWW Virtual Library
Indiana University School of Law—Bloomington
web-site: <http://www.law.indiana.edu/v-lib/>

Yahoo!Groups Net-Lawyers
web-site: <http://groups.yahoo.com/group/net-lawyers/>

CHAPTER 2

Designing the Course

Teaching demands contemplative organization. The chef confirms well before dinner is to be served that he has the necessary ingredients and utensils so that he has adequate supplies. He's planned his preparation so that the courses are ready in the appropriate sequence. The professor similarly is expected to arrive for each class session with an organized plan for what will be covered in that period, premised upon careful planning for its contextualization within the semester, predicated upon reading assignments, and arranged to build incrementally on foundational instruction in prior sessions.

Whether you're assuming responsibility for a required course with a specified text and format, teaching a new course or one offered for the first time under your tutelage, or varying a course you taught previously, you'll want to consider the overall design of the course. This necessitates delimiting course objectives and articulating specific themes to be addressed during the course of the semester. There are several components to this task, including crafting a course description so that students are positioned to understand the general nature and scope of the course, preparing the course syllabus to set out a "roadmap" of the assignments and topics to be covered, choosing or devising a text, and deliberating about the type of evaluative techniques you'll utilize. Certain courses, such as required first-year courses, may have specific guidelines relating to these matters so you'll want to check your school's policies. You may not have discretion to require a paper in lieu of a final exam in a first-year Contracts course, for example.

Defining Objectives and Drafting the Course Description

Students generally select elective courses from a course bulletin, compiled and distributed by the registrar. If you're teaching a required course, its general parameters likely will be delineated by the school's administration. If you've been asked to prepare a course description, you'll want to draft a brief summary of the topics to be covered. Students rely on the description as they select their courses, so it's important to give a concise but accurate picture of the nature of the course offering. Course descriptions in registrar's bulletins typically set forth the following:

- the title of the course
- the professor's name
- a brief description of the course's subject matter
- the number of available credits
- course requirements (such as a paper and/or a final examination)
- prerequisites, if any
- enrollment limitations, if any

Here's an example of a course description:

> *Negotiation Skills and Analysis* (3 credits)
> Professor Jane Jones
>
> This course is designed to improve negotiation skills and to increase the ability to resolve conflicts in a multitude of diverse situations. Students will examine the complex dynamics that occur before, during, and after negotiations and the theories underlying different approaches to problem solving through methods other than litigation. Practical application of negotiation strategies will be emphasized throughout the course. Students will participate in simulation exercises throughout the semester. Topics to be covered include distributive and integrative bargaining; preparation tactics; negotiations involving multiple parties with disparate and possibly conflicting interests; and a comparison of mediation and arbitral proceedings.
>
> Grading will be based on class participation, evaluation of participation in a negotiation, and a final exam.
>
> Enrollment is limited to 25 students.

If you've been asked to prepare a description of each elective course you'll be teaching, you'll need to submit it to the registrar's office well before the semester is scheduled to begin. This will afford the dean an opportunity to review the description and allow adequate time for the registrar's bulletin to be assembled, printed, and disseminated to students.

Along with the course description, you may be asked to submit a brief biographical sketch that the school may use for such purposes as informing students of your background and qualifications. The biographical sketch should include your educational background, professional experience, and publications. This sketch may be requested even though much of the information will have been provided to the school in your faculty application.

The registrar's office will endeavor to accommodate your preferences regarding the time and day your classes will meet. Note, though, that the registrar must coordinate a considerable number of courses and professors' preferences while working with constraints on classroom size and availability. If there is a particular time and day that you cannot teach, you should discuss the conflict with the registrar well in advance of his preparation of the course bulletin. There may be certain periods during which classes are not scheduled in order to facilitate faculty meetings, lectures, and the like, and thus requests for those time slots will be denied.

Once your classes have been assigned, you should carefully check the academic calendar for the semester. The calendar usually is posted on the school's web-site. Note that even though your classes have been assigned for particular days, they may be scheduled to meet occasionally on alternative days to accommodate holiday breaks. For example, one of your classes may be assigned to meet on Thursdays, but because classes are not held on the Thursday on which Thanksgiving falls, your class may meet on a Monday one week during the course of the semester.

Formulating the Course Curriculum

Determining the scope of the substantive subject matter to be covered in each course plainly is the most important part of designing the course. As an expert in the field, you'll already have some well-defined ideas of particular topics and caselaw that will comprise key components of the class. But you'll need to ensure that the components work together to form a comprehensive, cogent, and well-ordered course that can be arranged in separate albeit connected lessons.

Creating the Syllabus

The course syllabus can take a variety of forms and your school may require or recommend a template for you to follow. A syllabus typically includes, at a minimum, the following:

- the title of the course
- the professor's name
- a reference to the semester (e.g., "Spring Semester 2006")

- the text and/or other materials assigned
- the reading assignments for each class session
- the classroom location
- the day(s) and time the class is scheduled to meet

Additional information that many teachers set forth on syllabi include the following:

- contact information for the professor (telephone number, facsimile number, e-mail address, and office address)
- the professor's office hours
- course requirements
- recommended readings
- the academic calendar

Many professors specify other information as well, depending on how they envision the syllabus will be used and the means by which they make other information available to their students. Sometimes, this simply is a matter of semantics. Some professors, for instance, embed their syllabi with links to reading assignments and related materials, while others regard such links and materials as a section of their faculty web-sites separate from their syllabi. One professor might encompass a study guide within his syllabus, while another may include such a guide in a separate hand-out or make it available in another part of his web-site. Still another might dispense with a study guide altogether, deeming it within the province of students' responsibility to formulate such a guide.

A syllabus may be conceptualized as a road map for the course, helping students navigate the inter-relationship between topics and reading assignments. Depending on the nature and structure of your course, you may want to include topic headings with each reading assignment to help your students contextualize the substance of the course. Even the visual design of the syllabus can offer perspective about broad concepts; indenting sub-categories in outline form or listing case captions under headings suggests thematic relationships amongst the reading assignments. Indeed, even the use of an elliptical frontispiece on an on-line tutorial (*see infra* at 58) "to navigate the tutorial awakens the user's spatial orientation and serves to heighten recall of the material."[1] You might even want to remind students to look over the syllabus at

1. Peter A. Hook, *Creating an Online Tutorial and Pathfinder*, 94 Law Libr. J. 243, 253 (2002).

the conclusion of the semester when they've completed the reading assignments to reflect on how the assignments relate to the themes explored.

Despite your careful planning, it may be appropriate to make some adjustments to the syllabus during the course of the semester. You might want to add a reading assignment, for example, if during the course of the semester an appellate court issued an important decision or a journal published provocative scholarly commentary about a matter you're covering. Perhaps a class session was cancelled because of inclement weather or maybe an active discussion or some confusion by your students precluded completion of an entire lesson plan. In addition, "the teacher can amend the syllabus regularly, mid-course, to account for the revealed strengths and weaknesses of students in the course."[2]

Some professors encourage student feedback about the syllabus during the course of the semester. Particular areas of interest might help shape the course's direction and scope.[3] Whether instigated by student comment or by the professor, it's important to continually reflect on the syllabus as the course progresses to confirm that material is appropriately allocated throughout the semester so that the class is suitably paced.

Faculty may also use the syllabus as a means of addressing questions that often arise or of placing students on notice of course requirements so that papers, exams, and the like, as well as the standards that will be used to evaluate them, are prominently displayed. Clear explication of the due date for a mid-term paper and a statement regarding your policy on penalties for late submissions helps students understand your expectations as well as the consequences of their failure to meet them. It also serves as something to which you can refer the student if he professes that you weren't clear about a due date or if he expresses disappointment that he was penalized because his submission was untimely. If the information is to be set forth in a separate section of a web-site, the section may be delineated as a set of frequently asked questions ("FAQs") and responses. Some professors include a statement of course goals, study tips, grading procedures and standards, and sample exam questions. Policies regarding absences and late arrivals to and early departures from class may be indicated as well.

As you prepare your syllabus, it's important to be mindful of the prerequisite classes your students will have attended prior to your class so that you can address their level accordingly. Also bear in mind that law school courses

---

2. Joel Atlas, *The Student-Driven Syllabus,* Institute for Law School Teaching, The Law Teacher (Spring 2001), *at* <http://law.gonzaga.edu/ilst/Newsletters/spring01/atlas.htm>.

3. *See* Paula E. Berg, *Using Distance Learning to Enhance Cross-Listed Interdisciplinary Law School Courses,* 29 Rutgers Computer & Tech. L.J. 33, 47 (2003).

are meant to be academically rigorous. Your school may have specific policies, but as a general guideline, students are expected to spend time not only attending classes but preparing for each.

If you're preparing a syllabus for a newly-offered course, the task can seem a bit challenging at first. You might begin by simply listing on the left-hand side of a page the themes that occur to you randomly, without initially focusing on the order in which they are to be assigned or even on the degree to which they may overlap or inter-relate. Look over the list, and on the right-hand side of the page, next to each theme, jot down the cases, statutory excerpts, journal articles, and other materials that you want to assign that pertain to each of the themes. As you do this, do additional themes occur to you? If so, go ahead and add them to the left-hand column. Are some themes without any materials in the left-hand column? Can those themes be combined with other themes, either because they're encompassed within broader themes or because they're ancillary to them and can be addressed together?

Then look over the two lists to see how they might be logically ordered. This, too, can be broken down so that the task seems a bit less daunting. Just start by considering the first two themes; which of these would be discussed first? Then look at the third entry; where does that theme fit within the first two? As you continue the process, you'll see that you've basically developed your syllabus and formulated a course plan.

As an alternative approach or in conjunction with review of your draft syllabus, you can peruse casebooks' tables of contents. The authors of the books have spent considerable time organizing the materials into a comprehensive and logical flow. Many casebooks have a summary table of contents, affording a more cursory overview of the books' contents. These summaries provide an informative outline perspective of the course to which the casebook relates. The more detailed table of contents (which immediately follows the summary table of contents) lists more specifically the selected court decisions, statutory and regulatory excerpts, and scholarly writings included in the book. Reviewing the selected excerpts also may suggest additional materials you'll want to assign. While casebooks, particularly lengthy editions, usually are not assigned in their entirety, consideration of the table of contents may help you avoid an inadvertent omission of a topic intrinsically related to your course.

Some teachers' manuals that accompany casebooks include sample syllabi. It can be helpful to consult these to see how the material has been organized, to assess whether and how the order for presentation deviates from the structure of the casebook, and to take into account the volume of readings the casebook authors deem appropriate. Sample syllabi that are tailored to particular casebooks may be especially useful if you've decided to use the related text.

It's also helpful to consult syllabi crafted by other professors who are teaching similar courses. If your course has a predecessor whom you're replacing, request a copy of the syllabus from him or from the school's registrar. You might confer with other professors at your school who have taught similar courses to review their approaches. Many professors (possibly including your predecessor if you have one) post their syllabi on-line. You can search for professors' sites through such search engines as Google.[4] If you know the school with which a professor is affiliated, you can search for the school's site and then access the site's faculty pages. Or you might try searching particular law schools' sites for the course you'll be teaching; such a search may yield additional syllabi, or, at the very least, a list of assigned readings or a description of the subject matter to be covered.

You also may want to consult various resources to locate specific law school faculty who specialize in your field. One helpful site is the Jurist Legal Intelligence site,[5] which offers a compilation of syllabi that you can access according to subject matter. In addition, WashLawWeb[6] links to law-related materials on the Internet and hosts listserv discussion groups that may be of interest and stimulate thought about current topics relevant to your course.

While it's doubtful that your syllabus will replicate precisely that of another professor, you'll likely gain considerable insights from your review of other versions. You'll probably get a better sense of the scope of the subject matter covered, the topics routinely or occasionally omitted, and the amount of material apportioned to each class session.

You'll want to have the syllabus completed before class begins. You may decide, depending on your school's procedures, to furnish just the reading assignment for the first class session to the registrar's office before the semester starts. In either event, copies of syllabi should be distributed or otherwise made available to students during the first class session.

The Faculty Web-Site

Information technology can render professors more accessible to their students through electronic means and enhance the breadth of resources rec-

---

4. *See* <http://www.google.com>.
5. *See* <http://jurist.law.pitt.edu/lawteaching.htm>.
6. *See* <http://washlaw.edu>.

ommended to students for further reading. Amongst the ways that the Internet may be exploited is through the creation and development of a faculty web-site. In addition to using computer technology to enhance in-class presentations (*see infra* at 109), a faculty web-site can expand and facilitate content delivery and promote interactive and direct access to the student's professor and classmates.

A professor's site can be launched by the professor or can be incorporated into the school's existing site, located with an ".edu" top level domain name. Relevant to the design and scope of the site is whether it is devoted exclusively to a particular course or will cover all of the courses you'll be teaching as well as other school-related responsibilities you'll be assuming. In the latter situation, it's even more important to include clearly marked icons to enable visitors to navigate the site and locate information relevant to each course, your journal activities, upcoming conferences you'll be hosting, and the like. Of course, you'll want to include your name, title, and contact information, including your school, address, telephone number, facsimile number, and e-mail address. You also can include a variety of administrative-related materials, such as your office hours and a link to your syllabus.

Links to the school's policies, academic requirements, programs and conferences, and information about facilities ease student access to such information and can be used to emphasize particular items of interest. A professor who is teaching a seminar in Comparative International Law may want to alert students about an upcoming lecture to be presented by a visiting academician from a foreign country, for instance.

Posting such information reduces the time you'll need to spend during class sessions making administrative announcements. You also may find that the need to clarify your policies, such as those pertaining to late submissions of required course material, page limitations for assigned papers, and missed class sessions, is reduced. And you'll need to spend less time handing out brochures about conferences or substantive handouts absent students missed.

Faculty web-sites typically include a link to the professors' syllabi. This assists students enrolled in the professor's class who may wish to check an assignment or review the overall context of the readings. It also helps students who are contemplating their course selections; they can readily see beyond the more cursory description of the course supplied by the registrar (*see supra* at 41).

Many professors also post information about their biographical backgrounds. Students usually are interested to know a bit about their professors. The information may stimulate a conversation about some common ground that can help students establish a rapport with their teachers. You and a class member may have been born in the same town, have studied at the same college, or share an interest in fly-fishing.

Typically included amongst this information is a list of the professor's prior publications and possibly even his works in progress. This provides another indication of your areas of interest, especially because the courses you've been asked to teach during a particular semester may not be commensurate with all of the fields in which you specialize or about which you've written. This may help a student who wants to seek out a mentor in a particular field, inquire about various career options, or explore opportunities for an independent study project.

Because information on an Internet web-site is available beyond the school's student community, others may gain insights about your background, your writings, and the structure of your courses. You may be contacted by someone who has a common substantive interest such as another academician who would like to collaborate on a project or would like to solicit participants in an upcoming symposium. The site may act as a catalyst for shared thoughts about teaching similar courses or use of the same casebook. And if you've browsed other sites to get information about the schools' faculty, curricula, and course designs, developing your own site provides you with an opportunity to reciprocate.

In addition to posting administrative material and biographical information, the site may be used as a means of disseminating content for educational purposes. This can be done in order to comprise the totality of the class' reading assignments or to supplement a text because you want to add more recent material; tailor the text with additional or substitute reading assignments; or enrich the text with graphics, photographs, or other material not readily found in casebooks. Visual and aural material can be made available in digital format to augment lectures and text.

Web-sites also offer a wide range of material for background for a student who has not taken a course that, while not a formal prerequisite, would have provided helpful context. A brief capsule summary of a related subject can be presented, which is especially useful in an inter-disciplinary course. Or it may assist a student who is struggling to master a concept that wasn't readily comprehended through the required reading and class discussion. Some software programs even provide the means for interactive exercises to practice problem-solving and other tasks (*see infra* at 55). In addition, recommended readings can be set forth to accommodate students who wish to satisfy their intellectual curiosity in greater depth or whose interest on a particular topic has been especially sparked to write a journal article on the subject. It's important, of course, to be explicit as to whether readings are required or recommended, so that students are placed on notice as to what is expected of them and so that they don't feel overwhelmed by a misperception that optional material must be covered as well.

Linking to sites that include sources you'd like your students to peruse facilitates their access; a click of the mouse transports them to another resource without effort, consideration of library hours, or frustration due to the unavailability of limited copies of a source that has been borrowed by others. Using the Web as an educational resource is beneficial because of the Web's virtual perpetual availability. The student's autonomy over his schedule is thereby increased. Furthermore, if the material that you want your students to access is not in the public domain and would not constitute a fair use of a work protected by copyright (*see infra* at 63), a link may alleviate your need to clear permission from the copyright holder to distribute the excerpt.

Selection of Course Materials

You'll need to carefully consider the materials you want to assign to your each of your classes, taking into account the scope of the topics to be explored, the intellectual level of the readings, the nature of the material assigned (whether they should be predominantly caselaw excerpts, compilations of statutory materials, scholarly commentary, or factual case studies), and the volume of the material to be assigned. It's doubtful you'll find a single source that accommodates all of your requirements for every class. Your task basically is to find or develop one that comes as close as possible to your vision. You've got several options available from which to choose (*see* Fig. 1).

Casebooks

Print Editions

It's possible that your school may require or recommend particular texts or other materials for your course, especially if you'll be teaching a required class. Or you may be responsible for selecting the materials to be assigned to students. Obviously, you'll want to clarify this before you begin extensive work on the design and structure of your course so that you'll know the extent of your options as you select the sources that will be the basis of the students' reading assignments.

Legal publishers often accommodate professors by making a courtesy copy of texts available. You may wish to browse publishers' web-sites or contact individual publishers to inquire about texts suitable for your class. (Contact in-

Figure 1

Text Selection Options

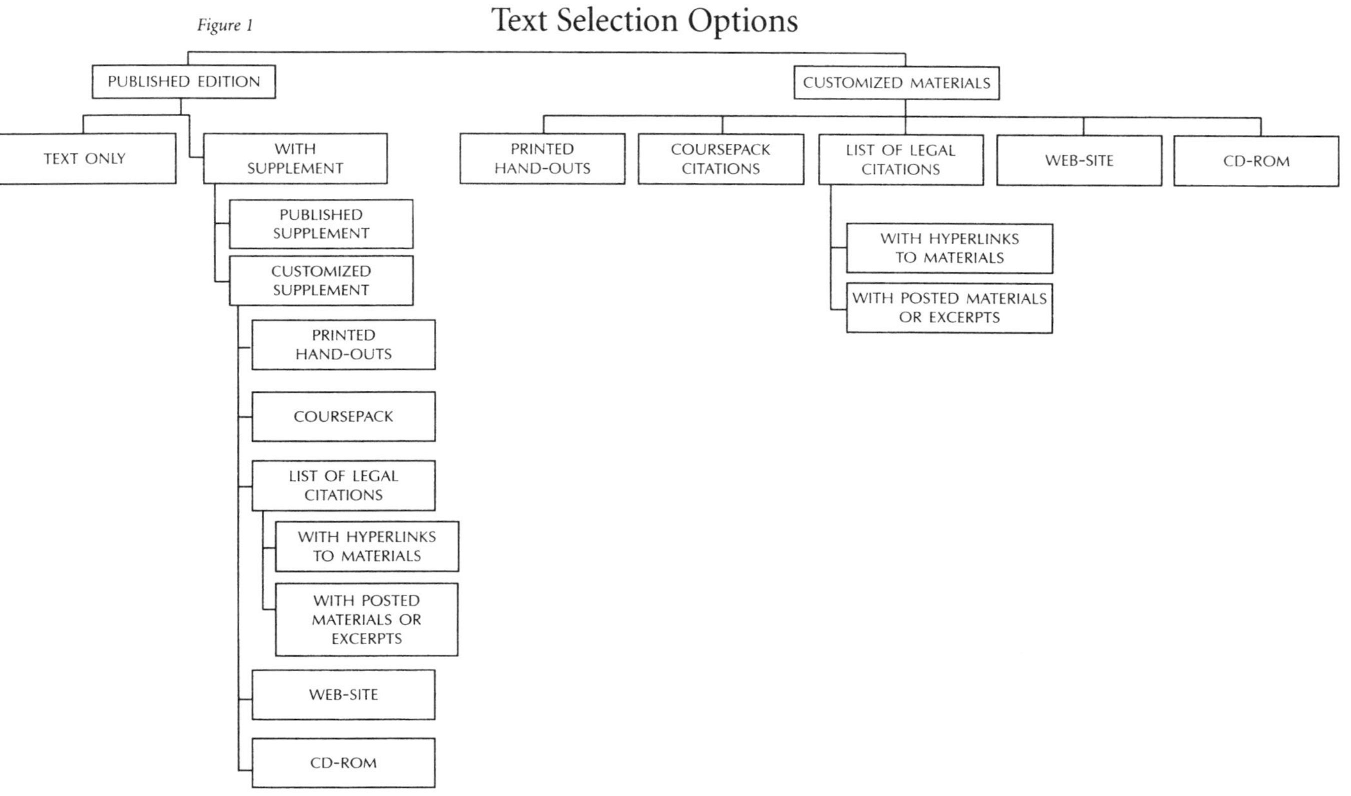

formation relating to prominent legal publishers is included in the Selected Resources section, *see infra* at 86.)

You'll also want to request any supplements to the texts you review. These provide additional materials that have been generated after the casebook was published. Occasionally, a supplement may include an excerpt of a case decision or other selection that was issued before the casebook was written but that gained additional significance because of subsequent legal developments.

Many casebooks have accompanying teachers' manuals that are available to faculty. You can request the manual that accompanies the casebook you're reviewing if one exists. While the manual won't be a viable substitute for your own diligent preparation, it can inspire you to consider another line of questioning during discussions, offer sample syllabi for you to consider, or refer to additional citations you may want to review.

Just as the organization and selection of material to be included in a book is subject to broad discretion, so, too, is a teacher's manual susceptible to disparate approaches. Some manuals briefly summarize aspects of excerpted cases, offer questions that may stimulate class discussion, and present brief hypothetical situations to encourage application of legal principles. These may be useful supplements to your notes or provide a means of considering additional permutations on course themes.

If you select a printed text, you'll probably be asked to complete a course book information request form, which alerts the school's bookstore which text you have chosen and allows the store time to order the book in sufficient quantities to meet the demands of your class enrollment. The bookstore usually coordinates with the registrar's office to ascertain the approximate enrollment of your class. All materials that are to be ordered for purchase by students enrolled in the class should be listed (e.g., any supplements to assigned texts). You should also note on the form whether each of the materials specified is required or recommended.

CD-ROMs

Another approach is the use of a CD-ROM. The Practising Law Institute offers CD-ROMs in an Interactive Courtroom series.[7] One of these, "Cross Examination: Evidence and Tactics with Terence MacCarthy," covers the use of leading questions, foundations for impeachment purposes, thematic (rather than chronological) approaches to cross-examination, and tips on refraining

---

7. Practising Law Institute, Upcoming Programs, *available at* <http://www.pli.edu/product/upprog_searchresults.asp>.

from making certain technically correct objections, as well as such evidentiary matters as those relating to relevance, hearsay, opinion, and privilege.[8]

Before choosing a CD-ROM as the text for one of your courses, confirm students' access to the requisite technology. You can check with your school to find out whether students are required to have laptops with CD drives or whether facilities are readily accessible through the school's library.

Customized Texts

If you haven't found a printed edition of a casebook that adequately suits your needs, you have other options. You can select the edition that comes closest to a compilation of materials you'd like to use and then customize it to tailor it to your needs or you can create your own materials.

Coursepacks and Handouts

You may want to distribute an anthology of materials, such as excerpts of court decisions, statutory provisions, and journal articles. These may be designed to supplement a printed casebook or in lieu of another text.

Your school may be able to assist you with the duplication of handouts and coursepacks. This option allows you to tailor the text by assembling the materials you want to assign. You could include excerpts of works that you've located but that are not readily available for sale because they're out of print, for instance. In addition, for large classes, West Law School Publishing can work with you to custom publish a coursepack, downloading court decisions and statutory provisions from Westlaw, binding them in the order you determine, and offering them for sale to students.[9] Another option is to enlist West Law School Publishing to help you clear permissions on a per-page fee basis from works to which it holds the rights; then you would assemble the materials in a coursepack.[10]

Note, though, that unless you're prepared to spend time editing works you want to include or wish to incorporate discrete portions of works in their entirety (such as an entire chapter of a book), you risk presenting your students with voluminous quantities of irrelevant material. Unlike a print edition of a casebook that includes edited selections of readings, a coursepack that merely

---

8. *See id.*

9. Telephone Interview with Alice Mitchell, Legal Editor, West Law School Publishing (Aug. 14, 2003).

10. *Id.*

compiles lengthy cases and statutes will include extensive extraneous matter. For example, a seminal case may have a lengthy discussion of the action's procedural history or an in-depth analysis of several claims that are irrelevant to your course's subject matter.

Another issue to consider is whether the materials you're contemplating including are in the public domain or whether you must clear permission to use them (*see infra* at 63). Determination about the materials' copyright status and the acquisition of any necessary permission can be time-consuming and, depending upon the nature of the material and the permission fees demanded, quite costly. You'll want to allow adequate time for this process and to ascertain the scope of your budget in advance.

You'll also want to be mindful of the aggregate cost of the materials you require students to access. If you are assigning a casebook, mandatory purchase of a lengthy coursepack supplement as well may be quite costly. If the materials you want to assign aren't voluminous, your school may have the means to absorb the cost of duplication for distribution to your class. Or you may want to provide students with a list of readings and the citations, which they may access either through a law-based software program such as LexisNexis or Westlaw or through Internet sites.

Another option, particularly when duplication of material (such as audio and videotape material) is cumbersome, is to make the material available to your students through the school's library as a faculty loan. Note, however, that such an approach does not afford you a means of ascertaining from the library whether the entire class diligently accessed the materials for review; laws relating to libraries may preclude you from securing from the library the identities of the students who have signed out or otherwise accessed the materials. Nearly all states have enacted laws that protect the names and other personally identifiable information regarding patrons of public, university, and other libraries. The American Library Association[11] and individual libraries have policies promoting privacy and confidentiality.

Web-Based Books, E-Books, and Tutorials

Hypertext functionality can enhance course materials by expediting access to legal sources, overcoming temporal and geographic constraints imposed by

---

11. *See Questions and Answers on Privacy and Confidentiality*, American Library Association (Jan. 22, 2003), *available at* <http://www.ala.org/Content/NavigationMenu/Our_Association/Offices/Intellectual_Freedom3/Challenge_Support/Dealing_with_Challenges/qandaonprivacyandconfidentiality.pdf>.

physical repositories. In addition, hypertext electronic materials can promote associative thinking by emphasizing, quite viscerally, the "link" between various concepts. Even the integration of substantive topics within a course, across multiple courses, and amongst multiple disciplines can be emphasized.

There are various ways to electronically distribute educational materials. A "Web-based book" may be understood to refer to material or a compilation of materials for use in a single law school class (which may, of course, extend over more than one semester depending on the number of credits) that is based on content acquired or derived from or accessed through the World Wide Web. "Electronic casebooks," often called "e-books," may refer to an electronic version of a book that can be read on a computer screen or an electronic device. Such works can be created by converting digitized text into a format readable by computer software. Educational content may be made available in CD-ROM form, on a web-site, or through an e-book device. A software program may have been used to assist in the work's creation. Certain works utilize electronic functionality to enable the reader to engage in such tasks as annotating, highlighting, bookmarking, and searching the works. This facilitates research and other scholarly uses.

Web-based material also may include tutorials or lessons. A tutorial can be structured to explain material and provide tips on locating relevant information, perhaps demonstrating research techniques. LexisNexis offers several legal research and on-line writing exercises in which students engage interactively.[12] Westlaw has an Instructional Aids Series, comprised of modules to view or download.[13] Professors sometimes design tutorials to cover not only substantive legal principles but also related processes. Gretchen Van Dam, an Adjunct Professor at the Chicago-Kent College of Law and the Circuit Librarian of the Seventh Circuit Court of Appeals, devised a tutorial regarding the federal legislative process, delineating the process from the introduction of a bill to enactment.[14] Amongst the tutorial's benefits were expanded classroom time, the ability of students to work at their own pace, the capacity for remote access, and an "inject[ion of] some visual pizzazz into the teaching of legal research...."[15]

12. *See* LexisNexis Tutorials, *at* <http://www.LexisNexis.com/lawschool/tutorials>.

13. *See* Westlaw Instructional Aids Series, *at* <http://lawschool.westlaw.com/research/InstructionalAids.asp?SecondaryPage=3>.

14. Gretchen Van Dam, *Web Tutorials for Teaching Legal Research,* Jurist Legal Intelligence, Lessons from the Web, *at* <http://jurist.law.pitt.edu/lessons/lesmay01.htm>.

15. *Id.*

The Center for Computer-Aided Legal Instruction ("CALI") Library of Lessons "is a collection of over 270 interactive, computer-based lessons covering 28 legal education subject areas[,]...designed to augment traditional law school instruction."[16] They may be integrated into other course materials as supplemental readings or as study guides after the material has been covered in class. These lessons are available in a range of subject areas, including Arbitration, Business Associations, Legal Concepts and Skills, and Remedies. The CALI Lesson in Corporations, for instance, includes materials on, amongst other topics, Business Financing and the Federal Securities Laws, the Business Judgment Rule, Company Research, Corporate Acquisitions, Corporate Distributions, Issuance of Shares, Judicial Review of Director's Conflicting Interest Transactions, Shareholder Agreements Under the Revised Model Business Corporation Act Section 7.32, Shareholder Inspection Rights, and Voting Trusts and Voting Agreements. The CALI Library includes Topic Grids that categorize subject areas that correlate to CALI Lessons.[17] CALI also offers teacher manuals designed to complement use of the CALI Lessons.[18]

Tutorials can fill gaps in students' relative backgrounds, affording a means to gain understanding of basic principles covered in a course that is not a formal prerequisite. This can help promote parity amongst students when some have taken a foundational course and others have not. If you're covering legal issues relating to domain names in an E-Commerce class, for instance, you may not have required a course in Trademarks as a prerequisite. Some students who haven't studied Trademark Law may find the discussion relating to claims grounded in trademark infringement and dilution a bit challenging. Or they may see others in the class refer to cases or concepts not included in the assigned readings, resulting in a disturbing perception of disparity in background knowledge. An optional tutorial, perhaps through hyperlinked materials relating to basic Trademark principles, can offer guidance. Students can then work at their own place to learn or review.

Depending upon how the terminology is used and the technology has been applied, e-books may be more static than Web-based books in the sense that, notwithstanding potential annotation of an e-book by the reader, the mate-

16. CALI Lesson Catalog, The Center for Computer-Aided Legal Instruction, *at* <http://lessons.cali.org>.

17. CALI Topic Grids, The Center for Computer-Aided Legal Instruction, *at* <http://www.cali.org/fellows/grids/>.

18. CALI Teachers Manuals, The Center for Computer-Aided Legal Instruction, *at* <http://www.cali.org/TeachersManuals/>.

rials basically have been packaged; it is the reader, not the author, who modifies the work. This is analogous to borrowing the hardcover copy of a book another has purchased; you may see that the reader has highlighted passages, made notes in the margins, and perhaps stapled a press clipping onto a particular page. But the basic composition of the book you borrowed will be identical to that purchased by another reader of the same edition. A list of several e-books and electronic supplements is available on the Jurist Legal Intelligence site.[19]

By contrast, Web-based books may be customized by a professor. Such customization might delete a case that has been overruled or add a newly-issued decision or a recently-enacted statute. Some educators use e-books as a means of supplementing a print edition of a casebook in order to include legal developments that occurred after the casebook's publication. Gary Neustadter, Professor of Law at Santa Clara University School of Law, remarked that the use of electronic casebooks is "akin to the power boosts added to fruit drinks at currently fashionable juice bars. The technology provides a variety of very useful tools for navigating, reading, and manipulating the printed word, but has not altered the materials themselves."[20] Thus, Web-based books may augment another text, regardless of its form, that is assigned to students, by offering additional readings that help the professor tailor the primary text to his particular course.

Web-based books may include links to other aspects of the work as well as to additional web-sites. This facilitates research of related issues, review of material for study purposes, and perusal of foundational or ancillary concepts necessary for more thorough comprehension of the material.

Some professors rely on Internet access as a means of engaging students. Such access may present an irresistible distraction, especially if your class happens to meet, say, during the final game of the World Series when updates about each inning are readily within a student's reach. Patrick Wiseman of Georgia State University College of Law quipped, "What with the lure of websites, instant messaging, email, and games, it is a wonder that students with in-class Internet access pay any attention at all."[21] Sometimes, though, when I'm lecturing and I hear the tap, tap, tap of students hunched

---

19. *See* <http://jurist.law.pitt.edu/e_books.htm>.

20. Gary Neustadter, *Rethinking Electronic Casebooks,* Jurist Legal Intelligence, Lessons from the Web, Jurist Legal Intelligence, *at* <http://jurist.law.pitt.edu/lessons/lesjun98.htm> (footnote omitted).

21. Patrick Wiseman, *Internet Access in the Classroom: Who Needs It?,* Jurist Legal Intelligence, Lessons from the Web, *at* <http://jurist.law.pitt.edu/lessons/lesmar02.php>.

over their laptops, I console myself that they're not trying to memorialize my every word but instead are instant messaging one another.

Web-based tutorials can utilize multi-media interactive elements to provide general information about a topic. A related tool, "pathfinders," can furnish more specific information about ways to research detailed information. Peter Hook, Electronic Services Librarian at Indiana University School of Law, notes that "[t]he World Wide Web's multimedia environment allows two-dimensional, static, page-based tutorials to become interactive, sensory-rich learning environments capable of appealing to several different learning types concurrently."[22] Because people process and retain information in various ways, access to on-line tutorials can be tailored to accommodate disparities in cognition and learning styles.[23]

Access to legal developments can be enhanced by captive or embedded searches, a type of hyperlinking that facilitates retrieval of a range of sources. The user effectively launches a pre-determined search for certain information.[24] Thus you might devise a site that includes a number of court decisions on a particular topic as well as material that is expected to change over time. Such dynamic search techniques can yield results more efficiently than a static link to a particular document.

Web design and training is available from several sources. The HTML Writers Guild, for example, offers on-line training on such topics as Dreamweaver, Flash, Photoshop, HTML, XML, CorelDraw, SQL, and JavaScript.[25]

Many professors have helpfully written about their experiences utilizing software and Web-based sources to devise Web-based books or e-books. Enrique Carrasco of the University of Iowa College of Law, for example, created an e-book on International Finance and Development. The book essentially was "a practical 'handbook' for lay people that could be distributed widely to communities around the world."[26] Markus Dirk Dubber of the State Univer-

---

22. Peter A. Hook, *Creating an Online Tutorial and Pathfinder,* 94 Law Libr. J. 243, 245 (2002).

23. *See id.*

24. *See generally LII Building Block: Using Captive Searches, at* <http://www.law.cornell.edu/blocks/captive.htm>.

25. The HTML Writers Guild, *Web Design Training and Certification, at* <http://www.hwg.org/>.

26. Enrique Carrasco, *The Creation of the E-Book on International Finance and Development: A Journey into Cyberspace,* Jurist Legal Intelligence, Lessons from the Web, *previously posted at* <http://jurist.law.pitt.edu/lessons/lesnov/98.htm>.

sity of New York (Buffalo) utilizes a web-site to teach seminars on Criminal Law, using hyperlinks and split-screen comparers to explore differences amongst Criminal Law systems and consider regulatory offenses in addition to serious felonious acts. Dubber even uses the site during class by projecting it onto a screen, displaying, for instance, two disparate penal code sections and a split-screen display of a definition to contextualize the provision's historical foundation. One of the advantages, Dubber concludes, is that "projecting the material under discussion onto a screen visible to all means that every one in the room is always on the same page."[27]

Pioneer efforts have begun in the context of collaborative Web-based projects, coordinating a group of contributing authors. In one situation, each contributor was assigned a subject module for purposes of assembling, editing, and analyzing pertinent materials, annotating the contribution with queries for discussion purposes. "This divide and conquer approach allowed each collaborating professor to devote the necessary time to direct their full attention to creating a concise set of readings for one aspect of the field of cyberlaw."[28] Web-sites may readily hyperlink to one another to connect threads and facilitate review of background and supplemental materials. At some point in the future, multiple e-books may be integrated, creating, in effect, a "Web of Webs."[29] If you assign (or supplement your reading assignments with) references to web-sites, you should try to monitor them throughout the semester to confirm that the sites remain accessible and the information you're targeting remains available, as sometimes sites are delisted or material is withdrawn.

There are several software programs available to help you craft a Web-based text. LexisNexis' faculty page offers two step-by-step guides (basic and advanced) to building Web courses in Blackboard 5.5.1, a software platform for Web-enabled classes. The technology allows the user to convert course content into Web-based instructional materials from existing wordprocessing and slide documents. Professors can link to LexisNexis material and external sites, post announcements, track site usage, access student feedback, and link to CALI Lessons. You can customize your site to ease navigation and even prepost materials for delayed transmission. An on-line gradebook is available to

---

27. Markus Dirk Dubber, *Webbing the Law,* Jurist Legal Intelligence, Lessons from the Web, *at* <http://jurist.law.pitt.edu/lessons/lesmay00.htm>.

28. Lydia Pallas Loren, *Collaborative Web-Based Course Materials: Bypassing Publishers and Benefiting Students,* Jurist Legal Intelligence, Lessons from the Web, *at* <http://jurist.law.pitt.edu/lessons/lesnov99.htm>.

29. *Id.*

assist you in weighting scores.[30] Interactive discourse can be promoted through e-mail or a discussion board (*see infra* at 121, 124) and you can arrange to enter a virtual classroom.

Westlaw offers The West Education Network, commonly known by its acronym, "TWEN." The software, accessible through the section of Westlaw's site that offers help to professors, is described as an "online extension[ ] of your law school classroom."[31] TWEN enables you to create document pages for content distribution; establish forums for on-line discussion; host live discussions; link to Westlaw, CALI, and Internet sites; create exams; disseminate a course calendar; and set e-mail options.

Devising an e-book, Web-based text, or tutorial can be labor-intensive. Amongst your considerations as you contemplate such a project should be the level and needs of your class or user group; the development of "a rigorous and well-defined conceptual underpinning and organizational schema;"[32] informational architectural considerations such as navigation, branding, and cross-platform design issues; printing capabilities; and accessibility to disabled persons. Note that the Copyright Act exempts certain uses of works from otherwise available copyright protection when they're used by individuals who are prevented by special circumstances from attending class.[33]

Experimentation is appropriate, as variable success rates are to be expected. Electronic Services Librarian Peter Hook is but one of many who deliberated extensively about the design and scope of his multi-media project before it was launched, nevertheless concluding thereafter that he might have constructed it somewhat differently. He considered enabling display through the tutorial of archetypical documents on the elliptical frontispiece with a corresponding time component to indicate a legislative timeline or include mark-up transcripts (a record of proposed amendments to the original bill at the sub-committee and committee stages and members' voting records) on a subsequent iteration of the tutorial.[34] It's as helpful to appraise the substantive compo-

---

30. *See* LexisNexis, *Building LexisNexis Web Courses in Blackboard® 5.5.1, at* <http://www.lexisnexis.com/lawschool/faculty/webcourses/>.

31. *See* Westlaw, *Creating a TWEN Course, at* <http://lawschool.westlaw.com/help/professor/twenmenu.asp?Unit=twenmenu&appflag=53.8>.

32. Peter A. Hook, *Creating an Online Tutorial and Pathfinder,* 94 Law Libr. J. 243, 256 (2002).

33. 17 U.S.C. § 121.

34. Peter A. Hook, *Creating an Online Tutorial and Pathfinder,* 94 Law Libr. J. at 254 nn.60, 61.

nents of the electronic resources you create as it is to periodically assess the technological and navigability aspects.

An essential part of devising an electronic text or supplement is careful editing. Print editions of textbooks include excerpts of judicial decisions, statutes, and scholarly articles. The ease with which one can copy or link to such materials should not tempt wholesale inclusion. If you're teaching a substantive law course, you may be far more interested in having the class focus on the court's discussion of the *prima facie* elements of a claim than on the proceeding's procedural history. Or a plaintiff may have asserted some claims that bear no relation to the subject matter of your course. It will be difficult for students, confronted with unlimited access to such materials, to parse through what you intended to emphasize. Conscientious students may presume that because all of the voluminous readings were assigned, they deserve comparable attention. Thus the educational utility of electronically available materials can be readily subverted if students are confronted with copious amounts of information that simply have been uploaded to the Internet.

While the ease with which you can upload material can overwhelm your students, ironically, technological options may also sharpen the focus and enrich your presentation. Electronic agent technology, for example, can increase the visual appeal and possibly even aid in students' retention of the content. An electronic agent basically is a set of programmable software services that supports the presentation of interactive animated characters. Microsoft describes its agent as a "set of software services [that] developers can [use to] easily enhance the user interface of their applications and Web pages with interactive personalities in the form of animated characters."[35] Animated cartoon characters, known as "bots," can be added to your project to audibly make announcements through synthesized voices with a text-to-speech program that includes options for inflection and volume and even synchronizes the character's lips to the utterances made. Bots also can be designed to make gestures and even move about the screen to direct the viewer's attention, retrieve Web pages, or simply to serve as background images. A bot can be used to automate the collection of student responses to a question posed by the professor or send e-mail messages to students in preparation for an upcoming class, inviting them to ask questions for the professor's advance consideration. An example of an AI-based bot can be found on the Jurist Legal Intelligence site; the bot, named "Alex," is programmed to help locate basic legal infor-

---

35. Microsoft Agent, *at* <http://www.microsoft.com/msagent/default.asp>.

mation on-line and can be heard audibly through a program available to be downloaded.[36]

Setting a bot to "rotisserie" mode means that the bot will initiate a question and then re-route each pupil's initial answer to a classmate to solicit evaluation; by the end of the process, each class member will have offered and received targeted feedback from a classmate, providing the foundation for threads in a Web archive that can further stimulate thought and discussion. Wendy Seltzer, a Fellow at the Berkman Center for Internet & Society at Harvard Law School, recounts an application of a bot that "collected abstracts to students' planned research papers, and distributed those, to ask second-round recipients for suggestions and possible references."[37] The Berkman Center has been refining the bot's program as part of its H2O project, touting the rotisserie as an innovative on-line tool that "encourages measured, thoughtful discourse in a way that traditional threaded messaging systems cannot. In contrast to the completely asynchronous, broadcast-to-broadcast model of existing threaded messaging systems, the Rotisserie adds structure to both the timing and the flow of the discussion."[38] The discussion is broken down to semi-synchronous rounds so that users can choose the timing of their postings but publication is delayed until the deadline for the round of postings expires. Thus, students are able to take more time to deliberate about their responses without feeling pressured that their point will be usurped if they delay. Parity of participation is promoted because the system controls the distribution of responses in order to ensure that each participant has one item for response. An integrated discussion also may be conducted amongst multiple classes at different schools.[39]

One advantage of agent technology relative to streaming video (*see infra* at 95) is the disparity in required equipment; using bots requires "[n]o cameras; no microphones; no recording studios."[40] Agent technology also can be used with smaller files to facilitate transmission over the Internet even to those using slower connections. From a content standpoint, agent technology offers significant capacity for editing, a task for which those designing streaming or other video are dependent upon available equipment.

---

36. *See Ask Alex,* Jurist Legal Intelligence, *at* <http://jurist.law.pitt.edu/alex.htm>.

37. Wendy Seltzer, *Teaching with the Bot,* Jurist Legal Intelligence, Lessons from the Web, *at* <http://jurist.law.pitt.edu/lessons/lesmay02.php>.

38. *Id.; see also* H20 Project, The Berkman Center for Internet and Society, Harvard University School of Law, *at* <http://h2oproject.law.harvard.edu//>.

39. *See id.*

40. Ray August, *Animating Web Lectures with Agent Technology,* Jurist Legal Intelligence, Lessons from the Web, *at* <http://jurist.law.pitt.edu/lessons/lesfeb01.htm>.

Legal Considerations for Authors

Intellectual Property Considerations

If you've created or are in the process of creating a work, you'll want to be mindful of intellectual property considerations. Such laws come into play two ways in connection with teaching endeavors. First, if you're going to use others' works such as in a text, Web-based book, or e-book you're creating, you'll want to be sure that you're not infringing another's copyright rights.[41] You'll also want to properly attribute your use of others' works so that irrespective of the actionability of a copyright infringement claim, you don't commit plagiarism (*see infra* at 218). Conversely, you'll want to understand your rights if another requests permission to use material to which you hold the rights.

Using Others' Works

Humorist Andy Borowitz facetiously indicated that he avoids the tedium of original creation of expression by "[buy]ing an already written book and... crossing out the words [he has] no intention of using."[42] Of course, as is the case with students, faculty are expected to respect the intellectual property rights of others, and you must ensure that you have secured all necessary permissions to reproduce and distribute materials. There is a web of legislation and caselaw that relates to intellectual property issues. Special rules apply to photocopying and archival activities by libraries, for instance.[43]

Is the material subject to copyright protection? Your first task is to determine whether the work is subject to copyright protection. Many expressive works are protected by copyright, but some material is not even eligible to be copyrighted. Copyright protection extends to "original works of authorship fixed in any tangible medium of expression."[44] Copyright subsists in such creative works of expression as literary works; plays; pantomimes and choreographic works; pictorial, graphic, and sculptural works; motion pictures; musical works, audiovisual works, and sound recordings; and architectural works.[45] The copyright owner enjoys exclusive rights to reproduce the work, to create derivative

---

41. Another body of law, Patent Law, applies to your use of others' useful, novel, and non-obvious inventions as to which a patent has been granted. For example, your use of computer software my implicate patent rights. Academic institutions typically secure necessary licenses.

42. Andy Borowitz, *The Secret to Writing a Successful Book*, N.Y. Times, Jan. 1, 2002, at A23.

43. *See* 17 U.S.C. § 108.

44. 17 U.S.C. § 102.

45. 17 U.S.C. § 102(a).

works, to distribute copies of the work, and to perform and display the work publicly.[46] The fact that material is readily and freely accessible does not necessarily mean that it is devoid of copyright protection. Thus original authorship appearing on a web-site may be protected by copyright.

Simply because a work was created by another does not necessarily mean that it is subject to, or remains subject to, copyright protection or that portions of it may not be permissibly used. Certain material, such as ideas, are not subject to copyright,[47] which protects only the *expression* of ideas. Nor are "scénes á faire" subject to copyright; these are scenes that necessarily result from the selection of a setting or situation because of plot, genre, or storytelling. Historical incidents and "facts do not owe their origin to an act of authorship;"[48] thus there is a distinction between creation and discovery. But a factual compilation may be eligible for protection if it features an original selection and arrangement of those facts because although the protection does not extend to the facts themselves, it may cover the selection and arrangement of those facts.[49]

Works that are in the public domain likewise may be used without authorization. The copyright laws expressly exclude from eligibility for protection "any work of the United States Government,"[50] which includes "work[s] prepared by an officer or employee of the United States government as part of that person's official duties."[51] This approach renders publicly-financed work readily available to the citizenry. Thus the federal government holds no monopoly on such official records as federal statutes or court decisions. As is the case with virtually every other legal rule, there are nuances, such as the fact that memoirs written after a federal official leaves office could be copyrighted[52] or that the federal government may receive and hold copyrights transferred to it by assignment or bequest.[53]

Has the copyright for the work expired? Even if you've determined that the work is subject to copyright protection, the material may now be in the public domain if the copyright has expired. Copyright lasts for specified terms; determination of the applicable term depends on several factors, such as whether the work has been published, and if, so, the date of first publication. Copyright

---

46. 17 U.S.C. § 106.

47. 17 U.S.C. § 102(b).

48. *Feist Publications, Inc. v. Rural Tel. Serv. Co.*, 499 U.S. 340, 347 (1991).

49. *Id.* at 350–51.

50. 17 U.S.C. § 105.

51. 17 U.S.C. §101.

52. *See Harper & Row Publishers, Inc. v. Nation Enters.*, 471 U.S. 539 (1985) (ruling on a copyright infringement claim arising from publication of portions of memoirs by former President Gerald Ford).

53. 17 U.S.C. § 105.

statutes have been amended over time, creating permutations for determining whether a work's copyright has expired and thus is now in the public domain. Currently, publication is not the determinant for federal copyright protection as was the case under a prior statute, the Copyright Act of 1909, but publication determines the duration of copyright protection for anonymous and pseudonymous works and works-made-for-hire and can implicate other aspects of copyright law. There are some general guidelines (*see* Fig. 2), but various factors, such as whether the work is of foreign origin, may affect a work's copyright status.

Figure 2

Applicable Date	Attachment of Protection	Duration of Protection
before 1923	none	in the public domain
published or registered between January 1, 1923 and December 31, 1963	upon publication with notice	28 years plus 67 years if renewed before the end of the first term
published between January 1, 1964 and December 31, 1977	upon publication with notice	28 years plus automatic renewal for 67 years
created before January 1, 1978 but never published or registered before January 1, 1978	January 1, 1978	the greater of life plus 70 years or December 31, 2002; for works published on or before December 31, 2002 no expiration before December 31, 2047
created on or after January 1, 1978	upon creation	life plus 70 years • if anonymous or pseudonymous, or a work-made-for-hire, the shorter of 95 years from publication or 120 years from creation • if a joint work, measured by the life of the longest lived author

Copyright rights may be transferred by the owner through a conveyance, by assignment, by operation of law (such as through a bankruptcy sale), or bequeathed by will.[54] Transfers may be on an exclusive or a non-exclusive basis; the former can be conveyed only through a writing describing the transfer and signed by the copyright owner or his authorized agent unless the transfer occurs by operation of law. Not only may a non-exclusive license be granted orally, it may be implied from conduct that evidences intent to grant permission for a license. Note that a non-exclusive licensee cannot transfer his license or grant a sub-license unless he has the licensor's permission.

54. 17 U.S.C. §201(d)(1)–(2).

Therefore, you'll want to review uses on a case-by-case basis and consider consulting with the school's counsel or a copyright specialist. In addition, the U.S. Copyright Office's web-site[55] is highly informative. Illustrative of the fact that the site's "Frequently Asked Questions About Copyright" most assuredly is based on empirical review of questions in fact often received by the Office is the query, "How do I protect my sighting of Elvis?" (The answer: "Copyright law does not protect sightings. However, copyright law will protect your photo (or other depiction) of your sighting of Elvis. Just send it to us with a Form VA application and the $30 filing fee. No one can lawfully use your photo of your sighting, although someone else may file his own photo of his sighting. Copyright law protects the original photograph, not the subject of the photograph.")[56] Another helpful resource is the treatise by Intellectual Property specialists Bruce Keller and Jeffrey Cunard, entitled *Copyright Law: A Practitioner's Guide,* which includes "decision trees" relating to the duration and termination of copyright rights.[57]

You can investigate whether a work is subject to copyright protection and the salient facts relating to any such copyright in order to ascertain the person or entity from whom you must secure permission. Examine a copy of the work to search for a copyright notice, date and place of publication, name of author, and identity of publisher. Information relating to copyright ownership also is available through the copyright databases of Westlaw and Lexis-Nexis. Additionally, you can search the Copyright Office's catalogs and records or, for a fee, request that the Copyright Office undertake a search for you. Commercial search organizations also can perform searches for a fee. Although the results of these efforts may not be conclusive, they often lead to useful information. Note that simply acknowledging or attributing the source of copyrighted material does not satisfy any applicable requirement that permission be secured from the copyright holder.

Does the contemplated use constitute an infringement? If you've determined that a work in fact is subject to copyright protection, and your contemplated use is of protectible elements, the next step is to consider whether such use would constitute an infringement.

Is the contemplated use a "fair use"? The fair use doctrine is codified in the Copyright Act[58] in order to balance the need to protect the author's interest

---

55. *See* <www.copyright.gov>.

56. Library of Congress, U.S. Copyright Office, *Frequently Asked Questions About Copyright, at* <http://www.copyright/gov/help/faq/faq-protect.html>.

57. Bruce P. Keller and Jeffrey P. Cunard, *Copyright Law: A Practitioner's Guide,* 7–35, 7–36 (Practising Law Institute 2002).

58. 17 U.S.C. § 107.

in his work with the public's interest in promoting robust discourse. Thus, limited amounts of a protected work may be used without the copyright holder's permission for certain purposes, such as criticism, comment, news reporting, teaching, scholarship, and research.

There is no bright-line test for determining when a use qualifies as "fair." The task, "like the doctrine it recognizes, calls for case-by-case analysis."[59] Courts are statutorily directed to consider four non-exclusive factors in evaluating the use:

(1) the purpose and character of the use, including whether such use is of a commercial nature or is for non-profit educational purposes;
(2) the nature of the copyrighted work;
(3) the amount and substantiality of the portion used in relation to the copyrighted work as a whole; and
(4) the effect of the use upon the potential market for or value of the copyrighted work.[60]

All four factors "are to be explored, and the results weighed together, in light of the purposes of copyright."[61] Nor are the factors the exclusive determinants of the fair use inquiry. Rather, they are designed to provide guidance to courts as they undertake fact-specific inquiries in each case; "[s]ince the doctrine is an equitable rule of reason, no generally applicable definition is possible, and each case raising the question must be decided on its own facts."[62] The statute expressly states that the fact that a work is unpublished does not alone bar a finding of fair use.[63] Note that the statutory preamble expressly cites as illustrations such purposes as criticism, comment, news reporting, teaching, scholarship, and research, which are typical uses by professors in an academic environment. Therefore, it may be permissible to quote an excerpt in a review or criticism for purposes of illustration or comment or in a scholarly or technical work; to use in a parody some of the content of the work parodied; or for a teacher or student to reproduce a brief portion of a work to illustrate a lesson.

Is the use permissible as classroom copying? The legislative history of the Copyright Act of 1976 establishes Congressionally-endorsed guidelines relating to classroom copying in not-for-profit educational institutions with re-

---

59. *Campbell v. Acuff-Rose Music, Inc.*, 510 U.S. 569, 577 (1994) (citations omitted).

60. 17 U.S.C. § 107.

61. *Campbell v. Acuff-Rose Music, Inc.*, 510 U.S. at 578.

62. United States Copyright Office, Circular 21, *Reproduction of Copyrighted Works By Educators and Librarians* at 6, *available at* <http://www.copyright.gov/circs/circ21.pdf>.

63. *See* 17 U.S.C. § 107.

spect to books and periodicals.[64] For example, a single copy of a chapter from a book; a newspaper or periodical article; a short story or short poem; or a chart or graph from a book, periodical, or newspaper may be made by or for a teacher upon request for his scholarly research or for use in teaching or preparing to teach.[65] The guidelines contemplate that multiple copies of up to one copy per student may be made for classroom use or discussion, so long as the copying satisfies standards of "brevity" and "spontaneity," is not cumulative, and includes a copyright notice.[66]

The brevity guideline for a complete article or essay is fewer than 2,500 words or an excerpt from prose of the lesser of not more than 1,000 words or ten percent of the work (which is a minimum of 500 words); for a complete poem is fewer than 250 words printed on not more than two pages or of no more than a 250-word excerpt from a longer poem; or, with respect to illustrations, one chart or drawing per book or per periodical issue.[67] The spontaneity guideline is satisfied if the copying is at the instance and inspiration of the individual teacher and the decision to use the work and the timing of its use for maximum teaching effectiveness are so close in time that it would not be reasonable to expect a timely reply to a request for permission.[68] The copying also must not be cumulative, meaning that the material is for only one course in the school in which the copies are made, guidelines are respected as to the number of works by the same author that are copied, and there are no more than nine instances of multiple copying for one course during one class term.[69]

Notwithstanding all this, copying cannot be used to create or replace anthologies or collective works.[70] Nor may "consumable" works be copied; such works are exemplified by workbooks and standardized test booklets.[71] Further, copying cannot substitute for the purchase of books, be directed by "higher

---

64. Agreement on Guidelines for Classroom Copying in Not-For-Profit Educational Institutions With Respect to Books and Periodicals, U.S. Copyright Office, Circular 21, *Reproduction of Copyrighted Works By Educators and Librarians, available at* <http://www.copyright.gov/circs/circ21.pdf>; *see also* <http://www.publishers/org/conference/pubinfo.cfm?PublicationID=3>.

65. *Id.* at §I.

66. *Id.* at §II.

67. *Id.* at §II, Definitions, Brevity, (i)–(iii).

68. *Id.* at §II, Definitions, Spontaneity, (i)–(ii).

69. *Id.* at §II, Definitions, Cumulative Effect, (i)–(iii).

70. *Id.* at §III(A).

71. *Id.* at §III(B).

authority," or be repeated with respect to the same item by the same teacher from term to term.[72] Only actual photocopying costs may be charged to the students.[73]

Representatives of the Association of American Law Schools and the American Association of University Professors criticized the guidelines, particularly insofar as they addressed multiple copying. The groups deemed the guidelines unduly restrictive with respect to classroom situations at the university and graduate levels.[74] The guidelines represent a negotiated consensus amongst groups of interested parties and are designed " 'to state the minimum and not the maximum standards of educational fair use.' "[75] The agreement relating to the guidelines acknowledges that there may be instances in which copying may be permissible as a fair use even if not in accordance with the guidelines.[76]

Is the use through digital technologies for mediated instruction? The Copyright Act of 1976 includes an exclusive right to perform and display the work publicly.[77] The relatively expansive copyright protections were mitigated by exemptions relating, amongst others, to face-to-face teaching activities, certain instructional broadcasting of a performance of a non-dramatic literary or musical work, and transmissions directed to the visually or aurally impaired.[78]

In 2002, President George W. Bush signed into law the Technology, Education and Copyright Harmonization Act, commonly known by its acronym, the "TEACH Act."[79] The TEACH Act expands coverage of the Copyright Act's extant expemtion[80] to allow the delivery of authorized performances and displays by non-profit accredited educational institutions through digital technologies. The Act "limits the amount that may be used in these additional categories to 'reasonable and limited portions' and emphasizes the concept of 'mediated instruction' to ensure that the exemption

---

72. *Id.* at § III(C).

73. *Id.* at § III(D).

74. *See id.*, Discussion of Guidelines, at 9–10.

75. *See* Agreement on Guidelines for Classroom Copying in Not-For-Profit Educational Institutions With Respect to Books and Periodicals, U.S. Copyright Office, Circular 21, *Reproduction of Copyrighted Works By Educators and Librarians, available at* 10 (quoting Ad Hoc Committee on Copyright Law Revision), *available at* <http://www.copyright.gov/circs/circ21.pdf>.

76. *See id.*

77. 17 U.S.C. §§ 101, 106(4), (5).

78. *See* 17 U.S.C. §§ 110(1), (2), (8).

79. Pub. L. No. 207–273, 116 Stat. 1758 (Nov. 2, 2002).

80. 17 U.S.C. § 110(2).

is limited to what is, as much as possible, equivalent to a live classroom setting."[81] The requirement of "mediated instructional activities" generally requires the supervision of an instructor and use as an integral part of the class experience that is analogous to the type of display that typically takes place in a live classroom setting and directly relates to and materially assists the teaching content.[82]

The law seeks to accommodate developments in distance education while preserving protections accorded to copyright holders. For example, the Act contains safeguards to limit special risks to rightsholders attendant to the use of works in digital format by requiring the application of technological measures to reasonably constrain unauthorized access, retention, and dissemination.[83] Thus the statute prohibits transmitting institutions from engaging in conduct that reasonably could be expected to interfere with technological measures used by copyright holders to regulate the retention and further unauthorized dissemination of protected works.[84] The institution must implement policies regarding copyright and compliance and make such information available to both faculty and students.[85]

Can you secure permission? If you conclude that you must secure permission to use rights enforceable by another, you can contact the publisher of the work if one exists, the author of the work, or utilize a copyright licensing service. The Copyright Clearance Center ("CCC")[86] provides such services and it's possible that an academic institution has worked out an annual licensing arrangement or that you can clear rights to duplicate works on a transactional basis. Another entity, the Harry Fox Agency, administers mechanical and synchronization licenses for publishers to whom the organization has been assigned copyright rights.[87] Performing rights societies, known as ASCAP, BMI, and SESAC, license performance rights to musical works of its members, either as a blanket license or as a per-program license for a single performance.[88] The Motion Picture Licensing Corporation ("MPLC") is authorized by the

---

81. *Regulatory Activities, Policy Assistance, and Litigation,* Copyright Office Regulations, Distance Education, *available at* <http://www.copyright.gov>.

82. 17 U.S.C. § 110(2), *see also id.* at §§ (A), (B).

83. 17 U.S.C. §§ 110(2)(C), (D)(ii)(I)(aa), (bb).

84. 17 U.S.C. § 110(2)(D)(ii)(II).

85. 17 U.S.C. § 110(2)(D)(i).

86. *See* The Copyright Clearance Center, *at* <http://www.copyright.com>.

87. *See* Harry Fox Agency, *at* <http://www.nmpa.org/hfa.html>.

88. *See* ASCAP, *at* <http://www.ascap.com>; BMI, *at* <http://www.bmi.com>; SESAC, *at* <http://www.sesac.com>.

major motion picture studios to grant umbrella licenses for public performances of videocassettes and videodiscs.[89]

When requesting permission, it's helpful to first consult with your school's legal and faculty support personnel, as they may be able to guide you as to umbrella arrangements made by the school and whether your use will come within licenses previously secured. Even if your contemplated use is not authorized under such a license and even though you've determined that it has not come within fair use guidelines, it can be beneficial to indicate when you're requesting permission that your use is primarily designed for educational, rather than for commercial, purposes. Educational uses may incur lower fees if charges are imposed.

Does an electronic use implicate other legal issues? Other aspects of intellectual property law may come into play. If you're contemplating creation of a Web-based text, on-line tutorial, faculty web-site, or the like, you'll want to consider issues relating to the acquisition and modification of the content and the use of special Internet-related technologies such as linking, framing, metatags, and domain names.

The Digital Millennium Copyright Act ("DMCA")[90] amends copyright law with respect to the Internet. Amongst the provisions of the DMCA relevant to authors of legal texts is the protection granted to copyright holders who use technological measures to control protected works. The statute prohibits, subject to exception, the circumvention of measures that control access to a work.[91] The DMCA also prohibits the alteration or removal of "copyright management information" with the knowledge that doing so will conceal such information or lead to infringement of a copyright. Copyright management information refers to information that identifies the work; the author, owner, or performer; and the terms and conditions for the use of a work.[92] Thus it is important to be mindful of the ways in which you gain access to and modify digital works that are subject to copyright protection.

Other laws may be relevant if you're planning to deploy linking technologies. Although hyperlinking generally does not implicate a violation of the exclusive rights of the copyright holder in an openly-accessible linked-to site, other types of related technologies may implicate intellectual property rights. "In-line links" bring an image contained in a separate file within the text and

---

89. *See* Motion Picture Licensing Corporation, *at* <http://www.mplc.com>.

90. 17 U.S.C. §§512, 1201–05, 1301–22 and 24 U.S.C. §4001.

91. *See* 17 U.S.C. §1201.

92. 17 U.S.C. §1202.

onto the page the user is viewing. The user typically is not automatically alerted that the image or text called up by the in-line link resides on a separate site. Like in-line links, "framing" technology brings content from one web-site within another, but the framed content appears in a window on the original framing site, allowing two or more web-sites to appear simultaneously on the user's screen. Such technologies may give rise to claims for commercial misappropriation, copyright infringement, or trademark dilution and infringement.[93]

"Deep linking" refers to the practice in which one links to a Web page within a web-site other than the latter site's home page. Peter Hook recommends that "a tutorial creator first get the permission of each private vendor before 'deep linking' to a particular page within a vendor's site."[94] It may be problematic to deep link when you're bypassing password protections or evading other technological controls; otherwise, as a general matter, it's conventional to rely on an implied license to deep link. Information Technology specialists Jeffrey Neuburger and Richard Raysman point out that deep linking in commercial settings have given rise to issues under copyright law but "[a]s a general rule, materials published on the Web may be viewed by all Internet users unless affirmative steps are taken to limit access. As a result, websites are widely linked without prior consent from website owners."[95]

"Metatags" are bits of embedded data that are not visible to the end user, but allow description of web-sites so that search engines can retrieve the site in response to the user's inquiry. Some sites use keyword metatags to achieve favorable positioning in the indices produced by search engines and thereby encourage traffic to their sites. Legal disputes have arisen notably in the context of the use of metatags that consist of trademarks held by another. Although titles, names, short phrases, slogans, and familiar symbols and designs are not subject to copyright protection, trademark law be implicated. The U.S. Patent and Trademark Office has a helpful site that may be of assistance.[96]

---

93. *See, e.g., Bernstein v. JC Penney, Inc.*, 50 U.S.P.Q. 2d 1063 (C.D. Cal. 1998); *Futuredontics, Inc. v. Applied Anagramics, Inc.*, 45 U.S.P.Q.2d 2005 (C.D. Cal. 1997), *aff'd*, No. 97–56711, 1998 U.S. App. LEXIS 17012 (9th Cir. July 23, 1998), *aff'd*, No. 98–55801, 1999 U.S. App. LEXIS 26257 (9th Cir. Oct. 14, 1999); *see also Washington Post v. Total News, Inc.*, 97 Civ. 1190 (PKL) (S.D.N.Y. complaint filed Feb. 20, 1997).

94. Peter A. Hook, *Creating an Online Tutorial and Pathfinder*, 94 Law Libr. J. 243, 257 (2002).

95. Jeffrey D. Neuburger and Richard Raysman, "Internet Law," Carole Basri and Irving Kagan, eds. *Corporate Legal Departments*, App. 9 at A9–12–A9–13 (3d ed. 2003).

96. *See* <http://www.uspto.gov/>.

If you're creating a web-site, as opposed to adding a Web page to an existing site operated by your school, you'll also want to consider issues relating to domain names. Information about domain name registration can be accessed by contacting an accredited registrar of the Internet Corporation for Assigned Names and Numbers, commonly known as "ICANN." ICANN is a not-for-profit organization that manages a domain name system for generic top-level domains ("gTLDs") and administers the assignation of domain names.[97]

Use of Your Work By Others

Although currently you need not register your work in order to secure a copyright, timely registration affords special protections, such as satisfaction of the condition precedent to initiation of an infringement suit for U.S. works, *prima facie* evidence of the validity of the copyright and the facts set forth in the certificate, and the ability to pursue a claim for statutory damages and attorney's fees. Copyright registration is a legal formality that makes a public record of facts attendant to the copyright in a particular work.

Only the author or those who derived their rights through the author can rightfully assert a claim to copyright. Simply because another owns a copy of a book you wrote or is the person to whom you wrote a letter does not render him the copyright holder; the transfer of ownership of the copy does not itself convey copyright rights.

Whether you are the appropriate person from whom another must seek permission to use material depends not only on whether the proposed use would constitute an infringement (*see supra* at 66), but also on whether you transferred your rights to another. Work done within the scope of your employment or commissioned in a signed writing may belong to another as a "work-made-for-hire." Specifically, the Copyright Act defines a "work-made-for-hire" as either a work prepared by an employee within the scope of his employment or a work specially ordered or commissioned for use as a contribution to a collective work, as part of a motion picture or other audio-visual work, as a translation, as a supplementary work, as a compilation, as an instructional text, as a test, as answer material for a test, or as an atlas, if the parties expressly agree in a written and signed instrument that the work is to be considered a work-made-for-hire.[98]

---

97. *See* <http://www.icann.org/>.

98. *See* 17 U.S.C. § 101. A "supplementary work" is one prepared for publication as a secondary adjunct to a work by another author in order to introduce, conclude, illustrate, explain, revise, comment on, or assist in the use of the other work. Illustrations of supplementary works include forewords, afterwords, pictorial illustrations, maps, charts, ta-

Notwithstanding that professors technically may be employees of the educational institution for whom they work, the rights to academic writings generally rest with the professor. This common law rule is sometimes referred to as the "teachers' exception." Although the Copyright Act of 1976 does not address the matter in its legislative history, many universities contractually or as a matter of policy exclude writings by professors as works made for hire. Keller and Cunard state that the "long common-law tradition...has been carried forward under the 1976 [Copyright] Act, hold[ing] that the copyright in academic writings belongs to the professor."[99] Rationales for "this seemingly anomalous result" include the lack of supervision by the academic institution of faculty in their preparation of academic writings, questionable resources to exploit such writings, and the relative mobility of many professors that would encumber clearance of rights for lectures or the subsequent preparation of a book or other work derived from notes.[100]

It's possible, however, that you assigned the rights to your work to another, on an exclusive or non-exclusive basis, or, as is the case with certain scholarly journals, transferred a right of first publication. In such events, you'll want to review agreements (including employment agreements) you've entered into to determine whether it's appropriate to refer the individual who is requesting to use the material to another person or entity.

If you collaborated with another as a joint author, you each own an undivided interest as a tenant-in-common of the completed copyrighted work. A "joint work" is one prepared by two or more authors who intend their contributions to be merged into inseparable or inter-dependent parts of a unitary whole.[101] Therefore, you each have an independent right to use or license the copyright without the permission of the other, subject to an obligation to account to the other author for any profits.

Defamation and Privacy Issues

You'll want to be aware of other potential legal issues as you make statements about others and if you prepare textual material for distribution. Defamation is a tort that addresses damage to reputational interests. The defamatory statement may be oral, in which case the claim is denoted a "slan-

---

bles, editorial notes, musical arrangements, answer material for tests, bibliographies, appendices, and indices. *See id.*

99. Bruce P. Keller and Jeffrey P. Cunard, *Copyright Law: A Practitioner's Guide,* §3.2.3[A][2] at 3–17 (Practising Law Institute 2002).

100. *Id.*

101. 17 U.S.C. § 101.

der," or it may be written, in which case the claim is denoted a "libel." In general, a defamation is a communication to a third party that tends to hold the plaintiff up to hatred, contempt, or aversion, or to cause him to be shunned or avoided. A communication is defamatory if it tends to so harm the reputation of another as to induce an evil or unsavory opinion of him in the community.[102]

The Restatement (Second) of Torts lists the elements of an action for defamation as (1) a false and defamatory statement concerning another; (2) an unprivileged publication to a third party; (3) fault amounting at least to negligence on the part of the publisher; and (4) either actionability of the statement irrespective of special harm or the existence of special harm caused by the publication.[103] First Amendment expert Judge Robert Sack characterizes this list of enumerated elements as "deceptively simple."[104] Application of these elements to each case's salient facts requires the integration of an extensive body of caselaw with an impressive constitutional gloss.

While naturally you'll strive to create accurate works and presentations, from a legal standpoint, you'll want to be especially mindful of statements that attribute criminal conduct, unethical behavior, financial or professional irresponsibility, or other negative attributes to living persons to be sure that they are accurate or based on reasonable research for accuracy. If you indicate that someone has been convicted of a crime, for example, it's helpful to point out that the conviction was reversed on appeal. Note that omitting the subject's name doesn't necessarily preclude a finding of liability; third parties may recognize him from other details in the work that identify him.

With respect to common law invasion of privacy, there are four types of torts. While all four torts use the lexicon of "invasion of privacy," they are founded upon disparate legal doctrines and theories. As is the case with defamation claims, state law varies with respect to privacy torts; the following are general principles.

One of these claims is the "false light" invasion of privacy claim. The gravamen of this cause of action is that the claimant has been placed in a "false light;" that is, in a manner that would be highly offensive to a reasonable person or a person of ordinary sensibilities. The tort is closely analogous to defamation, but is designed to redress false speech that injures feelings rather than damage to reputation. Thus, the statement in issue need not necessarily be defamatory in order

---

102. *See generally* Restatement (Second) of Torts, §559, cmt. e (1997).

103. Restatement (Second) of Torts, §558 (1997).

104. Robert D. Sack, *Sack on Defamation: Libel, Slander, and Related Problems* §2.1.1 (3d ed. 1999).

to be actionable but nonetheless must be "offensive." Elements of false light claims include publication of the statement in issue; a statement that is "of and concerning" the plaintiff (i.e., about the plaintiff); a statement that is substantially false; and a showing that the defendant acted with the requisite degree of fault.

Another invasion of privacy claim arises from the publication of highly embarrassing private facts. Unlike a defamation claim, a claim grounded in publication of private embarrassing facts is premised on the unauthorized revelation of *true* information about a living person. If such facts have not been made public previously and would be highly offensive to a reasonable person, they can give rise to a claim unless their disclosure is of legitimate concern to the public.

The tort of misappropriation is premised upon a showing that one has appropriated to his own use or benefit the name or likeness of another.[105] The tort most frequently is asserted to protect from appropriation the valuable property right in names and likenesses. This right often has been blurred with references to a "right of publicity," which signifies a property right in the value of an individual's personality. The claims typically are inapposite in the educational context when the use is not for commercial or advertising purposes.

The final common law invasion of privacy claim is known as an "intrusion on seclusion" claim. Intrusion claims are predicated on an allegation that the plaintiff's right to seclusion has been transgressed. An intrusion claim is the only invasion of privacy tort that arises in the context of gathering, rather than disseminating, information. Generally, intrusion claims have not been advanced in the context of scholarly research and writing as such endeavors typically depend for their sources on legal databases, openly available web-sites, and published textual material.

Professional Ethics and Professional Responsibility Issues

As a lawyer engaged in academic endeavors, you still are subject to the canons of professional ethics operative in the relevant jurisdictions. It's important to remember that you're not only working to comply with professional norms and the regulations and policies of the institution by whom you are employed, but also that you are serving as a role model for your students. "[T]he law school experience provides the student's first exposure to the profession and...professors inevitably serve as important role models for stu-

105. *See generally* Restatement (Second) of Torts, §652C (1977).

dents;" accordingly, the American Bar Association's Commission on Professionalism states that "the highest standards of ethics and professionalism should be adhered to within law schools."[106]

Note that privileged matters are not insulated from waiver simply because you're disclosing a confidential client communication in order to further your students' education. You'll want to respect the confidentiality of privileged and proprietary information that you have not been authorized to disclose. Lawyers who are representing or have represented clients are ethically-bound to maintain certain confidences. Members of the judiciary who are engaged in teaching activities are constrained from discussing pending cases over which they're presiding.

As one acting in a lawful and moral fashion, you'll also want to avoid engaging in discriminatory conduct based on such factors as race, religion, national origin, gender, sexual orientation, disability, or age. Divergent political beliefs are worthy of respect. You'll want to work to establish and foster a hospitable and tolerant academic environment that eschews prejudice.

Such sensitivity should extend to efforts to promote access to scholarly resources. For instance, you can confer with your school's Information Technology department and Library services personnel to inquire about on-line information retrieval systems accessible to those who are visually impaired. In 1997, Congress amended the Copyright Act to allow certain not-for-profit organizations and governmental organizations to reproduce or distribute copies or phonorecords of previously published, non-dramatic literary works in Braille or other specialized formats that accommodate blind persons or persons with other disabilities.[107] (The exemption requires, amongst other things, a notice that reproduction or distribution in other formats constitutes an infringement and does not apply to tests or to computer programs.[108]) You might also consult the Web Accessibility Initiative, an organization that, in coordination with international organizations, pursues accessibility of the Web through technology, guidelines, tools, education and outreach, and research and development.[109]

As a professor, you are in a superior hierarchical position relative to your pupils and must not sexually harass students by, for example, inducing a stu-

---

106. American Bar Association, Commission on Professionalism, *In the Spirit of Public Service: A Blueprint for the Rekindling of Lawyer Professionalism* 19 (1986) ("The Stanley Report"), *available at* <http://www.abanet.org/cpr/pubs/561-0081.html>.

107. 17 U.S.C. § 121(a).

108. *See* 17 U.S.C. § 121(b)(1)(B), (b)(2).

109. *See* <http://www.w3.org/WAI/>.

dent to enter into an unwanted sexual relationship. The AALS Statement of Good Practices by Law Professors in the Discharge of Their Ethical and Professional Responsibilities advises that sexual relationships between a professor and a student who are not married to one another or are not in a pre-existing analogous relationship are not appropriate if the professor is charged with furthering the student's education or is

> otherwise evaluating, supervising, or advising a student as part of a school program. Even when a professor has no professional responsibility for a student, the professor should be sensitive to the perceptions of other students that a student who has a sexual relationship with a professor may receive preferential treatment from the professor or the professor's colleagues. A professor who is closely related to a student by blood or marriage, or who has a preexisting analogous relationship with a student, normally should eschew roles involving a professional responsibility for the student.[110]

Likewise, senior faculty should be mindful of their position relative to their other colleagues. Robust intellectual exchanges are to be encouraged, but not at the expense of pressure to capitulate to a point in order to avoid adverse personnel ramifications. As a general matter, you can work as a model from which your colleagues and students may emulate civility, avoiding acrimonious conflict as a means of generating intellectual discourse. As William Shakespeare said in *The Taming of the Shrew*, adversaries in law "strive mightily, but eat and drink as friends."[111]

You'll also want to preserve the integrity of your contributions to legal scholarship by disclosing potential conflicts of interest and placing others in a position to assess your work impartially. If your paper was sponsored by an industry group, for example, or you were compensated for your work, indicate that fact to the reader if it's not otherwise readily apparent. If you have been advocating a specific legal position in the course of representing a client, it may be appropriate to so disclose. Similarly, you may need to expressly indicate that you are speaking on behalf of yourself and not the school by whom you are employed or any firm, company, or other entity with which you are affiliated.

---

110. American Association of Law Schools, *Statement of Good Practices by Law Professors in the Discharge of Their Ethical and Professional Responsibilities, available at* <http://www.aals.org/ethic.html>.

111. William Shakespeare, *The Taming of the Shrew*, act I, scene 2.

Course Requirements

As you formulate your courses, you'll need to consider the nature and scope of their requirements. There almost assuredly will be a slate of reading assignments that you'll specify students must complete for each course. In addition, you'll need to enumerate the requirements for grading purposes. One or more of your course requirements may be mandated by the school, particularly in required courses in order to standardize the expectations amongst the student body. Course requirements typically include one or more of the following: a mid-term and final examination or a final examination; a paper; presentation of a paper; class attendance; and/or class participation. It's important to explicitly advise students of the course requirements during the first session of the class. This affords an important opportunity, at least for upperclassmen who have some discretion as to the courses they may select, to assess the extent of their workload relative to the balance of their other electives.

Written Requirements

Written submissions provide a critical evaluative instrument. Such tasks demand foundational substantive knowledge and effective articulation of the application of legal doctrine to factual situations. There are a number of options available (*see* Fig. 3).

Examinations

Law school final and midterm exams sometimes consist, at least in part, of multiple choice or short-answer questions. Typically at least a significant portion of the exam is comprised of essay questions. Certain courses may be more conducive to an exam that consists exclusively of essay questions. (With respect to the crafting and grading of examinations, *see infra* at 195, 200.)

Final exams generally are administered over a three-hour period for a three or more credit course, and over a two-hour period for shorter courses. You'll want to check your school's guidelines. If you want your exam to be of a different duration than the school's routine practice, you may need to coordinate with your school's registrar before the semester even begins.

Papers

Requirements for papers likely will vary, and you should clarify whether you prefer a particular format, whether external legal research is expected (as opposed to reliance exclusively on the assigned readings), and other require-

Figure 3

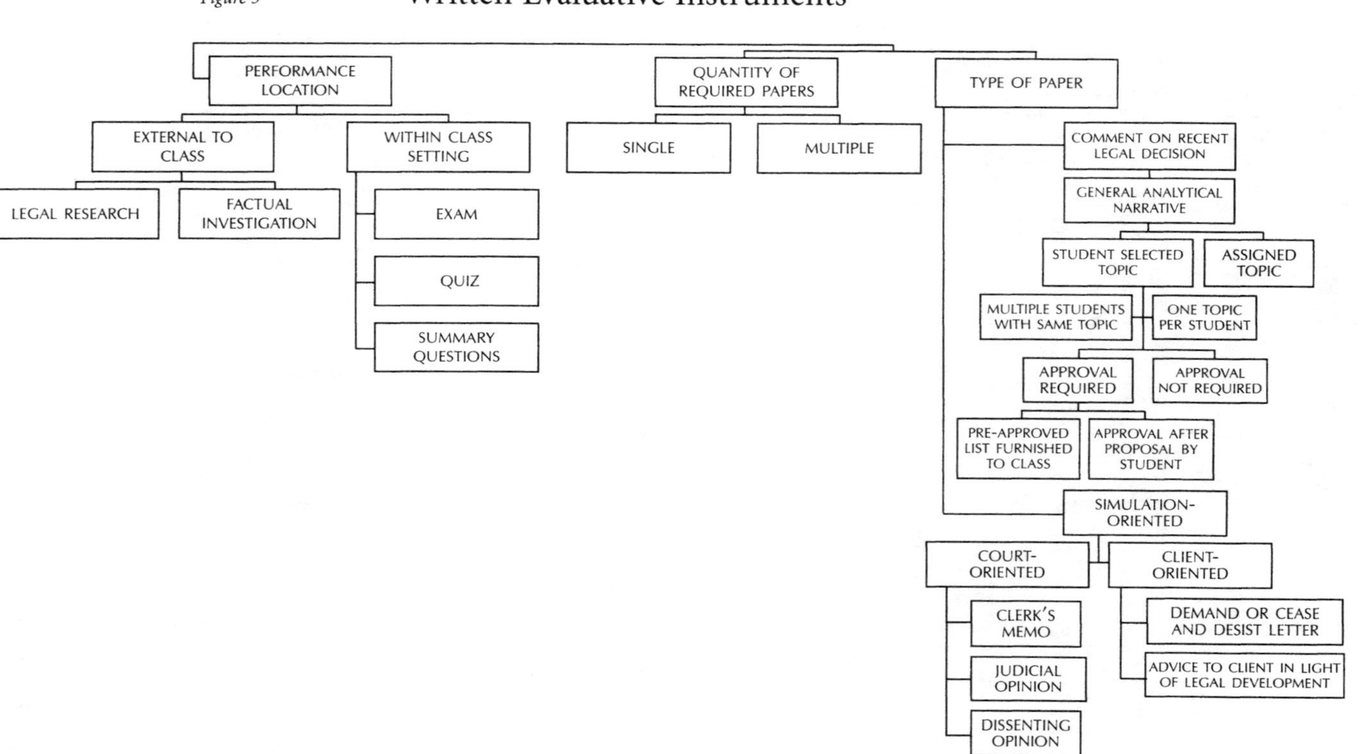
Written Evaluative Instruments
PERFORMANCE LOCATION
EXTERNAL TO CLASS
LEGAL RESEARCH
FACTUAL INVESTIGATION
WITHIN CLASS SETTING
EXAM
QUIZ
SUMMARY QUESTIONS
QUANTITY OF REQUIRED PAPERS
SINGLE
MULTIPLE
TYPE OF PAPER
COMMENT ON RECENT LEGAL DECISION
GENERAL ANALYTICAL NARRATIVE
STUDENT SELECTED TOPIC
ASSIGNED TOPIC
MULTIPLE STUDENTS WITH SAME TOPIC
ONE TOPIC PER STUDENT
APPROVAL REQUIRED
APPROVAL NOT REQUIRED
PRE-APPROVED LIST FURNISHED TO CLASS
APPROVAL AFTER PROPOSAL BY STUDENT
SIMULATION-ORIENTED
COURT-ORIENTED
CLERK'S MEMO
JUDICIAL OPINION
DISSENTING OPINION
CLIENT-ORIENTED
DEMAND OR CEASE AND DESIST LETTER
ADVICE TO CLIENT IN LIGHT OF LEGAL DEVELOPMENT

ments (*see infra* at 202). It's often helpful to suggest a page limit as a guideline. It can be quite disconcerting for a pupil to wonder whether his classmates are submitting three-page or 30-page papers. Papers submitted in satisfaction of the course's requirement should be original work that has not been previously submitted to another course, journal, or the like; nor may the paper satisfy requirements of a course the student is taking contemporaneously. Graduate students may be required to write a thesis that is distinguishable from other writings by the student; thus, generally neither a thesis nor portions of its contents may be used to satisfy a writing requirement of another course.

Your school likely has established policies regarding the last date of the semester on which papers may be submitted. Before you agree to a request to extend the due date, check your school's policies. Note that extending the due date will afford you less time to grade the paper.

If a paper is assigned, rather than a uniform final examination hypothetical or series of hypotheticals, the professor probably will be asked to suggest paper topics and should advise the class members whether they are required to have their topics approved. Professors may wish to consult, and contribute possible topics and refer students to, Lawtopic.org,[112] a site described as "A Clearinghouse for Legal Paper Topics" that categorically lists topics for legal papers according to subject matter.

The Writing Requirement: The professor who assigns a paper as either a course requirement or as an optional submission (e.g., in lieu of a final exam at the student's election) likely will be asked by students whether the paper may be used to satisfy the school's writing requirement. Many schools require that students participate in a program of supervised writing after they complete the first year curriculum. Check your school's requirements regarding writing requirements. Such projects typically involve significant research and writing under faculty supervision, based on a topic approved by a faculty member after the latter's review of an outline and rough draft. The final paper usually is required to demonstrate significant research and original analysis. The school may impose a required minimum page length. Special requirements may apply to writing projects that are undertaken in connection with specific courses or seminars.

Law Journal Submissions: Students also may inquire as to whether it's permissible for them to use the paper as the basis for publication in one of the law school's journals. Some schools allow students to subsequently submit a paper to a student law journal for publication at the discretion of the professor. Again, it's important to check your school's policies to make sure you're compliant.

---

112. *See* <http://www.lawtopic.org>.

Independent Study: Students may be able to engage in independent research under the supervision of a faculty member. Your school likely has policies regarding the minimum requirements students must satisfy to be eligible for credit. Independent study projects typically are arranged by consultation between the student and the individual faculty member and in coordination with the school's registrar.

Class Contribution

Attendance

Under certain rules governing admission to the bar, the law school must certify that bar applicants were in "good and regular attendance," and took and successfully completed the prescribed course of instruction required at the school for the law degree. A student may be subject to dismissal when his attendance becomes so erratic that the faculty deems it a bar to certification of the required "good and regular attendance" standard or considers it otherwise unwise to permit the student to continue.

Factoring in class attendance in students' grades is important for another reason. It helps motivate students to attend class, which in turn provides a larger pool of students to stimulate dialogue, respond to questions posed by the professor, and ask questions from which the professor may draw meaningful inferences about the students' level of comprehension of the material covered. When questions are asked of the professor, there is an opportunity to identify areas that generated confusion. As well, questions and class discussion reveal areas of particular interest to students which, within logical parameters, may help the professor shape the course by emphasizing matters of special interest.

Professors may find it especially helpful to emphasize the importance of attendance in classes that require papers so that students are not tempted to choose a topic and then absent themselves from the class. Of course, no penalty should be imposed on any student who is absent from class because of religious observance, illness or injury, or a death in the family. If a student has not been attending class regularly, you may want to seek out the student to inquire as to whether he is experiencing some difficulty or contact the school's dean of student affairs to suggest that he establish contact (*see infra* at 245).

Logistically, you can take attendance by calling students' names from your class roster or seating chart. Or you can circulate or post a sign-in sheet on which students can note their presence. The latter option may be especially helpful for larger classes if calling out a number of names would usurp valuable class time.

Class Participation

For similar reasons, taking into account class participation encourages students to engage in class discussion. In addition, when students are expected to meaningfully participate, they may have a greater incentive to prepare for class. Some have opined that "[l]earning is enhanced when it is more like a team effort than a solo race.... Sharing one's own ideas and responding to others' reactions sharpen thinking and deepen understanding."[113]

Students who are a bit reserved may find the classroom a more comfortable forum in which to risk making oral contributions than they will find other situations, such as when as practitioners they will be asked to conduct meetings or argue in court. One way to encourage the class to experiment with efforts to articulate their thoughts in the class setting is by explaining that doing so will better prepare them for the times when they're required to speak to a group as a practicing lawyer.

It's helpful to deliberate before classes begin as to whether you'll solicit participation by calling on students and about your policy in the event they're unprepared to respond. You may be fortunate enough to rely nearly exclusively on voluntary participation, but even when the discussion flows quite well because the majority of the class is engaged, you'll want to elicit involvement from more reticent students. Controlling class participation helps equalize student involvement, mitigates dominance over the discussion by a few, and ensures that more reserved students aren't disengaged. Occasionally calling on those who don't generally volunteer may motivate more diligent preparation for class, lest students fear embarrassment or adverse impact on their grades if they're caught unprepared.

Some professors allow students to indicate before the class session begins that they're not prepared by submitting notes, sending e-mail messages, or so indicating on a sign-in sheet or seating chart. This promotes attendance because a pupil who hasn't finished the reading assignments can resist the temptation to miss class in order to avoid being called on but still feel that he won't be asked to recite facts or explain a principle that he's not yet fully

---

113. Arthur W. Chickering and Zelda F. Gamson, *Seven Principles for Good Practice in Undergraduate Education,* 39 American Association for Higher Education Bulletin, 3–7 (1987).

grasped. Furthermore, students who routinely prepare for class effectively are rewarded because they won't have notified the professor that they're not ready. The policy also accommodates the exceptional situation when a student has a legitimate reason for failing to complete the homework assigned and avoids a distorted impression if he were called on that he is routinely unprepared.

Assessment of a student's contributions should consider the degree to which the statements reflect a working knowledge of the assigned reading, whether the student listened attentively to his classmates or was merely reiterating previous contributions, and the degree to which the student's expression of his views evinces respect for classmates with whom he disagrees. The quality of the students' comments is far more significant than the frequency of participation. It's important, too, to explain this to the class when you delineate the course requirements at the outset of the semester so that class members don't mistakenly assume that the mere act of volunteering to contribute will enhance their grades irrespective of the content of their remarks.

Discussion Leaders

Of course, some students still are more inclined to volunteer than others. Sometimes a member of the class may, despite the professor's best efforts to enlist the entire group, monopolize the discourse or may inadvertently intimidate other students to feel that their contributions may not be as meaningful. One technique to promote parity amongst students, and to try to encourage students who might be a bit more reticent, is a "discussion leader" requirement. Under this approach, the entire class is encouraged to participate, but each student is assigned a particular day on which he, perhaps along with a few of his classmates, is designated a "discussion leader." On that day, the student is expected not only to attend the class and have completed all of the reading assignments, but also to make it a point to meaningfully contribute to the class dialogue. Discussion leaders might, for example, read a concurring or dissenting opinion that was not assigned with a majority court opinion, investigate the prior or subsequent history of a case, or research a related or contrary decision. A student may be more willing to volunteer to speak during the particular class session in which he is designated a discussion leader if he is permitted to choose a date that suits his schedule.

This technique was utilized in an inter-disciplinary course on public health that encompassed both public health and law students. The professor assigned one or two students with each type of background to be "'on-call experts'" each week, "responding to questions or initiating discussions in their respective forums."[114] The approach can therefore help bridge students' gaps in background knowledge.

I've used the discussion leader technique in Law of Internet Speech classes. Amongst other ways students can contribute is by identifying a web-site that reflects a relevant legal issue. This helps stimulate reflection about the actual, pragmatic application of principles to practice.

Making the students' grade dependent in part on class attendance, and possibly also on class participation and as a discussion leader, rewards the student who has demonstrated a diligent commitment to the course throughout the semester. In addition, it alleviates the pressure students feel to perform on a single evaluative session of a final exam, and avoids a potentially distorted perception of a grade based solely on a final examination.

Student Presentations

The professor also may require students to orally present their papers or the results of their legal research. Oral explanation of legal concepts can be considerably demanding, arguably requiring a more comprehensive grasp of the material than is the case when one has the luxury of writing, reflecting, and re-drafting.

Explicit guidelines are important. Students deserve to know in advance the amount of time allotted to their presentation so they can guide themselves accordingly. You, too, will want to allocate time equitably amongst all class members and reserve adequate time for your instruction through lecture and discussion. Indicate whether you expect the presenting student to field questions from you or his classmates. If the presentation is an oral explication of a written paper, emphasize that each student should present the highlights of his paper without reading directly from it. You might also try to encourage attentiveness to the students' classmates as they present by indicating that aspects of the presentations may be included on a final exam if one is to be administered.

If you have access to the necessary facilities and resources, you may want to videotape students' presentations. The results could be viewed independently by the individual student presenter. If more than one presentation is expected of the student during the course of the semester, videotaping both can offer an opportunity for the student to assess whether he has improved based on his prior experience and your subsequent constructive feedback.

---

114. Paula E. Berg, *Using Distance Learning to Enhance Cross-Listed Interdisciplinary Law School Courses*, 29 Rutgers Computer & Tech. L.J. 33, 40 (2003).

Selected Resources

Legal Publishers:

Aspen Law & Business
Aspen Publishers, Inc.
1185 Avenue of the Americas
New York, NY 10036
tel.: 800–950–5259
fax: 212–597–0335
web-site: <http://www.aspenpublishers.com>

Carolina Academic Press
700 Kent Street
Durham, NC 27701
tel.: 919–489–7486
fax: 919–493–5668
web-site: <www.cap-press.com>

Foundation Press
11 Penn Plaza
New York, NY 10001
tel.: 877–888–1330
fax: 212–367–6799
web-site: <http://www.fdpress.com/fdpress/facsupp.htm>

LexisNexis Matthew Bender
1275 Broadway
Albany, NY 12204
tel.: 800–533–1646
fax: 800–643–1280
web-site: <www.lexisnexis.com>

West Law School Publishing
610 Opperman Drive
Eagan, MN 55123
tel.: 800–313–9378
fax: 651–687–4464
web-site: <www.west.thomson.com>
information pertaining to custom publishing:
tel.: 800–328–9378, ext. 85893
fax: 651–687–4464

Course Materials and Computer Assisted Learning Resources:

AALS Sections
AALS National Office
tel.: (202) 296–8851
web-site: <http://www.aals.org/sections/index.html>

Ray August, *Delivering Lectures Over the Internet, at* <http://august1.com/lectures/HowTo/slides/home.htm>

The Center for Computer-Aided Legal Instruction
web-site: <http://www.cali.org>
Lesson Catalog: <http://lessons.cali.org>
CALI Topic Grids: <http://www.cali.org/fellows/grids/>
CALI Teachers Manuals: <http://www.cali.org/TeachersManuals/>

Corinne Cooper, *Getting Graphic 2*™, Institute for Law School Teaching, *at* <http://law.gonzaga.edu/ilst/PubsResources/getgraph.htm>

Michael A. Geist, *Developing a Law School Web Culture Through Online Law*, Jurist Legal Intelligence, Lessons From the Web, *at* <http://jurist.law.pitt.edu/lessons/lesmar99.htm>

Peter Hook, *Creating an Online Tutorial and Pathfinder*, 94 Law Libr. J. 243 (2002) (Appendix: Bibliography—Information Architecture and Web Usability)

Hot Potatoes Half-Baked Software
web-site: <http://web.uvic.ca/hrd/halfbaked>

Jurist Legal Intelligence, Law School Courses
web-site: <http://jurist.law.pitt.edu/cour_pgs.htm>

Justice Web Collaboratory
Chicago-Kent College of Law
Illinois Institute of Technology
565 W. Adams Street
Chicago, IL 60661–3691
tel.: 312–906–5000
fax: 312–906–5280
web-site: <http://www.kentlaw.edu/jwc/>

Lawtopic.org
web-site: <http://www.lawtopic.org>

LexisNexis Tutorials
web-site: <http://www.LexisNexis.com/lawschool/tutorials>

Westlaw, Creating a TWEN Course
web-site: <http://lawschool.westlaw.com/help/professor/twenmenu.asp?Unit=twenmenu&appflag=53.8>

Intellectual Property Resources:

U.S. Copyright Office
web-site: <http://www.copyright.gov/>

Frequently Asked Questions About Copyright
web-site: <http://www.copyright.gov/help/faq/>

Copyright Forms
web-site: <http://www.copyright.gov/forms/>

U.S. Patent and Trademark Office
web-site: <http://www.uspto.gov/>

Copyright Clearance Center
222 Rosewood Drive
Danvers, MA 01923
tel.: 978–750–8400
fax: 978–750–4744
web-site: <http://www.copyright.com>

Fair Use Considerations Worksheet, Copyright Training Materials, North Carolina State University, *at* <http://www.ncsu.edu/provost/governance/standing_committees/2001_2002/CopC/fyi>

Lolly Gasaway, *When Works Pass Into the Public Domain, at* <http://www.unc.edu/~unclng/public-d.htm>

Georgia Harper, *Copyright Law in the Electronic Environment, at* <http://www.utsystem.edu/ogc/intellectualproperty/faculty.htm>

Internet Corporation for Assigned Names and Numbers
web-site: <http://www.icann.org/>

Bruce P. Keller and Jeffrey P. Cunard, *Copyright Law: A Practitioner's Guide* (Practising Law Institute 2002)

The TEACH Toolkit: An Online Resource for Understanding Copyright and Distance Education, *at* <http://www.lib.ncsu.edu/scc/legislative/teachkit/overview.html>

University of Texas, Crash Course in Copyright, *at* <http://www.utsystem.edu/ogc/intellectualproperty/cprtindx.htm>

Copyright Registration Procedures:

Library of Congress
Copyright Office
101 Independence Avenue, S.E.
Washington, DC 20559
tel.: 202–707–3000
fax: 202–707–2600
web-site: <www.copyright.gov>
listserv: NewsNet (subscription is available by sending a message to LISTSERV@LOC.GOV that states in the body of the message "SUBSCRIBE USCOPYRIGHT" or by completing an on-line subscription form by accessing <www.copyright.gov/newsnet>)

CHAPTER 3

CONDUCTING CLASSES

Extensive preparation for the design and scope of the course is necessary before the semester even begins. There also are a number of logistical and pedagogical matters to consider so that you and your students feel comfortable in the classroom setting, those who may be collaborating with you in the teaching enterprise are effectively assimilated in the curriculum, and any electronic or media techniques are appropriately and productively integrated. In addition, the material for the course must be suitably allocated to each session, lectures must be intellectually challenging, and discussions must be stimulated effectually and well-managed.

Even when the subject matter and textual materials are identical from one course to another, no two classes will be the same. The diversity of student composition and its synergistic impact on the ensuing dialogue will render each class unique. As you prepare to conduct classes, there are a number of pedagogical techniques you can choose amongst. As you become more acquainted with your class, you can determine with even greater insight which approaches work best for you and your students.

Logistical Aspects

Classroom Facilities

It's obviously helpful to ascertain in advance which classroom you've been assigned and where it's located. While some schools may expect you to check in with the registrar's office just before the first session begins or leave a note regarding classroom assignment in your faculty mailbox, usually you can simply call or send an e-mail to the school's registrar to get the information.

There's a reason why litigators visit the courtrooms in which they'll be appearing before their scheduled hearing or trial date. And why even professional athletes feel more comfortable playing on their home turf. Being able to visualize yourself in the classroom setting makes you feel more prepared for the onset of the semester.

You'll also want to confirm the classroom's facilities if you're contemplating the use of any electronic, visual, or aural media during the course of the semester (*see infra* at 109). If you've been assigned a particularly large classroom, you may want to see if a microphone is available; if so, it's helpful to know whether it's portable or whether you'll be tethered to a particular spot.

Most importantly, take a moment to locate exits and stairways. You'll want to be sure that you can help direct students and others in the event of a fire or other emergency. Also note the location of entrances and other facilities for disabled persons so that you can assist not only in emergent circumstances but also help with students, other faculty, or guest lecturers who may have special needs.

Registration

The size of your class may be determined by the registrar if it's a course required of first-year students, for example, or possibly determined by the registrar in consultation with you if it's an elective course. Clinical programs and certain advocacy courses may be confined to smaller enrollments than other courses. The number of students enrolled in classes in which professors supervise the preparation of papers in satisfaction of an upper-class writing requirement may be restricted in order to afford more direct communication with individual students. Such enrollment limitations similarly may apply to courses in which the students have an option to submit a paper in lieu of taking an exam.

Prior to your first class, you should obtain your class roster. You'll want to confirm that all those who attend your class are accurately listed on the roster and promptly advise the registrar's office of any discrepancies.

Oversubscribed Classes

If more students have signed up to take your class than have been authorized by the enrollment limit or than the classroom can accommodate, the students who have not been admitted to the class will be placed on a wait list by the registrar. Students usually are permitted to add and drop classes during the first week of the semester.

Selection from a wait list typically is made by class priority, meaning that preference is given to the most senior students. Within each class, selection from the wait list may be done randomly, rather than on a "first come, first served" basis, depending upon your school's policy. If there are more students in the priority class than there are open places in the course, a random selection of students may be made by computer. If there are additional open places in the course after the highest class priority is considered, then students in the next class priority are considered.

You may wish to consider expanding the class enrollment to accommodate one or more students on the wait list, assuming that there is adequate classroom space. You'll first want to confer with the registrar before granting any student admission to your class, so that students who have been wait-listed may be accommodated in the appropriate order.

Requests to Audit Classes

From time to time, you may receive a request from a student on behalf of a friend or from a colleague to audit your class. Assuming that there is adequate classroom space, you probably can just exercise your discretion to accommodate a request to attend a particular lecture. If you receive a request to audit an entire (or substantially all of a) semester, you'll want to refer it to the registrar or confer with the registrar. In any event, a student enrolled in your class should not be displaced by an auditor.

Seating Arrangements

Some schools may assign seats to students or may assign seats with respect to certain courses such as required first-year courses. You may want students to take the same places routinely in order to help you learn their names and more readily determine absences. Blank seating charts may be available from the registrar's office for this purpose. If you do decide to assign seats, consider whether you want to announce your intention to do so at the first class session and wait to make the assignments until the second class session so as to give students an opportunity to deliberate about their seat selection. This may be important, for example, for those who have difficulty seeing the chalkboard or screen and thus prefer to sit closer to the area of the classroom where visual material will be shown.

Seating arrangements in which students routinely assume the same places also can facilitate the monitoring of class participation. If you're factoring in participation in class grades (*see supra* at 83), you may find it easier to keep track of those who have volunteered or responded during class sessions if they routinely sit in the same places. Just as significantly, you can gain a sense as to who has *not* participated actively so that you can enhance your efforts to engage them.

Depending upon the size of the classroom, the configuration of the students' seats and desks or tables, and the level of your class enrollment, you may have some more flexibility to modify the arrangement you encountered when you first arrived. It's possible, however, that other restrictions may operate, as when classes are scheduled very close to one another and yours follows right after or immediately precedes another with special needs or one led by a professor that has other preferences.

Your classroom may have a physical lay-out that you're not able to adjust, perhaps because the students' seats are bolted in place or because of the means of access to electrical outlets to power students' laptop computers. Your mobility likewise may be restricted because you need to access overhead transparencies and the projector can be placed in only one location, or because your class is so large that you need to use a microphone to amplify your voice and the one provided is fixed in place. You may prefer a fairly structured class environment, in which case the lack of options for alternative seating arrangements won't present much of a problem. If, however, you prefer a more casual atmosphere, you'll simply do your best to make your students as comfortable as possible and rely on techniques other than seating configurations to reduce the more formalized structure of the class environment.

If you do have some options open to you, the primary determinant of the seating configuration, it seems to me, is what you believe will best facilitate an attentive audience, render your comments and those of your students audible to the entire class, and make the class sufficiently comfortable to focus on the discourse that evolves. For some professors, this means arranging students in a circle or "doughnut" type design. This pattern may be most conducive to seminars and classes in which you anticipate extensive contributions by students to the class dialogue. When such an arrangement is used, there's a subtle implication of informality and possibly even an expectation of participation by virtue of the logistical parity of the seating, placing the professor on a physical par with the students.

Once again, you'll want to first consider whether you'll be employing any media devices so that you can ensure that a screen will be visible to all of the class' participants. It can be quite disruptive to have students adjust their chairs during a presentation in order to see the screen, and doing so may mean that they're deprived, at least temporarily, of access to a desk or table for use as a writing surface, possibly encumbering their note-taking.

Recordation of Class Lectures

Students may be prohibited by school policy from tape-recording or videotaping lectures unless the professor grants permission. If you decide to allow the student to do so, you may want to clarify that students are responsible for providing their own recorders and tapes and making any other necessary arrangements or coordinating with the school's administration to do so.

Some professors videotape their lectures in order to make them available to students as a faculty loan to the library or through streaming technology. These tapes can be a helpful resource for a student who has missed class, for review and study purposes, or as a means of engaging in distance education (*see infra* at 117). In addition, as Gregory Maggs of the George Washington University School of Law pointed out, videotaped tutorials alleviate the need to conduct multiple review sessions during office hours on the same topic.[1]

One consideration if you're contemplating videotaping lectures is your capacity to edit. It's helpful to know before you begin the project whether you'll be able to splice in clips of other tapes for illustrative purposes. Editing capabilities also will affect whether you'll be able to delete a "flub," one of those occasional stumbles or flights of syntax we all experience. Conversation and even more formal oral presentations seem more susceptible to excusable transgressions of grammar and instances of imprecision than those created as a permanent record. Maggs notes that his experience with the recordation process was tedious because he wasn't able to easily edit the tapes. He remarked that his "appreciation for glib talking heads on television has grown enormously."[2]

Note that if you decide to make the video material available through streaming technology, bandwith may be a factor because such files are voluminous and more cumbersome than textual material to transmit. You'll want to get a sense of the relative parity of equipment to which students have access.

All of this takes special equipment, so unless you have the budgetary resources or access through your school to recording and possibly editing functionality, cost will be a factor. At least one professor found the experience so frustrating, he abandoned the project after recording a single lecture.[3]

Collaborative Teaching

Collaborative teaching techniques can take a variety of forms, such as appearances by guest lecturers, team teaching, the employment of teaching as-

1. Gregory E. Maggs, *Creating Law School Review Videos and Slides and Putting Them on the Internet*, Jurist Legal Intelligence, Lessons from the Web (offering technical instructions in an appendix), *at* <http://jurist.law.pitt.edu/lessons/lessept01.htm>.

2. *Id.*

3. *See* Ray August, *Animating Web Lectures with Agent Technology*, Jurist Legal Intelligence, Lessons from the Web, *at* <http://jurist.law.pitt.edu/lessons/lesfeb01.htm>.

sistants, or the joint efforts of students to assist one another. When the logistics are carefully planned, expectations by participants are confirmed, and participation is assimilated within the class curriculum, collaborative pedagogical techniques can enhance students' experiences by incorporating divergent viewpoints and a greater depth of expertise.

Guest Lecturers

One of the more commonly used examples of collaborative teaching is the integration of guest lecturers. This approach has the advantage of exposing the class to diverse viewpoints and pedagogical styles. And to some degree, it can reduce the demands on the professor primarily entrusted with the course to prepare as thoroughly as might otherwise be necessary.

As with other approaches to teaching, guest lectures should be used purposefully. Each guest should be invited because he'll contribute something meaningful to which the class might not otherwise have access. Is the guest an experienced academician at another institution who might offer different insights? Did the guest litigate a relevant landmark case and thus can explain some of the tactics and background not readily discernible from the published decision? Perhaps the guest was involved as a non-lawyer who had input into or an impact on how the law ultimately developed. A prison inmate who was released only after subsequent DNA testing established that he hadn't been at the crime scene might well have a dramatic and long-lasting effect on students' ultimate commitment to factual investigation in criminal proceedings. When Susan Hanley Kosse incorporated discussion about *The Buffalo Creek Disaster* by Gerald Stern into her legal writing course (*see infra* at 158), she invited the author to meet with her class; he critiqued a few student papers and discussed his career as a public interest lawyer.[4] Such guest appearances benefit the class and afford you insights into alternative instructional approaches.

The guest lecturer has a discrete but meaningful opportunity to experience the task of teaching. He may be gratified to have the chance to offer his views about a particular matter. A practitioner may benefit as well by eliciting reaction to his client's position in an ongoing dispute. While the professor may use the factual circumstances outlined by the guest as a foundation for the en-

---

4. Susan Hanley Kosse, *Buffalo Creek Prevents Legal Writing Class Disaster,* Institute for Law School Teaching, The Law Teacher (Spring 2003), 13, 14, *at* <http://law.gonzaga.edu/ILST/Newsletters/Spring03/Spring03Newsletter.pdf>.

suing legal discussion, the practitioner is the beneficiary of feedback that otherwise might be available through costly focus groups or shadow juries.

While it may initially seem that you're basically relieved from having to prepare and conduct the class session at which the guest lecturer will appear, this isn't quite the case. You'll actually increase certain logistical tasks because you'll need to coordinate your guest's schedule with your course plan. You'll want to avoid having his lecture disrupt the flow of the progression of the course. And you may want to prepare the lecture as though you'll be leading the session alone in the event the guest has a sudden scheduling conflict. You'll also handle administrative matters, directing him to the location of the school and your particular classroom and making any necessary arrangements for computer or other equipment, duplication of hand-outs, and the like. And possibly your greatest investment of time will result from efforts to reconcile disparate pedagogical approaches and ensure that the specific lecture is integrated effectively into the course.

It's important to furnish a copy of your syllabus to your guest well before his scheduled session so that he can see how his presentation fits into the course contextually. You'll also want to work with the guest lecturer prior to the class session to give him some basic background about the progress of the class and advise him of the scope of the material you'll already have covered. And you'll want to collaborate on the excerpts to be assigned; as an expert in some way, your guest will have helpful suggestions. Ideally, you will have reviewed the proposed readings for the entire course with the guest lecturer before the semester even begins to ensure that he's comfortable with the approach and to get his input into the curriculum so that you won't have to modify the assignments after you've distributed the syllabus.

If you're inclined to participate in the discussion during the sessions, discuss this with the guest in advance to be sure he won't regard it as a distraction. You won't want to throw his plan off course by raising a topic that he intended to cover at a later point. Conversely, if you intend to simply turn the class over to the guest, confirm that he understands that he'll be leading the session. In either event, request a copy of the guest's curriculum vitae or biographical sketch so that you can fashion an introduction for the class.

It will be up to you to integrate the guest lecture into the course. You may do this during the session itself if you're participating, assimilating the material covered with themes previously discussed. You might allude to a related court decision, for instance, to suggest an analogy or tie together an emerging legal principle with caselaw reviewed by the guest. After the session, either as it concludes or at the next session, you can help orient the class, filling in gaps in the material to be covered in the course.

Team Teaching

A more expansive variation of a collaborative approach that uses one or more professors to conduct the course is commonly known as "team teaching" or "co-teaching." Team teaching can be, as it was for me, a helpful introduction to teaching. When I first started teaching, I joined an extremely knowledgeable, dedicated, and experienced professor who was familiar with the school's practices and policies and accustomed to teaching the course. He shared previous syllabi and exams and had a text in mind from prior use. A novice teacher can join a mentor, bridging inexperience with experience.

As you would expect, the key to the success of team teaching is effective communication and comparable expectations about responsibility. How will tasks be divided? Will each partner assume sole or primary responsibility for particular lectures? Does each expect the other to attend all of the class sessions or only those for which he has assumed primary responsibility? Does each partner have particular expertise or a special interest in the specific topics to be covered? As is the case with a guest lecturer situation (*see supra* at 96), it's also important to clarify in advance whether both co-professors will help lead the class discussions. How will the lectures be allocated?

Tasks relating to class assessment also should be coordinated. Who will be charged with creating the final exam or meeting with students as they select topics for a mid-term paper? One way to equalize the responsibility for these tasks is to develop an exam with two (or some other equal number) of parts; each co-teacher could then come up with, say, 25 multiple-choice questions and one essay to comprise a 50-question and two essay exam. Each professor would read the portion of the exam he devised. This approach facilitates the grading as well because each teacher's portion of the test would be designed to address the topics covered at the class sessions for which he had primary or sole responsibility, which helps ensure that the test doesn't inadvertently stray from the material covered.

Ideally, the relative commitment of the co-teachers to the course should be comparable. The best-run households probably are those in which each of the occupants presumes that he's solely responsible for each task; inevitably, the laundry gets done, there's fresh milk in the refrigerator, and the carpets are vacuumed. When one person cooks the dinner and clears the dishes afterwards, the other notices, feels relieved of the task, and appreciates the contribution to the household. Even when particular tasks, or days on which particular tasks are to be undertaken, are allocated to particular members of the household, things function well if the allocation is equitable – and, probably just as importantly, *perceived* to be equitable. Things seem to break down when one presumes that specific tasks are not within his province and tacitly expects the other to perform them.

So, too, in co-teaching, if both participants are diligent and committed to the preparation for each class session, the administrative demands, and student assessment, things likely will work quite well. A co-teaching enterprise's success also depends on whether the parties' respective preferences fortuitously complement each other, fostered, perhaps, by a bit of affability and compromise. One may enjoy perusing the text before the semester to carefully select and equitably apportion reading assignments throughout the semester, while the other may be content to read all of the assigned papers and compute course grades in accordance with the school's policies regarding curves. But as is the case with any other positive relationship, successful team teaching is dependent upon mutual respect, good communication, and a joint commitment.

While pedagogical styles amongst team teachers may vary considerably, the class may benefit from the diversity. But in addition to the logistical allocation of responsibility, co-teaching likely will be more susceptible to success when the partners have certain similar philosophies. One teacher may believe, for instance, that academic transgressions such as tardiness to class or missed deadlines for papers should be subject to severe penalties, while the other would not even take the deficiencies into consideration. It's helpful to discuss policies about such matters before the class begins to try to reconcile disparate approaches. One need not necessarily capitulate to the other's approach; each might adhere to his policies so long as the students are fully apprised in advance and both teachers are amenable to adjusting scores so that their policies are applied equitably.

Collaborative teaching techniques have been extended to remote participation. Although Professors Theresa Player, Michael Norwood, and Robert Seibel taught at different law schools, they jointly conducted a course by using Internet capabilities such as e-mail and listservs, a shared web-site, and a bulletin board service; utilizing video and audio conferencing; and engaging in telephonic conference calls amongst the faculty.[5] The collaborative technique may afford an opportunity for shared scholarly exchanges and camaraderie amongst faculty when one professor is charged with teaching a fairly specialized course and lacks geographically proximate peers with whom to exchange ideas. The acquisition of global perspectives to comparatively construe foreign law can be facilitated by collaborative effort with academicians who have

5. Theresa Player, Michael Norwood, Robert Seibel, *Internet Team Teaching,* Jurist Legal Intelligence, Lessons from the Web, *at* <http://jurist.law.pitt.edu/lessons/lesnov01.htm>.

expertise in their respective jurisdictions. Collaborative efforts also may assist with inter-disciplinary courses that demand expertise in multiple, disparate fields. Factors that may affect the efficacy of a collaboratively-taught class include the size of the class, the relative experience of the respective faculty members and their commitment to coordinating with one another, and the degree to which students are receptive to disparate pedagogical styles.

Teaching Assistants and Student Coaches

Teaching assistants sometimes may be made available to professors. Such assistants, known as "TAs," can be a source of valuable support, helping to grade papers and meet with students to clarify areas of confusion.

If you're going to enlist the help of a TA to grade papers, check your school's policies. While it's doubtful there will be a restriction if the TA is performing ministerial computations, as is the case with grading a multiple-choice exam, the school may prefer that discretionary or subjective evaluations, as is the case with reviewing essay exams, rest with you.

As with any other collaborative teaching arrangement, communication is key. The professor and teaching assistant should confer before the class even begins to define objectives and demarcate their respective roles. Throughout the class, regular consultation can help further the relationship as well as inform the professor about how the class is progressing and provide feedback about areas of class confusion.

If you're teaching a first-year course, you might consider investigating an arrangement with your school to invite assistance from student coaches. These might be upper-classmen or graduate students who have demonstrated proficiency in the subject matter of your class. Perhaps a third-year student, for example, excelled in the course you're teaching, took an advanced seminar in related subject matter, and is writing a journal article on a relevant topic. A student coach can help tutor a first-year student, review complicated legal concepts, and offer guidance about preparation for class and exams.

Study Groups

Some people absorb material and engage in creative and critical thinking most effectively when they have a period of solitude. Others work best in collaborative settings. A student who seems to be struggling on his own with complex legal concepts might benefit from working with others in a study group. Sometimes, "'[i]solation is the worst possible counselor.'"[6] You might suggest that the student try participating in a session or two of a group before committing as it's important to find the right composition and confirm that the members have similar objectives. Highly intense groups can increase a sense of competition, but just as problematically, a less motivated group may add to the student's sense of befuddlement.

Ideally, the study group should be a reasonable size, probably ranging between three and seven members. This renders the group less unwieldy, diminishes potential scheduling conflicts, and provides adequate opportunities for everyone to share views and express concerns. Although it's to be expected that students will gravitate towards those with whom they've become friends, it's also important that the study group retain a sense of professionalism so that pursuit of academic objectives formulated by the group is achieved. Encourage students to discuss their expectations with the group to ensure that all members are prepared to devote comparable amounts of time and effort. They might even sketch out brief agendas for each meeting in order to set goals and equitably delegate tasks.

You can remind students that study groups cannot substitute for individualized study and attentive commitment to class sessions. But exchanging ideas amongst peers can be especially helpful for students who are reticent to experiment with class participation. A study group provides an informal and relaxed setting in which a pupil can more openly concede confusion and foible. Testing concepts in a study group may provide an important forum for a relatively reserved student to gain confidence about the validity of his point, corroborate his understanding of the legal precept at work, and rehearse expression of his comment. Furthermore, the student may feel fortified by his ability at times to explain a point to another study group member. Ultimately, confidence may be inspired through reciprocal assistance.

Electronic technology offers another way study groups may be conducted effectively and in variant forms. Students may establish a discussion board or participate in a chatroom to review material. Or, rather than engaging in an on-line review of the entire semester's material, they can form a small group of peers with whom they can exchange e-mail messages targeted to points about which they have specific questions.

---

6. Cathaleen A. Roach, *A River Runs Through It: Tapping Into the Informational Stream to Move Students From Isolation to Autonomy*, 36 Ariz. L. Rev. 667, 667 (1994) (quoting Miguel de Unamuno, *Civilization is Civilism*, in Mi Religion y Otros Ensayos Breves 69 (Espasa-Calpe Argentina, S.A., 1945)).

Integration of Electronic and Media Tools

Now here's a bit of wisdom I can confidently impart: technology has changed over time. I know this because some years ago, I came across a box of old Beatles singles. "Do you want to see my old '45s?" I asked my kids. My son looked up, clearly appalled. Finally he managed to blurt out, "But, Mom, you never let us play with guns!"

Electronic and media tools increasingly play a role in legal education. Key to facilitating digital access is establishing adequate computer literacy in administrative support staff and ensuring the availabity of training for faculty and students.[7] In addition to the ways in which electronic technology can afford opportunities to enhance the scope of available materials (*see supra at* 47, 54), it can promote "creative interactions. ... Electronic technology enables instant access with a click of a mouse to pictures, video, sounds, and simulations, as well as textual information and, even more importantly, to others with whom to exchange, discuss, and refine new ideas."[8]

Much has been written about ways law schools can improve the use of information technology to reap educational benefits. Informal surveys have been undertaken regarding the efficacy of computer-based legal training. The Center for Computer-Aided Legal Instruction surveyed the availability of technology in schools, posting on-line the results of its 1998 and 1999 findings.[9] Data from more than 150 law schools was reviewed by the University of Georgia Law School to assess staffing for law school computer services.[10] A recent study at an Australian university investigated potential correlations between business students' performance in a commercial law course and the frequency of their visits to a web-site that posted the materials for the course.[11] The study concluded that the site was accessed more frequently than the teaching faculty had anticipated and that better-performing students accessed the site more often than others, especially when access occurred at the beginning of the semester.[12]

---

7. *See, e.g.*, Elmer R. Masters, *5 Steps Toward Improving the Use of Information Technology in the Law School*, J. L. Sch. Computing, *at* <http://www.cali.org/jlsc/masters.html>.

8. Rogelio Lasso, *From the Paper Chase to the Digital Chase: Technology and the Challenge of Teaching 21st Century Law Students*, 43 Santa Clara L. Rev. 1, 11 (2000).

9. CALI Technology Surveys, The Center for Computer-Aided Legal Instruction, *at* <http://www.cali.org/survey/>.

10. *Staffing for Law School Computing Services*, Alexander Campbell King Law Library, University of Georgia School of Law, *at* <http://www.law.uga.edu/library/stafcomp.html>.

11. Andrew Field, *Australian Study of Student Use of Course Web Site*, The Law Teacher, Institute for Law School Teaching (Spring 2003) at 1, 11, *at* <http://law.gonzaga/edu/ilst/Newsletters/Spring03/spring03Newsletter.pdf>.

12. *Id.*

The most important question is how media tools will be integrated into the course. A recent survey conducted by the Penn State University Center for Excellence in Learning & Teaching considered respondents' motivations for experimenting with computers. The majority, more than 60 percent, indicated that they decided to use computers as a means of providing an opportunity for practice; other rationales included use in order to clarify a difficult concept (comprising more than 24 percent of respondents), and to expand the boundaries of the classroom and access to information (roughly four percent).[13] Nearly 14 percent of the respondents indicated that they used a computer "[b]ecause it was there."[14] Such a rationale seems questionable at best.

The decision to integrate electronic tools, it strikes me, rests preliminarily on two key considerations. First, are you comfortable using the technological device you're considering? The answer to this likely depends on the particular tool you're contemplating using. You might have considerable experience making PowerPoint presentations, for instance, but never had an opportunity to design and launch a web-site. Even if you have often used an electronic or other technique in the past, you may want to consider your ability to troubleshoot in the event of a malfunction. If your idea of rectifying computer problems completely on your own is dialing your Information Technology department without asking your secretary to place the call, think about whether you'd be comfortable in the classroom if there was no one at the school to summon to assist you immediately. Inquire about the hours of the school's IT personnel and their typical response time. And ask about the availability of the classroom before your session starts so you can try to arrive before class to test the equipment and work out any "bugs" before your class starts.

You might also chat with those in the school's IT department and others savvy about technology. What kinds of problems do they believe arise most commonly, and how do they address them? As you "rehearse" your presentation, are there technical issues that recur? You could also consult a chart, prepared by the University of Oregon's Teaching Effectiveness Program, entitled *Troubleshooting Your Presentation*, that lists circumstances, results, and possible fixes designed to assist you as you trouble-shoot problems.[15]

---

13. Diane M. Enerson, *Using Computers as an Aid to Teaching and Learning from Existing Practice*, Center for Excellence in Learning & Teaching, Penn State University, *at* <http://www.psu.edu/celt/computer.html>.

14. *Id.*

15. *Troubleshooting Your Presentation*, Teaching Effectiveness Program, Academic Learning Services, University of Oregon, *at* <http://tep.uoregon.edu/technology/lecture/troubleshooting.html>.

Consider, too, the degree to which your students will feel comfortable with the technology and have access to IT assistance. Heavy emphasis on computer technology can pose challenges to the novice, and some have observed that in their experience, "Troubleshooting the technology was sometimes as common as the legal problem solving."[16]

Also reflect on whether you'll feel comfortable forging ahead with the class session if the technology fails completely. Perhaps you've been unable to resolve the malfunction or the IT folks simply could not get the program up and running or the university's network is down. Will you be able to turn to a print version of your notes and carry on?

Another, and more significant, question is whether the use of technology will enhance your presentation. In an increasingly digital world, saturated with impressive graphics and real-time exchanges of communication, it can be tempting to incorporate new media. Visual presentations can be arresting and impressive. But the fundamental question is will the use of digital, visual, or aural media likely increase learning potential? Or is it being used simply because it's available or seemingly renders the course material more current?

The decision to incorporate digital or other media likely depends on the nature of the particular media you're contemplating using and the purpose for which you intend to use it. The subject matter of your course bears on this determination. Integrating visual enhancements within your lectures helps illustrate and simulate phenomena that cannot be readily visualized from a description. It may be very useful to be able to play examples of two melodies that gave rise to a copyright infringement claim so the class can hear the comparison, for example. Having the opportunity in a Patents course to visually display images of inventions as you discuss the implications of their patentability and compare their novelty may be hugely beneficial. Laura Gasaway of the University of North Carolina School of Law pointed out, "When discussing a trademark and trade dress case involving Coach® bags and the hang tag labels, showing the handbags and tags to the class from a website makes a world of difference in the students' understanding of the facts in the case."[17]

By contrast, simply repeating lengthy texts of statutory provisions may be distracting, leading students to scribble down the text without fully paying at-

---

16. Johnny Burris, Debra Curtis, Steve Friedland, and Billie Jo Kaufman, *Venturing Into the On-Line Wilderness: Some Lessons Learned,* Jurist Legal Intelligence, Lessons from the Web, *at* <http://jurist.law.pitt.edu/lessons/lesfeb03.php>.

17. Laura Gasaway, *The Indispensable Web,* Jurist Legal Intelligence, Lessons from the Web, *at* <http://jurist.law.pitt.edu/lessons/lesaug99.htm>.

tention to the lecturer's points about the interpretation of the law by the courts. Michael Schwartz, Professor of Law and Director of Online Instruction at Western State University College of Law, described himself as "an unabashed course webpage enthusiast," nevertheless appropriately noting that "it is not the medium (the particular platform) that is the message. It's all about the content."[18]

The appropriate incorporation of media in course curricula has an important benefit: offering a means for knowledge and insight through a complementary format. Research in education and psychology suggests that people have different learning styles. Some may assimilate material through linguistic cognition and linear thinking. Others rely significantly on spatial learning; images can be especially helpful to such persons for eidetic detail. Some have even concluded that "[e]veryone learns more when information is presented both visually and verbally."[19] You may well reach more students or better exploit the learning potential of each member of the class with media enhancements.

Furthermore, demonstrating the capabilities of various media can help prepare students for the practice of law. Practitioners often use visual images to explain facts to judges and juries. Diagrams are used to explain the configuration of roads and the placement of automobiles in motor vehicle accident cases and images are used to explain anatomy in medical malpractice cases.[20] Courtrooms increasingly are becoming more high-tech; in the U.S. District Court for the Southern District of New York, the audibility of a sidebar conference is reduced when the judge activates sound-neutralizing white noise in the jury box by activating a touch-screen panel. Audio conferencing facilitates remote foreign translations, opening and closing arguments may include PowerPoint presentations, and the parties' counsel have the capacity to highlight evidentiary exhibits on flat-screen monitors. Video depositions may be viewed by the jury on monitors positioned in the jury box. Real-time court reporting, digital audio recording, and Internet access are available in certain high-tech courtrooms.[21] At an experimental court at the William and Mary School of Law, students "conducted a trial using immersive virtual reality, recon-

---

18. Michael Schwartz, *Using Course Webpages to Fill Gaps Within Traditional Law School Instruction*, Jurist Legal Intelligence, Lessons from the Web, *at* <http://jurist.law.pitt.edu/lessons/lesmar03.php>.

19. Richard M. Felder and Barbara A. Soloman, *Learning Styles and Strategies, at* <http://www.ncsu.edu/felder-public/ILSdir/styles.htm>.

20. *See generally* Thomas G. Collins and Karin Marlett, *New Tools Can Enhance Legal Writing*, N.Y. State Bar Ass'n, *Journal* (June 2003) at 10.

21. *See* Sherri Day, *Electronic Order in the Court*, N.Y. Times, May 29, 2003, §C at 2.

structing the scene of a crime with computer graphics. Wearing headsets and goggles, witnesses were able to view the scene as if they were there."[22]

Thus, another advantage of utilizing computer technology is that it promotes students' familiarity with resources that inevitably will be integral to their practice regardless of the specialty they pursue. Use of technology promotes digital literacy, a skill fundamental to the practice of law. Utilizing the Web helps students become more facile with technology that can enable them to conduct more effective legal and factual investigation.

Becoming more familiar with navigational techniques also builds confidence by implicitly teaching that information may be acquired and exchanged through various methodologies. "[U]sers who click through successive screens [of an informational site] should become aware that they are going deeper within the organizational structure of a particular topic."[23] Electronic research reinforces the notion that factual and analytical material may be acquired in multiple ways, leading to the implicit conclusion that there's rarely a single "correct" path to obtain information or for the resolution of a problem. Searches for information on the World Wide Web also help negate a propensity to believe that a subject has been comprehensively mastered; students are regularly reminded quite viscerally that there is a depth of information that they have not and may never access. Vividly confronted with the volume of Web pages relevant to his research and the fact that there are numerous links to yet other sources he has never accessed, the student is humbly reminded that there is a wealth of information that has not been tapped.

Archival capabilities also are enhanced. Threaded discussions that at one time could take place only within the exclusive province of the classroom setting are now less ephemeral. Even if such communicative exchanges are not deliberately and permanently archived, they may be printed out or otherwise saved by students. Note, too, though, that minor transgressions of grammar and syntax and imprecise phrasing of a legal principle sometimes seem more pronounced when they're committed to printed form.

As a report by the Penn State University Center for Excellence in Learning & Teaching concluded, "[c]omputers may be a new frontier, but they are not an educational panacea."[24] Creating a computerized enhancement for your class

---

22. *See id.*

23. Peter A. Hook, *Creating an Online Tutorial and Pathfinder,* 94 Law Libr. J. 243, 253 (2002).

24. Diane M. Enerson, *Using Computers as an Aid to Teaching and Learning from Existing Practice,* Center for Excellence in Learning & Teaching, Penn State University, *at* <http://www.psu.edu/celt/computer.html>.

entails a fair amount of effort. Depending on how technologically savvy you are, how interested you are in acquiring computer skills, and the degree to which your school has IT personnel available to assist you, the task may take a considerable amount of time. Using a computer as a teaching aid typically "is an iterative process involving considerable experimentation, planning, redesign, and persistence. Initial efforts are not always successful."[25] Reflect at the outset as to whether you have the requisite time, stamina, and interest. If you do, you'll likely learn quite a bit from the experiment and effort.

There are an ever-increasing number of ways to use Internet and other technology in a course. These range, at one end of the spectrum, from posting administrative announcements relating to the class on the school's existing web-site to the other end of the spectrum, teaching a virtual law school class. As you peruse the syllabi and frameworks of other professors' courses, particularly those in the same or similar subject matter as the ones you'll be teaching (*see supra* at 47), look at the ways in which they've incorporated media. Consider, too, the degree to which your school has modernized its facilities to accommodate technological developments. Suffolk University Law School, for instance, expended $70 million on a new 300,000 square foot hall, wiring each classroom for data and video to provide thousands of network ports, as well as touchscreen room controls.[26]

There are numerous organizations that offer informative instructional technology resources. While many of these are not targeted specifically to the study of law, they include guides to enhancing the quality of the course by incorporating technological devices. Case studies of teaching in categorized disciplines and extracts of published articles are available from DeLiberations, for example, which offers generic and subject-specific resources.[27] EDUCAUSE reports on the findings of a study on how faculty members have been using course management systems and sets forth information about upcoming conferences.[28] Horizon includes information about conferences and educational technology.[29]

The NODE Learning Technologies Network publishes information designed to give practical advice about using technology to teach.[30] Amongst these is a publication on incorporating on-line discussions into campus-based and distance learning classes. The Scout Report includes reports tangential to

25. *Id.*

26. *See* <http://www.law.suffolk.edu/video/index.html>. A virtual tour is available.

27. *See* <http://www.lgu.ac.uk/deliberations>.

28. *See* <http://www.educause.edu>.

29. *See* <http://horizon.unc.edu>.

30. *See* <http://node.on.ca>.

the study of law, such as math, engineering, and technology. But it also looks at the impact of research on education and includes information about such network tools as MacDICT 2.8, which offers users the ability to connect with databases on-line and provides access to translation services.[31] Teaching and Learning on the WWW is part of the Maricopa Center for Learning & Instruction and includes nearly a thousand examples of how the Web has been used as a means of learning.[32] Kathy Schrock's Guide for Educators is located on DiscoverySchool.com, comprising "a categorized list of sites on the Internet found to be useful for enhancing curriculum and teacher professional growth."[33] TeAch-nology "offers a wide variety of resources intended to bring educators into the world of teaching with technology. As a portal, it provides links to valuable and useful information relative to current and past practice in the field of education."[34] The University of Texas' World Lecture Hall links to pages created by faculty who are utilizing the Web in a variety of ways.[35]

Therefore, even those resources that are not focused primarily on legal education have valuable information about ways to integrate instructional technology. In addition, the inter-relationship between law and other disciplines often requires the professor to review or update information. One notable illustration is legal courses that implicate scientific principles. A Privacy Law class that includes the study of autonomous decision-making regarding procreative and reproductive issues, for instance, may necessitate a foundational understanding of the medical efficacy of different types of abortion procedures. Instructional learning sites may be an important source of substantive, graphic, statistical, and research material, as well as of exposure to the practitioner's options for digital and other means to present the material.

An obvious benefit of an openly accessible web-site is that it contributes to the free flow of information and intellectual discourse. To the extent one of your goals is to attract an audience beyond that of your class enrollment or even of your law school community, cursory empirical review of visitation suggests that a web-site can help. Doug Linder of the University of Missouri-Kansas City Law School recalled that when he began the labor-intensive task of launching an electronic compilation of trial records, images, essays, and other documents relating to famous trials, he was cautioned, "'It's like colonizing a planet in outer space.... You might create a beautiful world, but how

31. *See* <http://scout.wisc.edu/report/sr/current>.

32. *See* <http://www.mcli.dist.maricopa.edu/tl/brain.html>.

33. *See* <http://school.discovery.com/schrockguide>.

34. *See* <http://teach-nology.com>.

35. *See* <http://www.utexas.edu/world/lecture/>.

likely is it people will find it and stop by to visit?' "[36] But amongst the visitors to Linder's site were a student of Nathan Leopold, lawyers who worked on the "Chicago 8" trial, and the grandson of the legislator who authored Tennessee's anti-evolution statute.[37]

In-Class Lecture Enhancements

There are a variety of technological devices designed to enhance the visual presentation of your class sessions. These offer a means of complementing your lecture presentations in order to facilitate retention and comprehension of the concepts reviewed. The diversity of presentation of the material increases the chances that one of the means of explanations will resonate with each member of the class.

The Chalkboard, the Dry-Erase Board, and the Easel

Ah, technology even I can explain. To add material for display on a chalkboard, apply chalk. To delete images, rub an eraser over the chalk display. This format accommodates both text and graphics.

Before there was PowerPoint, there was the chalkboard. It must be a fairly successful device, because despite the proliferation of electronic media, it's still with us. (The chalkboard is analogous for our purposes to paper on an easel and dry-erase boards that use erasable markers.)

If you're only intending to post a change in your office hours or the pages for a reading assignment you've decided to add, the chalkboard is ideal. Why toil with setting up a computerized display if you're simply referencing a brief notation? If you've got just a bit more to display, such as a single sentence text of a statute for analysis, you might arrive a few minutes early if the classroom is available so that you needn't take time to write during the class itself.

The chalkboard has some disadvantages, all of which are pretty obvious. You can't prepare the material for posting in advance (other than arriving a bit early). This may be of special concern when you don't want the class to look at the material at the beginning of the class, unless the room has some sort of screen over the board that you can use to hide the writing. For example, you may want to try to elicit a three-prong test from your students and then have them review the way the court applied the test in a particular case.

---

36. Doug Linder, *Lessons Learned from Building the Famous Trials Website*, Jurist Legal Intelligence, Lessons from the Web, *at* <http://jurist.law.pitt.edu/lessons/lesjan01.htm>.

37. *See id.*

Unless there's a screen to hide the writing, you'll be tipping off your students if you've written the complete statement before they arrive. If you wait until you've teased the test from them during the class to display the court's statement, you'll use valuable class time to write the statement. Plus, I always feel a little self-conscious if I take much time writing on the chalkboard, knowing that the students are watching me invariably immerse myself in chalk dust.

You obviously can't save what you've written. Which means that if you want to refer to it again, you'll need another version of some sort. This also means that your students will be scribbling down whatever you write, likely assuming that if it's up on the board, it's of special significance. So the more you write on the board, the more likely you and your students may be distracted from the discussion at hand.

Of course, if even you have difficulty reading your handwriting, you'll need to make an extra effort to be sure your postings are legible. I'm routinely surprised when I do write a phrase across the board and then step back; it looks quite straight when I'm up close, but seemingly took on an upward tilt of its own. You'll need to exaggerate the size of your writing, especially if you've got a large class, so that the board will be visible to everyone.

Another somewhat commonsensical concern is audibility. Remember that if you continue to lecture as you write on the board, your back will be turned to the students and you'll need to raise your voice to be heard. Of course, you can just take a moment to write the phrase and then resume your lecture. It's usually once you step back, however, that the students are better able to see what you've written, and thus their scribbling begins, potentially distracting them from hearing your next thought.

If it's not unduly cumbersome, you could bring a tablet of prepared text or graphics to the classroom to display on an easel. Unlike the chalkboard, you would have discretion as to when to reveal the material, could retain it, and would avoid distracting students or usurping class time to write the content. The obvious disadvantage is that a tablet that is sufficiently visible to the entire class probably is too unwieldy to transport.

Overhead Transparencies and Graphic Presentation Programs

Compared to the chalkboard or dry-erase board, overhead transparencies are advantageous because they can be prepared in advance, and yet you can still annotate them or point to particular aspects while you're lecturing. They're readily transportable and they can accommodate graphics and illustrations. You can simply write on clear acetate with colored pens, or you can reproduce material on a duplicating machine that accommodates acetate; the latter may be available only in black and white or may be available in full-color. It's also possible to convert computer graphics files to transparencies on special printers, depending on the hardware and software to which you have access.

In today's technological environment, transparencies often are eschewed in favor of computerized slide presentations that use such software as PowerPoint, Presentation Slides, or Corel. You can create text, craft graphics, and scan in or download other material, including photographs, maps, charts, and other illustrations. The computer functioning allows you to save, edit, shift the order, and even add various visual effects. And of course the finished product isn't dependent upon the quality of your handwriting. Some on-line graphics providers offer a searchable database of images that can be incorporated, sometimes even without the need to clear permission from copyright holders.

Graphic presentation programs such as PowerPoint are thus a helpful option. Such programs can be used to create electronic slide shows based on templates for content and design, by creating a blank presentation, or by modifying an existing presentation. Clip art, charts, and graphs may be added to enhance the visual appeal of the presentation.

Another variation of slide displays is the use of a presentation system such as the SmartBoard that allows you to both project prepared material and annotate it during the class session through a touch-sensitive board. A word-processing document can be prepared in advance, projected during the class session, and edited with colored markers.

Such presentations often incorporate textual bullets designed to focus students' attention on key points during the lecture and facilitate their note-taking. Or you may want to use the aid to refer to new terms, especially if they have complicated spellings or are in a foreign language. It can also assist pupils whose first language is not English and are concentrating more intently to follow a lecture with unfamiliar jargon. Displaying the full name of a statute or regulatory agency that you invariably refer to by an acronym can be a useful reminder.

You'll want to anticipate students' heightened focus on the displayed material. There will be a presumption that if you've taken the trouble to devise bullet points and display them, they must be important. I often think that people naturally, albeit subconsciously, also assume that if something is typed, it must be accurate, or at the very least important; if it's printed, it will probably be credited with brilliance. This presumption may well be losing its vitality in light of the ubiquity of computers, through which users routinely communicate even informal, typo-laden, casual chat by keying their messages. But keep in mind that in the context of your lecture presentation, students will defer to you as an expert on the subject and imbue the slides with significance simply by virtue of your having prepared them in advance.

When you prepare your slides, consider, too, their overall design. Slides can be overwhelming if they're too dense; you can include a few summary bullet points with brief phrases that will be amplified by your lecture and the ensuing discussion. The slides rarely if ever should be a mere duplication of a prepared speech. An entire sentence is conventionally appropriate only when the phrasing of the sentence itself is of pivotal importance, such as when the class is charged with construing a statutory clause. You may decide to display a graph or chart with extraneous material because it would be difficult or too time-consuming to tailor it to your needs or because you want to use the primary source to emphasize adherence in order to enhance credibility. In such circumstances, you can highlight the relevant portions in order to focus attention on the aspects to be addressed. The typeface should be legible and of adequate size to be viewed by the entire class. Points deserving of emphasis can be scored or placed in variant colors, bold-face type, or italics.

Clarity of presentation is important. Visual depictions are readily susceptible to comparison and emphasis. Data can be compared by using contrasting colors, for example. Attention can be focused by using a marker (such as an arrow or a circle), gradations or variation in color, different typeface, or overlays. As with textual prose, you'll want to maintain the accuracy of your presentation so that facts aren't distorted through graphical depiction.

Reflect as well on how informative the slides will be after a lapse of time. Will the brief phrases adequately refresh your class' recollection of the discussion? Will students have had the time to annotate your bullet points with the corresponding class discussion to contextualize them? Professors sometimes resolve this concern by posting slides only after the class concludes so that they don't become a substitute for note-taking or preparation for the class.[38] Others use them as a means of summarizing the prior sessions' concepts, reducing the frequency with which students rely on commercially prepared outlines.[39]

Still others distribute or otherwise make available a copy of their presentations to students in advance of the lecture, perhaps by posting them on a faculty web-site for future consultation. Occasionally slide show presentations are placed on a CD-ROM that accompanies a casebook and are made avail-

---

38. *See, e.g.*, Gregory Sisk, *Using PowerPoint in Law School Classes and on the Web*, Jurist Legal Intelligence, Lessons from the Web, *at* <http://jurist.law.pitt.edu/lessons/lesnov02.php>.

39. *See id.* (comment by Rogelio Lasso).

able to faculty who adopt the book for use in their classes.[40] There are those who feel that the distraction likely engendered by copying information displayed during the class session is ameliorated by assurances that a set will be made available. Others feel that bullet points or similar items displayed in the presentation are a visual device designed to target students' attention and direct their focus, and that taking notes, making inferences, and integrating concepts should be left to the students.

Consider, therefore, whether the slides will facilitate your students' note-taking and develop their note-taking skills, or instead become, in effect, a proxy for their effort to do so. Because students will attribute special significance to your prepared presentation, they'll probably try to write down every item on every slide. You'll want to allow time for them to do so in order to avoid feelings of frustration or the inevitable chat of conferring with a neighbor to ascertain what was missed.

Videotapes, Film, and Audio Materials

It's possible that you'll want to show an excerpt of a videotape or film during a class. Maybe you have access to a recordation of a trial that was covered by the broadcast or cablecast press. Or you may have video or audio material that sets up a factual situation that you want to use to stimulate a discussion about the applicable legal claims and principles. Perhaps you have access to a work read in the author's voice. *New York Times* editorial journalist Verlyn Klinkenborg wrote about the utility of hearing great authors read their own works, remarking that otherwise "I hear the literature I read in the tonality of my own inner voice, a silent voice, mostly, enslaved by the eye."[41]

You might play excerpts of an oral argument in a seminal case. Perhaps involve the students by pausing the tape after a question is asked by the judge of the party's counsel to elicit the class' response. Then listen to the lawyer's reply and ask the class to assess its persuasiveness and legal foundation. This technique effectively combines aspects of simulation exercises (*see infra* at 158) and the Socratic method (*see infra* at 154).

A videotape or film might be used in an Environmental Law course to visually portray topography, beach erosion, or urban development. Or an ex-

---

40. *See, e.g.*, Norman Garland, *From Punch Cards to CALI: My Pedagogical and Scholarly Experiences Online*, Jurist Legal Intelligence, Lessons from the Web, *at* <http://jurist.law.pitt.edu/lessons/lesfeb00.htm>.

41. Verlyn Klinkenborg, *The Silence of the Past Gives Way, and Dead Writers Peak Once More*, N.Y. Times, July 5, 2003, at A10.

cerpt of a trial in which cameras were admitted could be shown in a Trial Advocacy class to demonstrate direct and cross-examination techniques.

Jan Constantine, Executive Vice President and Deputy General Counsel of News America Corporation, has conducted employment issues training seminars by first showing a scene from "The Mary Tyler Moore Show." The audience watches Lou Grant, Mary's eventual boss, conduct a job interview, inquiring about her religion (which Mary declines to answer) and then asking why she hasn't married. The scene continues as Mary then responds, "Presbyterian," and when Mr. Grant looks surprised, she indicates that rather than answer his question as to why she's still single, she's decided to answer the prior question.

The scene is entertaining and it's fairly brief and thus it doesn't usurp much valuable time for the session. Sometimes members of the audience chuckle at the very beginning and recall having seen the episode when it first aired. Thus, in addition to setting the stage for a discussion about issues pertaining to discrimination, there's a subtle reminder that when one has the benefit of legal training, a variety of incidents may be understood to implicate legal issues.

One professor, Robert Rains, reported showing the "Titicut Follies" film,[42] which depicts conditions of the Massachusetts Correctional Institution at Bridgewater to which persons deemed mentally ill or charged with crimes had been committed. The film was said to include "a hodge-podge of sequences... depicting mentally ill patients engaged in repetitive, incoherent, and obscene rantings.... The film is excessively preoccupied with nudity.... [N]aked inmates are shown desperately attempting to hide...their privates with their hands.... There is a scene of [a priest] administering the last rites of the church to a dying patient [and] the preparation of a corpse for burial.... A...patient, grossly deformed by...congenital brain damage, is paraded before the camera."[43]

The Massachusetts Attorney General objected to the film, amongst other reasons, on the ground that it invaded the privacy of those depicted.[44] The film was ordered suppressed from general audiences but the court declined to uphold the injunction with respect to "legislators, judges, lawyers, sociologists, social workers, doctors, psychiatrists, students in these or related fields,

---

42. *See* Robert E. Rains (quoted in Gerald F. Hess and Steven Friedland, *Techniques for Teaching Law,* 115 (Carolina Academic Press 1999)).

43. *Commonwealth v. Wiseman,* 249 N.E.2d 610, 612, 617, 356 Mass. 251, 252, 261 (1969) (citation omitted), *cert. denied,* 398 U.S. 960 (1970).

44. *Id.*

and organizations dealing with the social problems of custodial care and mental infirmity.[45]

The case raises important questions about free speech generally and whether in particular the court's segregation of the audience based on the training of its constituent members and presumptively ostensible professionalism is a principled basis on which to determine access to the film.[46] Showing an excerpt of the film undoubtedly would generate visceral reaction in a Privacy Law class from which a spirited dialogue would ensue about the tension between access to information that helps enlighten the citizenry about important matters of legitimate public concern and the privacy interests of especially vulnerable individuals.

Rains showed the film to students in a Disability Law Seminar. "I want students to feel what long-term institutionalization meant for mental patients," he explained.[47] Such a vivid portrayal helps sensitize students to the conditions to which the patients were subjected in a way that mere textual descriptions cannot.

Of course, in an academically rigorous environment like law school, tape and film are rarely if ever a reasonable substitute for class discussion or lecture. They should consist of a brief clip or excerpt that you've pre-screened to illustrate a point or serve as a foundational fact pattern so that they are intrinsically related to and readily integrated into the class session.

Interactive Learning Devices and Computer Assisted Information

The World Wide Web can allow you to extend the dialogue you stimulate during class beyond the assigned class hour and offer a way to reinvigorate traditional approaches to legal education. There are a variety of ways to accomplish this while still being mindful of ensuring that students do not become overwhelmed by the amount of time they're required to put into the course. As Barbara Glesner-Fines of the University of Missouri at Kansas City School of Law observed, "web authoring tempts adding more teaching to the package. The risk is student overload."[48]

---

45. *Id.*, 249 N.E.2d at 617-18, 356 Mass. at 261-62.

46. *See* Madeleine Schachter, *Informational and Decisional Privacy*, 200 (Carolina Academic Press 2003).

47. Robert E. Rains (quoted in Gerald F. Hess and Steven Friedland, *Techniques for Teaching Law*, 115 (Carolina Academic Press 1999)).

48. Barbara Glesner-Fines, *The Rewards and Risks of Authoring a Web Site*, Jurist Legal Intelligence, Lessons from the Web, *at* <http://jurist.law.pitt.edu/lessons/lesaug98.htm>.

Certain courses in particular may pose special demands on the accessibility of a teacher. Appellate advocacy, legal reasoning, and writing and research seminars often generate ongoing questions from students who seek more regular contact with their instructor.[49] Interactive functionalities, used purposefully, can streamline professors' responses to repeatedly asked questions.

You also can exploit technology to offer a global perspective to the study of law. A professor who teaches International Law observed that "[g]lobalization is infiltrating every legal domain, whether in the commercial, nonprofit or governmental sectors, even fields as seemingly 'local' as family law."[50] Some professors have invited persons who are not affiliated with the academic institution to participate in electronic exchanges as a means of soliciting views from foreign lawyers and others. A "Joint Privacy Project," an international collaboration between professors at the Catholic University of America in Washington, DC and Bond University in Queensland, Australia, was used as a way to familiarize students with technologies that are increasingly used in "a technically sophisticated world."[51] If you've established a discussion board (*see infra* at 121), for example, you can grant guest access to one who wishes to audit the class or contribute to the dialogue.

Interactive learning devices promote a shared learning environment and provide a locus for collaborative work. An interactive discussion "allows each participant to speak as often as any other member of the group, and the physical trappings of the usual classroom, which make the teacher the center of attention, are absent."[52] University of Maryland School of Law Visiting Scholar Paula Monopoli noted that browsing the Web lacks "the same tactile satisfaction as picking up dusty old books and skimming their yellowed pages, [but it has] the benefit of being able to engage in an activity without ever leaving [one's] desk."[53] Interactivity also can mitigate the insularity that might otherwise exist with distance education.

---

49. *See, e.g.*, Spencer S. Boyer and Gregory Alan Berry, *Unlikely Buddies: Faculty Websites Can Help Bridge the Seniority Gap and Promote Collegiality,* Jurist Legal Intelligence, Lessons from the Web, *at* <http://jurist.law.pitt.edu/lessons/lesoct99.htm>.

50. Donna E. Arzt, *Teaching to the Not Yet HTML-Converted,* Jurist Legal Intelligence, Lessons from the Web, *at* <http://jurist.law.pitt.edu/lessons/lesjun99.htm>.

51. Susanna Fischer, *Choosing Appropriate Web Courseware for Your Law School Class,* Jurist Legal Intelligence, Lessons from the Web, *at* <http://jurist.law.pitt.edu/lessons/lesapr01.htm>.

52. Peter Tillers, *There is Something Foul in Legal Education. And the Internet is Part of the Cure,* Jurist Legal Intelligence, Lessons from the Web, *at* <http://jurist.law.pitt.edu/lessons/lesdec00.htm>.

53. Paula A. Monopoli, *The Evolution of PortiaLaw,* Jurist Legal Intelligence, Lessons from the Web, *at* <http://jurist.law.pitt.edu/lessons/lessept00.htm>.

The Virtual Law Class and Distance Education

"Distance education" has been defined by the American Bar Association as "an educational process characterized by the separation, in time or place, between instructor and student."[54] Such training includes courses that are primarily offered through technological transmission (such as via the Internet, open broadcast, closed circuit, cable, microwave, or satellite transmission), audio or computer conferences, video, or correspondence.[55] The ABA notes that, ironically, distance education methods "present[both] special opportunities and unique challenges for the maintenance of educational quality."[56] Distance legal education has been offered for specific courses and as a law school in its entirety; both implicate accreditation issues.

Accreditation is significant because in order to secure a license to practice law in the United States, most law school graduates apply for admission through a state board of bar examiners that is an agency of the jurisdiction's highest court or associated with the state's bar association. Eligibility to take the bar examination (or, as many refer to the process, to "sit" for the exam) generally requires that the applicant hold a degree from a law school that meets specified educational standards; such determinations typically are made by relying on ABA approval.

Although the ABA's standards state that "a law school shall not grant credit for study by correspondence,"[57] there are certain exceptions to course offerings. The standards contemplate credit for distance education courses provided their content, pedagogy, and student evaluation methods are approved as part of the school's regular curriculum approval process. Credit for such courses may be counted toward the requisite instruction time for regularly scheduled classes at the law school so long as the courses include "ample interaction with the instructor and other students both inside and outside the formal structure of the course throughout its duration;" and "ample monitoring of student effort and accomplishment as the course progresses."[58] Even when distance education courses do not meet these standards, they may be taken to satisfy permissible study outside the law school.[59] The aggregate num-

54. American Bar Association Standards for Approval of Law Schools, ch. 3, standard 306(b).

55. *Id.* at 306(b)(1)-(4).

56. *Id.* at 306, Interpretation 306-2.

57. *Id.* at 304(f).

58. *Id.* at 306(c)(1) & (2); *see also id.* at 306(a).

59. *See id.* at 305(a).

ber of credit hours of a student's courseload for courses in which two-thirds or more of the instruction are conducted through distance education, computed over the course of the semester and over the course of the law school career, are constrained.[60] Further, distance education courses may be taken only after significant credit hours already have been accumulated.[61] More specific criteria may be set by the respective state boards of bar examiners.[62]

As of mid-2003, the ABA had not accredited law schools offering a Juris Doctor degree through on-line study. As Professor Steve Sheppard observed, "One reason to continue to require personal instruction rather than automated access will be a technical requirement of state bar licensure, that law faculty representatives certify the character and fitness of their students to practice law."[63] Reservations about the quality of distance legal education were notably expressed by Supreme Court Justice Ruth Bader Ginsburg. While lauding the integration of Internet functionality into the legal education experience, Justice Ginsburg expressed uneasiness about a completely virtual legal education. "'So much of legal education and legal practice is a shared enterprise, a genuine interactive endeavor. The process inevitably loses something vital when students learn in isolation, even if they can engage in virtual interaction with their peers and teachers,'" she stated.[64] In a similar vein, Professor William Slomanson of Thomas Jefferson School of Law expressed doubt that the Socratic method could be replicated on-line.[65]

Proponents of distance legal education counter that interactivity between faculty and the student body is enhanced, pointing out that "'many law schools still have first-year classes of 70 or 80 people in which a student has very little interaction with the professor.'"[66] Professor Paula Berg of the City University

60. *See id.* at 306(d).

61. *See id.* at 306(e).

62. *See* American Bar Association, *Comprehensive Guide to Bar Admission Requirements; ABA Network* (2003), <www.abanet.org/legaled>.

63. Steve Sheppard, *The Role of the Professor in the High-Tech Law School,* J.L. Sch. Computing, *at* <http://www.cali.org/jlsc/sheppard.html>.

64. Justice Ruth Bader Ginsburg (quoted in Katherine S. Mangan, *Justice Ginsburg Raises Questions About Internet-Only Law School,* The Chronicle of Higher Education, *at* <http://chronicle.com/free/99/09/99091302.htm>).

65. Pam Mendels, *Skepticism About Online Law Degrees from a Supreme Court Justice,* N.Y. Times, Oct. 1, 1999, *available at* <http://www.nytimes.com/library/tech/99/10/cyber/cyberlaw/01law.html> (quoting William Sloamanson).

66. Jack R. Goetz, Dean of Concord University School of Law (quoted in Katherine S. Mangan, *Justice Ginsburg Raises Questions About Internet-Only Law School,* The Chronicle of Higher Education, *at* <http://chronicle.com/free/99/09/99091302.htm>).

of New York Law School noted that distance learning techniques may be especially useful in inter-disciplinary courses; they "facilitate teaching at different levels to students from two different disciplines" such as public health and law; "enhance interdisciplinary interaction and collaboration;" and lower "barriers associated with time and place constraints."[67] Engaging students may be facilitated through deliberate and targeted discussions with all members of the class so that some aren't lost amongst more vociferous participants.

Graduate law degrees are available through distance education from St. Thomas University School of Law, which offers an L.L.M. degree in International and Offshore Tax Planning; and the Shepard Broad Law Center of Nova Southeastern University, which offers a masters degree in Health Law. Specialist certificates are awarded through on-line study in Financial Markets by the Center for Law and Financial Markets of the Chicago-Kent College of Law, and in Legal Aspects of E-Commerce, also by the Chicago-Kent College of Law.

The Concord Law Center in California, which, as of mid-2003, was not accredited by the ABA, offers both a masters degree in Health Law and a J.D. degree. The school is accredited by the California Bureau of Private Post-Secondary and Vocational Education, which is recognized solely by the California State Bar, rendering graduates eligible to practice law in California (and possibly states granting reciprocity).[68]

In 2003, the first Web-trained lawyers were graduated from the Concord Law Center, where students attended lectures through audio streamed in real time. Class discussions were conducted via chatrooms. Concord's initial class was comprised of 33 students, of which twelve graduated on schedule. By 2003, 1,200 students were enrolled in the school.[69]

Law courses are available from the Berkman Center for Internet & Society of Harvard Law School. Interactive computer programs offered by CALI Lessons (*see supra* at 56) and the Bridge Project of Harvard Law School provide on-line instruction. Individual courses have been offered through long-distance learning. Multi-user dungeon object-oriented ("MOO") technology, for instance, enables virtual space to be shared electronically.

The LexisNexis Web course (*see supra* at 59–60) includes a virtual classroom page that enables real-time lessons and perusal of prior sessions. Guest speakers can be admitted. LexisNexis suggests "grouping students into several

---

67. Paula E. Berg, *Using Distance Learning to Enhance Cross-Listed Interdisciplinary Law School Courses,* 29 Rutgers Computer & Tech. L.J. 33, 36 (2003).

68. Bob Sullivan, *First Net-Schooled Lawyers Pass Bar,* MSNBC.com, *at* <http://www.msnbc.com/news/920131.asp>.

69. *See id.*

small groups to keep the conversation manageable" if a session is overwhelmed with too many users.[70]

Some law professors who have taught virtual courses have helpfully shared their thoughts about their experiences. Susan Brenner of the University of Dayton School of Law, for example, taught a Criminal Law seminar in 1998, creating a web-site[71] and requiring students to collaborate on a draft of a model state computer crimes code.[72]

Virtual education can utilize technological devices designed to enhance student participation and promote meaningful communication with classmates, the professor, and even external faculty and commentators. But, as Professor Joan Bullock of Florida A&M University College of Law remarked, there's a disparity between connections with students in classroom and in on-line settings. In the former, she noted, "much can be learned from the student—how well he or she is learning the material, how motivated, etc., from body language, eye contact, class participation, or lack thereof. In the online environment, [the professor is]...not able to see the student in order to gauge whether the material [is] 'sinking in' or assess the student's level of motivation."[73] Kathy Marcel, a former law professor who works as a curriculum and implementation consultant for an educational media company, concluded after taking and developing on-line courses that "the best online instruction, like the best law courses, are instructor-facilitated, student-centered, and interactive. The role of the instructor in an online course, as with the role of a law teacher, is not to impart knowledge but rather to design an experience and guide students through a process of discovery through his experience."[74] Recall the comments other professors made about what most inspired them to teach law (*see supra* at 9). Mark Dubois of the University of Connecticut School of Law "could not have imagined the joy of being there when the light finally clicked on...."[75] While it may still be possible on some level to divine epiphanies from students'

---

70. *See* LexisNexis, *Building LexisNexis Web Courses in Blackboard® 5.5.* (Advanced Instructor Manual), *at* <http://www.lexisnexis.com/lawschool/faculty/>.

71. *See* <http://www.cybercrimes.net>.

72. Susan Brenner, *Teaching a Virtual Law Class,* Jurist Legal Intelligence, Lessons from the Web, *at* <http://jurist.law.pitt.edu/lessons/lesmay99.htm>.

73. Joan R. Bullock, *Online Education: No Substitute for the Classroom,* Jurist legal Intelligence, Lessons from the Web, *at* <http://jurist.law.pitt.edu/lessons/lesjan03.php>.

74. Kathy Marcel, *Can Law Be Taught Effectively Online?,* Jurist Legal Intelligence, Lessons from the Web, *at* <http://jurist.law.pitt.edu/lessons/lesdec02.php>.

75. Mark Dubois, *Why I Teach,* Institute for Law School Teaching, The Law Teacher (Spring 2002), *at* <http://law.gonzaga.edu/ilst/Newsletters/Spring02/dubois.htm>.

electronic postings, query whether they offer the same rewards as face-to-face observation of moments of clarity and comprehension.

In any event, distance education does allow students to engage in educational endeavors according to their preferred schedules and at their own pace. Such instructional devices are highly portable, available wherever the student transports his computer and has an Internet connection.

Asynchronous Methods

Interactive dialogue with the class can be achieved with reduced disruption to schedules through asynchronous methods. Such communication does not necessarily occur simultaneously. This means that the professor and students post messages that can be read by one another but does not presuppose contemporaneous responses. Asynchronous on-line environments can be supported through e-mail and discussion boards to create a shared workspace, support document uploading, and facilitate concurrent and multiple notification of administrative matters. Ronald Staudt, a Professor of Law at Chicago-Kent College of Law of the Illinois Institute of Technology and Vice President for Technological Development of LexisNexis, observed that "ubiquitous connectivity delivered by local area networking and the introduction of the Internet added interactive communications power that paper could never offer. Asynchronous communication with the professor or the study group with precise reference to the texts in question could make the electronic casebook itself a repository for electronic discussion."[76]

The Discussion Board

Classroom learning can be enhanced through a discussion board, sometimes referred to as a compilation of "threads," which allows a professor or discussion leader to pose a question or outline a hypothetical. Students can then respond, eliciting further replies from the professor and other students and so perpetuating a dialogue. The message and its threads can be stored in a forum. A LexisNexis Web course built with Blackboard 5.5.1, for instance, can incorporate a discussion board to promote collaborative learning.

One obvious advantage of this device is that it extends the discourse beyond the temporal confines of the class setting. Of course, the professor should be mindful of the requirements he imposes on students' time, lest the

---

76. Ronald Staudt, *In Search of the Origins of the Electronic Casebook,* Technology: J.L. Sch. Computing, Center for Computer-Assisted Legal Education, The Law Teacher (Spring 2002), *at* <http://www.cali.org/jlsc/staudt.html>.

course become unwieldy. Conversely, it also may be important to establish guidelines about how much participation is permissible. An eager student may inadvertently intimidate his classmates by dominating a conversation, who may infer from extensive postings that they, too, should be exceeding the stated requisite or recommended level of participation. As is the case with a physical classroom setting, the class' discourse must be carefully navigated by the professor.

Professor Michael Geist pointed out that "discussion groups can be used to regulate class tension. Particularly emotional topics can result in frayed nerves in the traditional classroom dynamic. Discussion groups allow students to vent their frustrations and force them to carefully consider their responses, since writing e-mail is far different from speaking in class."[77] Discourse on polemical issues arguably can benefit from more deliberation before views are exchanged.

Used judiciously and applied with parity, a discussion board can also help the professor gain perspective about the comprehension level of the class or of individual pupils. Comments that reflect a misapprehension about a rule of law can suggest that the teacher review a topic or clarify a principle, either through a posting or during the next class session. The board also affords the professor time to deliberate, a luxury that is often absent during a lively class discussion. You can re-read a student's question to try to better divine the source of his misunderstanding without having to instantaneously reply as you would during a class session. You likewise have time to reflect about how to steer the discussion. There's more opportunity to consider ways to acknowledge students' input and guide the dialogue to stay focused than there is during a class session when you're endeavoring to be responsive to questions that seek clarification but begin to veer off course.

You can supplement a point raised during a class discussion or muse about a tangential issue through a "blog," a Web page typically comprised of frequently updated posts set out in journal form. You might, for instance, summarize a court decision rendered during the course of the semester, indicating that while the case is not assigned, it bears on theories covered in the course.

As you review the class' postings to assess their relevance and credence, you may see that you've elicited a greater diversity of viewpoints by virtue of having the means and the time to gather comments from more students than you feasibly could do during a single class session. When you pose a question during a class, your lesson plan may accommodate time to solicit responses from

---

77. Michael A. Geist, *Where Can You Go Today?: The Computerization of Legal Education from Workbooks to the Web*, 11 Harv. L.J. & Tech. 141 (1997), *available at* <http://jolt.law.Harvard.edu/articles/11hjolt141.html>.

just a few students. There's an understandable temptation to move on if a class member answers the question with a thoughtful, reasoned response. In doing so, though, you may not only miss an opportunity to ascertain whether any pupils don't understand the comment, but also fail to elicit comments from those who disagree or have another meaningful or creative contribution.

Students, too, have more time to deliberate about their comments when they participate in a discussion board. This may be especially important for an individual who finds it challenging to formulate and articulate his thoughts orally in a large classroom setting. Such a reaction may be exacerbated in situations when the student is called upon and taken a bit off guard. Using a discussion board may enhance the quality of the discussion because students can pause a bit to think about the question and the responsiveness and relevance of their reply.

Again, though, you want to encourage your class to participate in the discussion board without spending undue time agonizing over the phrasing of their comments. If you sense that the board is usurping too much of their time, you might consider announcing that you don't expect them to focus on such matters as the citational form they use as they refer to cases; you'd prefer that they work to review the prior remarks and formulate a response promptly.

Imposing time constraints may be even more productive. You might, for instance, state that the board is "open" for response only for a certain amount of time after the student has accessed it. The class member therefore must respond to the postings within a confined period of time from the moment he has logged on. This approach has the added benefit of ensuring that the discussion board doesn't impose excessive demands on students who are, of course, juggling multiple classes and possibly outside employment, scholarly, or other activities.

You may, however, be confronted with the opposite situation, in which you find that your students are not actively participating in the board or are spending inadequate time reviewing the postings. If it's important to you to integrate the discussion board within the course's curriculum, you might clarify to the class that their participation is expected as it is a pivotal component of their educational experience. Of course, reiterating that the grade is partially dependent on their participation likely will serve to motivate, too.

There's also the challenge of ensuring that a student doesn't participate solely by repeating his classmates' comments. Explain that simply indicating that you agree with another posting is not adequate if it is done on a regular basis. One way to deal with this issue is to rotate the task of responding first to a question so that the same student or the same few students don't routinely jump in while the others hold back. Or you might indicate your feedback only after a threshold number of students have posted comments in order to allow others in the class to opine or to explain why they believe a remark is unfounded.

E-Mail Messages

A variation on the discussion board is the exchange of e-mail messages. E-mail similarly presupposes that communications are not necessarily contemporaneously exchanged, which affords you and your students time to deliberate about a response and allows flexibility about the availability of you and your students to participate. Some programs allow for a closed loop on the server so that all of the messages relate to the course and permit sorting of the messages.

Unlike an open and communal discussion board, however, you can arrange these communications privately so that you're communicating with the class on a one-on-one basis. This alleviates concerns that a single class member might dominate the discourse or that some are not participating. You can easily include more students in the discussion if you'd like, simply by adding their e-mail addresses when you send or reply.

It also means that you can address a concern with a student confidentially. You might indicate that a student's posting touched on the subject but didn't reflect a thorough understanding of the assigned reading. Or you can encourage a student who has been reserved in class by emphasizing the positive aspects of his postings and even affirmatively suggesting that he reiterate them at the next session because the entire class would benefit from hearing his thoughts.

Newsgroups, Mailing Lists, and E-Conferencing

Distributed message databases, such as Usenet newsgroups, are exemplified by user-sponsored newsgroups. They consist of open discussions but are not necessarily conducted in real-time. A mailing list, sometimes referred to as a "listserv" or "listproc" because of the software programs on which they are run, is similar to a Usenet newsgroup. Both function like electronic bulletin boards, facilitating postings for others to read and enabling access to the messages posted by others. "Majordomo" is a term used to refer to one who speaks or makes arrangements for another from the Latin root "*major domus*" meaning "master of the house."[78] Such community-supported file software programs automate the management of Internet mailing lists, performing such functions as moderating lists, enabling archival maintenance of messages, facilitating remote retrieval, digesting messages, and confirming that access is restricted to subscribers.

---

78. *See, e.g.*, Great Circle Associates, *at* <http://www.greatcircle.com/majordomo/>.

A law list can assist with the dissemination of information and include an electronic discussion group, an e-mail list, and perhaps even a bulletin board.[79] Subscribers may be able to access a digest of messages and search archives. Lawprof, for instance, is an Internet listserv that resides on the Chicago-Kent College of Law site, designed as a discussion group for law faculty who teach in universities and professional schools.[80] A listserv's message is directed to one's e-mail account, whereas access to a newsgroup is dependent upon the individual's navigation of the newsgroup.

E-conferencing likewise enables many users to conduct an on-line discussion group in a centralized fashion. Like newsgroups and lists, e-conferences typically focus on a particular theme. E-conferences also may permit users to establish new themes within the conference to stimulate another discussion.[81] E-conferences can include audio, video, and/or Web-conferencing and may be conducted synchronously as well (*see infra* at 128).

Not only might you participate on a faculty law list or newsgroup to stay current about legal developments and share insights with your peers (*see supra* at 33), but you can also use this technology to allow the entire class to see messages regarding matters raised by the professor or students. (Guidelines to establishing a list are available from several sources.[82]) Some professors have broadened the composition of the class by adding others to the listserv. You might, for instance, allow a student who would like to audit the class to participate or observe, or grant access to non-academicians who are practicing, writing, or developing policy in the relevant substantive area. A member of a legislative body in a foreign country who is looking at similar issues may help broaden students' cultural perspectives about disparities in international law by participating in the list.

In addition to the advantages and disadvantages outlined above regarding other asynchronous communications, you might notice that a newsgroup posted an initial problem or question that generated numerous lines of re-

---

79. *See generally* Lyonette Louis-Jacques, *Law Lists on the Internet,* Legal Information Services, 3 L. Tech. J., *at* <http://www.law.warwick.ac.uk/ltj/3-2f.html>.

80. Subscription to the list requires a message directed to <listproc@chicagokent.kent law.edu> with the message "SUBSCRIBE LAWPROF" and a brief reference to your name and institution.

81. *See, e.g., Web-Conferencing,* Teaching Effectiveness Program, Academic Learning Services, University of Oregon, *at* <http://tep.uoregon.edu/technology/discussion/motet. html>.

82. *See, e.g., Electronic Mailing Lists,* Teaching Effectiveness Program, Academic Learning Services, University of Oregon, *at* <http://tep.uoregon.edu/technology/discussion/ lists.html>.

sponses. Organizing these and tracking the responsiveness of multiple messages to different points can be challenging. It may be helpful, at least to some degree, to encourage participants to include and modify subject lines of their messages as they post. If two students have expressed different ideas virtually simultaneously, a respondent might, for instance, add to the subject line of his reply something like, "picking up on Jenny's point" or "more on the policy considerations."

Remind your students that even if access to an interactive electronic device is restricted through screened subscription, they should not automatically presume that their comments will be kept confidential. Also caution your class to consider whether it's appropriate to confine a response or remark to you or another individual, rather than replying to the entire list. The basic criterion should be whether the posting or question likely will further the dialogue or is relevant only to one person or a couple of people. A request for an extension of time to submit a paper, for instance, concerns only the student making the request. Etiquette considerations also should be taken into account; if the student feels that a debate has deteriorated into opprobrious comments, you may want to have a private electronic, face-to-face, or telephonic conversation with the individuals involved. Mutual respect for diverse viewpoints should be accorded in comparable fashion to the atmosphere fostered in a physical classroom setting.

Synchronous Methods

Software programs also are available to enable real-time (or virtually real-time) conversation through Internet relay chat and Web-based conferencing. Access may be unrestricted, allowing all to participate; private, restricting participation; or semi-private, enabling some to listen only or others to speak.

Chatrooms

The chatroom is a real-time communication device, allowing communication to appear almost immediately on remote computers. On-line chats facilitate contemporaneous communications, essentially mirroring the classroom experience in electronic form. Of course, as with other electronic devices, you miss out on all the non-verbal cues to which you'd otherwise have access. You won't see a student's perplexed frown, necessarily perceive an inflection suggesting emphasis of a particular point, or observe that an individual has become distracted.

Sometimes, however, access to mere textual remarks helps focus the recipient on the content of the statements. It also may diminish an inadvertent tendency to misread verbal cues, as when a student nods after the point is clarified but remains confused.

Like other discussion devices, you'll be able to track the chatroom's participants, allowing you to monitor which students have logged on and to attribute comments to each in order to assess their value. As with other methods, you'll want to be clear with your students about whether their participation is mandatory. You might, for instance, use the device as a surrogate for office hours. Your availability in a chatroom during the school's reading period before exams may be especially appreciated by students who want to ask a few questions or see the extent to which they're following comments from their classmates. Chatrooms therefore can be an integral component of a course, a periodic offering, or an occasional forum upon student request or with the professor's advance notice.

If you're contemplating use of a chatroom as an extension of the classroom discussion, you'll probably need to emphasize your expectations about the responsiveness of comments. The device might otherwise become a compilation of tutorials, lacking cohesiveness and requiring you to answer individual questions about matters that generated confusion. Also indicate that you expect students to be carefully reading one another's comments, lest you find yourself answering the same question repeatedly.

As with the classroom experience, you'll want to observe which students are participating, especially if you're expecting everyone to contribute. It can be easy for a student to sign onto the chatroom and then step away from his computer, suggesting attendance but missing out on the benefits of the discussion. Some call these "lurkers," referring to students who were electronically present but eschewed entreaties to become engaged.[83] You can, akin to the classroom experience, invite participation. "We haven't heard much from Joe," you might say. "What are you thoughts about Carolyn's last point?"

Chatroom discussions can be archived and thus made available for review by students for study purposes or in the event they were "absent" from the session. This also is important if you add a chatroom to the course without noting it in the registrar's bulletin because in order to conduct contemporaneous discourse, you'll obviously need to set a time for the chatroom; depending on the size of your class, at least some students may have a scheduling conflict that will preclude their contemporaneous participation.

---

83. Johnny Burris, Debra Curtis, Steve Friedland, and Billie Jo Kaufman, *Venturing Into the On-Line Wilderness: Some Lessons Learned,* Jurist Legal Intelligence, Lessons from the Web, *at* <http://jurist.law.pitt.edu/lessons/lesfeb03.php>.

Webcasts

Another synchronous method is webcasting. This involves recording a lecture or other live event and streaming it over the Internet. Audio and/or video transmissions are broadcast over the Internet. As is the case with some types of e-conferences (*see supra* at 125), webcasts can be conducted asynchronously as well, as when the lecture or event is archived for delayed viewing. Thus prerecorded or live lectures can be offered through webcasting, provided that users have the necessary multi-media applications to view them.

Class Sessions

Planning Course Sessions

Articulating Session Objectives

It's important to have a clear sense of the objectives of each session and a plan for achieving them. This requires you to fashion a structure for each class session.

Begin by thinking about the topic you'll be covering. From a high-level or macro perspective, what is the thesis you'll be addressing? What's the heading on your syllabus for this class? What's the primary focus of the session?

Next, try to set forth just a few basic themes. What four or five fundamental concepts do you want your students to take away from the session? What basic concepts comprise an understanding of the theses of the session?

During the class, you'll want to emphasize these key points. You can accomplish this in a number of ways. Reiterate the themes or explicitly indicate that they're significant. Demonstrate their significance by articulating the themes' inter-relationship. Verbally cue the class as to their importance; indicate, for instance, that "it's important to remember that...." Modify your inflection. Change your posture; if you've been sitting, stand up. You might gesture a bit with your hands. When you or another makes a relatively tangential point, indicate its status; "while that's merely one aspect of...."

As you list the themes under the session's overall thesis, what ancillary or corollary principles do you want to discuss? How might you illustrate each of these? What hypothetical situations or fact patterns might stimulate thought? Deliberate about the underlying policy rationales. Explore the fairness of the law as it has developed.

Then reflect on the reading assignments. Where does each fit in? How can you tie the excerpts to the themes and ultimately to the overall thesis?

Do you have visual or audio aids that you'll be integrating? Annotate your notes so that you'll know when to refer to a graph or annotate on your PowerPoint display when you plan to move to another screen.

Scrutinize the terms to which you'll be referring. Remember to reiterate new terms and their acronyms. Indicate that you're repeating yourself; you might say something like, "again, by 'SEC,' I mean 'the Securities & Exchange Commission.'" Spell unfamiliar nomenclature and possibly add a visual aid, such as a notation on the chalkboard or a slide.

Go back to the beginning of your notes. How will you introduce the session? Do you want to begin with a discussion of a reading assignment or present a hypothetical fact pattern? Think of all the novels and historical accounts you've read that begin in the middle of the story, grab your attention, and then go back to a chronological account to contextualize the introduction. Would this approach work for you? Or recall all those books you've read that use a "flashback" technique to interrupt a present-day account to depict a historical event. Might you start with the current state of the law pertaining to your thesis and work back to help the class understand how the principles evolved?

As you consider the methods you'll use to inspire your students and cultivate their analytical abilities, consider the *components* of your analysis. Suppose Ms. Jones wrote a note to Mr. Smith that said, "Maybe in a few years I'll sell you an acre of land." You've concluded, virtually contemporaneously with reading the sentence, that Mr. Smith cannot rely on the note as the basis of an enforceable agreement to purchase Ms. Jones' land. Now step back and think about how you so readily arrived at your conclusion.

Your students likewise may have an intuitive reaction that it wouldn't be fair to turn over Ms. Jones' land to Mr. Smith. They'll likely sense that the note is incomplete in some fashion. How will you take this mush of a conclusion and help them channel it through a prism of principled analysis?

What were the components of your conclusion that the agreement wasn't binding? Perhaps several concepts come to mind in seemingly free association. Lack of consideration. Absence of assent. No offer. Illusory terms (what price? which acre?). Statute of Frauds issues.

Can you organize these concepts in a logical sequence? Might you discuss principles relating to offer before probing what constitutes acceptance? Then would you turn to rationales for the existence of consideration? Is the Statute of Frauds aspect appropriately conceptualized as a requirement when real property is transferred or as an affirmative defense to be asserted by Ms. Jones?

Then can you tie each concept to applicable caselaw, branching out to explore nuances of principles that may be gleaned from the assigned readings?

As you consider these, what policy rationales support the criteria for a binding agreement?

After you've completed these exercises, you'll want to craft conclusions about the session's thesis and correlative themes. Wrapping up at the end of the session provides closure and context and offers an opportunity to segue to and entice interest in the next session (*see infra* at 184).

Allocating Course Material to Class Sessions

Conducting classes effectively necessitates suitable allocation of reading assignments and discussion stimulants to each course session. While you'll already have fashioned a syllabus that has ordered the sequence of the substance of the course and allotted reading assignments to each meeting of the class, you'll also need to pace your presentation. Nearly every professor who has been entrusted to teach a two- or three-hour session fears that he will have insufficient material. There the professor will stand, all eyes focused upon him, with absolutely nothing else to say. No hypotheticals to posit. No questions to answer. No other insights to convey.

Despite repetitive deep-breathing exercises, the professor will only be able to calm himself with assurances that there are extensive readings, numerous ways to provoke class discussion, and likely much interest amongst students to voice their own opinions. This most assuredly will take up class time. But wait. What if there's *too much* material to cover? What if you manage to review only the first three pages of a 50-page assignment? What if you have more to say, having diligently prepared thoughtful and incisive commentary, only to see your students gather their books and backpacks and leave skid marks and a cloud of dust as they exit the classroom?

The answer to all this is that, well, there is no answer. You can't time a class discussion with the same precision with which NASA launches a rocket. There's simply no way you can be absolutely certain how long it will take you to explain a concept or the number of questions and opinions your presentation will generate.

Besides, it might be quite stimulating to follow the flow of the class' interest and discourse. Despite your most exacting and thorough preparation, you can't necessarily anticipate what will intrigue or perplex your class. Classroom discussion inevitably varies from class to class, even when you've taught the same course with the same text in the past. While you're responsible for guiding the discourse, provoking student participation, and pacing the class session, you also need to be responsive to students' cues. When a few students seem confused by an aspect of the legal principles and theories covered in the course, it's sensible to pause and review the material. As Chris Iijima noted, prepared lectures will "veer off course occasionally – perhaps prompted by a student's question."[84] Sometimes the diversion results from a lively exchange or a provocative comment. At least some of those instances offer a chance to shift the focus a bit.

Sometimes you've invited friends over for dinner and elaborately set the table in the dining room, but everyone ends up eating and chatting in the kitchen. You can either contrive a migration back into the dining room, or (more sensibly, perhaps), you can shove aside the newspaper, the coupons, and the kids' homework and plop down in the kitchen with your friends. The key even with desultory class discussions is to continue to navigate the distractions and utilize diversions judiciously and purposefully, ultimately transitioning back to the course plan and resuming a telic orientation.

There are some specific things you can do to orchestrate the pacing of the class and help stay on track with your syllabus. You can, for example, actually time how long it takes you to espouse a particular point. Perhaps, quite admirably, your grasp of the material is so thorough that you need only a couple of brief phrases in your notes to prompt you. Your handwritten notes or your PowerPoint bullet points comprise an aggregate of, say, a dozen words. That doesn't look like very much when you view it on your screen or print it out. Now actually stand in front of a mirror, and, using a clock, explain the phrases as you would were you standing in front of the class. How long did it take you? Was the actual time it took the same as your estimate?

Another tip is that if you have to choose between having *too much* and having *too little* material prepared, go with the former option. It's far better to lament at the end of a class that you still have more you'd like to impart than to be standing in front of a group of eager pupils with 25 minutes left to go and not have much more to say.

Also, when you go to each session, bring your notes and other presentation materials for the next session. You can always introduce a new topic. Just be careful not to expect your students to have read the material for the next class. After all, the assignments are not yet due.

You can always take a break. This is reasonable if your class is more than two hours long. While your students search for coffee, extricate yourself from the classroom. (If you stay at the lectern, you may be accosted with such questions as whether something will be on the final exam. You need this time.)

---

84. Chris Iijima, *Four Distinctions and a Pet Peeve,* Institute for Law School Teaching, The Law Teacher, (Fall 2002), *at* <http://law.gonzaga.edu/ilst/Newsletters/Fall02/iijima/htm>.

Take a moment to look over your lecture notes and reflect on comments and questions the prior discussion elicited. Are there other hypotheticals you might pose? Are there analogies you might make? Do you want to go back and clarify a point? Is there some concept you want to review in order to emphasize it or lay a foundation for an upcoming discussion?

Consider whether it's appropriate to just end the class. If there's only a few minutes left, you might want to wrap things up. Especially if the alternative is to belabor a point. If you've covered what you set out to do, and the time remaining is relatively negligible, you can just indicate that the class will pick up again with the next theme to be explored.

In preparation for each class session, when you organize your lecture notes, you might divide each session into a grid and allocate material to proportional or even disproportionate segments of the class. Say your class consists of two-hour sessions. Divide the material in half, allocating one hour to each half. This doesn't mean, of course, that you must count up the pages of your notes and divide by two. Rather, it means that you're looking over your material to relegate thematic concepts to each half of the class.

Next, divide again in the same fashion. Keep doing this until you've allotted your material to 15-minute segments. As you prepare your lecture notes, consider inserting optional questions you might pose. You can even do this in colored pencil on your handwritten notes or in italics if you type your notes.

During the class session, try to track your progress. Glance at the clock occasionally, or if it's not visible, bring a wristwatch. (You'll want to take off your watch and place it next to your notes so that you can glance at it discretely. You won't want the class to see you turn your wrist to check the time. They might mistakenly infer that you're bored or have a pressing engagement that's making you eager to leave.)

If you see that an hour of your two-hour class session has passed but you're well past the halfway point of your lecture grid, ask some of your optional questions, referenced in your notes in colored pencil or italics. Or resort to a prepared list of virtually universally-applicable queries and other techniques for stimulating a dialogue (*see infra* at 138, 141). Conversely, if a quick glance at your grid reveals that you haven't covered the material within the time-frame you expected, skip your colored-pencil or italicized optional points.

Paradoxically, it also can be problematic to have too much material to cover. Students' attention may wander a bit as the class time comes to an end. You may hear a bit of backpack rustling as the final class hour approaches. Rather than rushing through your material, you can simply point out to the class that there are a few minutes remaining. Quickly glance at your notes or outline to determine how much more you reasonably can cover. Cue students about the progress of the session by saying something like, "and the final point I want to go over today is...." Segue to the next class session (*see infra* at 184) by referring to the material you'll pick up with next time.

Techniques for Lectures and Discussion Management

Teaching Through Lecture and Discussion

No matter how many times you've engaged in public speaking or how well prepared you are, it's quite common to feel a bit nervous as you begin each class. Even experienced teachers who have taught the same subject repeatedly can feel that way when they look out at a sea of faces. This feeling may be especially acute at the start of the semester when you begin each of your new classes.

There are a few things you can do to try to minimize that tension. First, careful organization and diligent preparation really are key. When you pause to think rationally about the cause of your feelings, to the extent there is some logic lurking about, it's likely that you feel concerned that you'll forget some important information, lose your train of thought, or be stumped by a difficult question. If you've carefully read the material, thoroughly reviewed the themes for the session, and deliberated about your approach, you'll feel more comfortable simply because you won't have to concentrate as hard on what to do next. If you're well prepared, it won't be as disruptive if you lose your place in your notes or need to revert to your planned discussion after a digression from a question.

You'll also feel that your mastery of the material will reduce the likelihood that you'll be asked a question to which you won't have some response. You can remind yourself, however, that in the event such a query is made, it's fine to say that you'd like to think about it a bit and will address it later (even if you don't get to it until the next session, after you've done some additional research). Remember, too, that sometimes the question itself, asked by a novice who is still working to master the course's subject matter, has a logical fallacy in it that complicates its very premise. You may need to clarify the question, which at the very least affords you more time to consider the matter. And you can indicate that you're not quite sure about the source of the student's confusion and so would prefer to take the matter up after class so that you can move on.

Because preparation will help reduce feelings of nervousness, consider memorizing the very beginning of your lecture. Sometimes the hardest part is simply getting started. If you've got that first paragraph down, you can focus less on formulating your thoughts with proper syntax and more on launching into the class discussion.

Remember that you and your students are collaboratively engaged in a learning enterprise. Some have recommended that you "[t]hink in terms of *communication* rather than *performance.* Your students are *not* theater critics waiting for you to flub a line. They're probably more empathetic rather than judgmental...."[85] If you stumble over a few words so that an incomprehensible mumble emerges, pause, chuckle, and start again. You can acknowledge the burble by saying something like, "Whew! Let me try that again."

Try to determine what makes you feel most comfortable as you position yourself to conduct the lecture. Do you feel a bit shielded by a lectern on which you can rest your notes? Is it easier for you to move about the front of the room without being tethered to a microphone?

There are some fairly conventional public speaking tips, all of which you've heard before. Speak slowly, audibly, and without mumbling. Don't allow your inflection to suggest a question when you're in fact making a statement. Sometimes it's helpful to just make a mental note to remind yourself of these basics before you begin the class session.

Maintain eye contact with the members of your audience. You can gain visual impressions as you lecture, getting a fairly accurate sense as to whether the class is engaged merely through the observation of non-verbal cues. Students who are attentive, interested, and comprehending often nod as you make a point and make regular eye contact with you. Negative indications include facial expressions such as frowning, looking at a neighbor's notes, or chatting with others. You can help minimize disinterest not only by offering respites from the monotony of lecture through discussion and the integration of media tools (*see supra* at 109), but also by consistently maintaining eye contact with class members, speaking colloquially as appropriate, and interrupting from time to time to solicit questions.

Maintaining eye contact is also important because it leads to considerable selfish rewards. The visual connections you make with your students afford unique and extraordinary glimpses into comprehension; you have special insight into the instant that separates confusion and clarity. As well, you get virtually contemporaneous feedback about aspects of the lesson that sparked special interest or generated bewilderment, enabling you to adjust your lecture a bit to accommodate the class.

Is it appropriate to read to the class from your notes? I've never understood the point of watching someone simply read aloud from a prepared speech

---

85. Teaching FAQs, Teaching Effectiveness Program, Academic Learning Services, University of Oregon, *at* <http://tep.uoregon.edu/resources/faqs/presenting/stagefright.html>.

without deviation or eye contact. It seems to me that he could just as easily have given me the prepared statement to read at my own pace, thereby also obviating my need to scribble frantically and spell unfamiliar names and terms phonetically. Uninterrupted reading can be monotonous even when there are variations in voice inflection and body language, rendering the content fairly easy to tune out. Your students undoubtedly are looking to connect with you and you'll deprive yourself of glimpses of insight and inspiration if you're unnecessarily focused on prepared comments.

An exception to efforts to eschew reading during lectures is when you want to emphasize that the words you're speaking are attributable to another. Perhaps, for instance, the argument being made is fallacious or seems particularly repugnant to you and you want to avoid an inference of endorsement. Or you may want to credit the statement to another, as when, for example, you want your students to be mindful that the Supreme Court as the nation's highest judicial authority issued the pronouncement. The phrasing of the statement may be especially eloquent and thus deserving of exact recitation. There also are times when the precision of the language is critical to an understanding of the legal doctrine in operation; guiding your students in a task of statutory construction may well depend on the very words used by the legislature.

Of course, it's quite reasonable to rely on notes or a lecture outline to some degree. Even when you're able to go through much of a class session or a speech without referring extensively to notes, it's comforting to know they're there; if you've been distracted from your train of thought by students' questions or discussion on a tangential issue, an indication as to which justices joined in the concurring opinion or a reference to the year a case was decided will be right there waiting for you. Notes can be especially important when you're teaching more than one course in the same semester, especially if the subject matter is inter-related or the reading assignments overlap. A quick glance at your notes helps orient you and reminds you of the session's lesson plan.

Try to remember as you proceed with your lectures that even if your students have diligently completed the reading assignments, the material, the concepts, and the skills of applying doctrine to facts are still new to them. Repeat new legal terms. Define acronyms multiple times. ("Again, when I refer to the 'NDA,' I mean the 'non-disclosure agreement.' ")

As you prepare your lectures, you might outline basic themes and, on a separate page or in the margins of your notes, refer to the issues and legal authorities relating to tangential points. If the discussion veers toward one of these corollary issues, you'll be poised to discuss it and then resume your overall lesson plan.

As you facilitate the class discussion, work to promote civility and respect. Learning is best facilitated in an atmosphere of mutual tolerance in which ideas can be exchanged without intimidation. Demonstrate this principle by respecting the views of others with whom you disagree. Point out contrary points of view with tact. Neither show nor tolerate disdain for others' opinions. Remember that you're effectively working not just as an instructor but also as a mentor. Chief Judge of the U.S. Court of Appeals for the Seventh Circuit Richard Posner points out that even as to student-edited law reviews, "editors, a subset of law students, are, like the rest of the law students, apprentice lawyers. It is natural for them to imitate their masters: lawyers and, especially because of proximity, law professors."[86] Your students may not consciously realize that they're watching how you interact with others, but they'll likely pick up on your approaches and inflection. This applies as well to your responses to those who misstate the applicable law, are unprepared, or whose reasoning is unsound. Of course, you don't want to leave the class with the impression that a misstatement is accurate or that being unprepared for class is acceptable. But neither do you want to be dismissive or disparaging of the student who made the comment.

You might respond to a student who made a misstatement by saying something about how many do believe that there's no deadline to assert a civil claim, but in fact it's interesting to note that there are statutes of limitations that address the matter. Then turn to someone else to ask, perhaps, about the policy underlying such statutes. You might return to the first student to follow up with a question as to whether he agrees with the proffered rationale or to probe for circumstances under which the rule could lead to an unfair result.

In connection with your efforts to promote robust debate and foster respect for disparate viewpoints, you may decide at times to withhold your personal opinions lest students presume that it will be beneficial simply to agree with you. This way, you can effectively urge students to draw conclusions independently of authoritative pronouncement. Pupils are thereby educated to strengthen and develop skills of reflection and analysis. But neither is it appropriate to suggest to your class that they should disagree with others solely for the sake of dissension. Independent but critical thinking is the goal.

You'll also need to monitor the responses of class members to one another. If there's an egregious instance of disrespect, you'll need to intercede, expressly indicating that the tone or statement is inappropriate. A fairly simply method of fostering respect is to affirmatively endorse positive demonstrations of such conduct. When a student courteously and correctly articulates a legal doctrine

---

86. Richard A. Posner, *Law Review Conference: The Future of the Student-Edited Law Review*, 47 Stan. L. Rev. 1131, 1135 (1995).

after an erroneous statement by another, acknowledge the former's tact by saying something like, "Thanks, Jim. Well said." If a student accurately states the point but seems to preen excessively, you might consider resisting the temptation to endorse the statement at that moment or to nod in acknowledgement. You can signal to the class shortly thereafter the substantive point that you want them to remember without necessarily approving the demeanor of the student. You will have sent a subtle message that disdain for others will not be rewarded.

Similarly acknowledge enthusiasm for the course but discourage tactics that are disruptive. If a student calls out or interrupts another, you can just motion to him to wait while you call on another. Sometimes this seems to be simply the product of where the student happens to be sitting in the class; he just may not realize that others behind him, out of his range of sight, also are volunteering to speak. If the situation persists, you can just address it directly by saying, "there are several with their hands up; I'm going to take some comments first from those who haven't yet spoken."

Indicate to your class that you expect them to prepare for class. You're effectively coaching your students through the process, cheering them on as they master new skills and concepts and instilling a sense of capability. Professor B. Glesner Fines concluded that learning is best fostered through the maintenance of high expectations; "high expectations are correlated with high achievement, low expectations with low achievement. Moreover, once expectations are established, they tend to be self-sustaining for both students and teachers."[87]

Sometimes a student will regard his comment as a contribution to the class when in fact it's merely the product of an intuitive reaction to a hypothetical or case study, rather than a reasoned response premised on legal principles culled from assigned case excerpts. You can gently challenge the student by asking him to tie his point to a court's ruling or statute.

Try, too, to listen carefully to students' questions. They may well reveal a common point of confusion, helping you determine what needs to be clarified or reviewed. Be prepared to defer a question or curtail a discussion if it veers off course dramatically. You can, however, offer to continue the conversation at some other point.

It's also useful to repeat questions before responding. This confirms that the student's query has been heard by the entire class and implicitly legitimizes the process of asking questions and the particular query. Students may, with-

87. B. Glesner Fines, *The Impact of Expectations on Teaching and Learning,* 38 Gonz. L. Rev. 89, 91 (2002-2003).

out even realizing they're doing so, infer much from your tone and receptivity as you address the question. They draw conclusions about whether you regard it as a breach of etiquette to interrupt the lecture with a question. And they form impressions about the degree to which you've scrutinized the student's inquiry to determine whether it was founded on deliberative reasoning culled from the readings or whether it's valid to be confused by a point that could have been readily resolved by careful attention to the content of the assignments.

Acknowledging the student by name when you repeat the question and formulate your response also helps remind you of those who have been participating. When you say something like, "Maria raised an interesting point," you're more likely to recall later that Maria had been engaged in the class discussion, a useful point not only as you work to learn students' names but also as you score class attendance and participation.

In addition, repeating the question gives you a bit of extra time to reflect on precisely what was asked and how you might be most responsive and also connect the query to the discussion to be resumed. You also can re-phrase a question so that the matter to be explored is stated a bit more clearly for the class.

Stimulating and Managing Class Dialogue

Class discussion is an essential part of the legal education experience. Through participation in a group dialogue, students learn to articulate legal principles and explain the analytical bases of their reasoning. An interactive discourse also promotes interest and attention; interspersing lectures with questions and explanations by students varies the rhythm and diversity of the class presentation. Discussion exposes students to different viewpoints and advocacy styles, helps students stay engaged and attentive, and provides insights for the teacher as to whether the material is being absorbed and comprehended.

It's also important to encourage students to listen to one another. Your response to one student may help inform and shape the ensuing dialogue. In addition, prepared students contribute meaningfully to the class dialogue. And students need to learn to distinguish between well-reasoned and inaccurate comments.

You can promote attention to the class generally by asking follow-up questions. "Let's pick up on Richard's point," you might say. Or you can repeat a remark that wasn't audible and preface it with an invitation to consider the matter further. Praising an insightful comment will stimulate attention, too, as the class will be eager to make note of a thoughtful statement. Creating an environment that's conducive to query will encourage the class at large to listen to questions and responses from students as well as from you, in case their classmates probe or clarify matters about which they, too, were puzzled.

The dynamics of your class will vary from semester to semester even if you're teaching the same material at the same law school. Such factors as the size of the class, the degree to which students are prepared for class, and even potentially synergistic effects of participation in class dialogue all contribute to the class composition and overall tenor. There are several techniques you may consider in order to stimulate class discussion, but it's not surprising to discover that some are more successful than others with particular classes, better suited to certain subject matter, or more consistent with your personal teaching style.

One way to generate a discussion is to throw out a question for response. If there are no volunteers, try making the question even more provocative, which may stimulate a reaction from a student. It also may be helpful to include an erroneous assumption in a statement in order to create an environment conducive to challenge.

Of course, there's the conventional approach of calling on students. Sometimes professors choose students randomly; other times they systematically call on students based on their alphabetical order on the class roster or their places according to the seating chart. Calling on students helps equalize participation so that more vocal students don't dominate a discussion at the expense of more reticent participants. When you call on students, either because you're selecting them from a seating chart or through some other means, or because you're acknowledging that a student has raised his hand to offer a contribution, consider vacillating between each side of the room and between front and back rows. This avoids generating the focus of the discussion to one cluster of students and helps maintain overall class attentiveness simply because students are seated adjacent to those who are speaking.

Occasionally, a teacher will call on a student who appears to be distracted in order to direct his attention back to the class and to deter him from drifting off in the future. If the student is otherwise generally attentive, this seems to me to be rather punitive. It may be a more valid technique, however, if the individual is routinely unfocused.

You might consider utilizing the "discussion leader" approach (*see supra* at 84) in which students are specifically assigned dates on which they're expected affirmatively to contribute to the class dialogue. Discussion leaders can assume even greater responsibility for class dialogue by being assigned a session in which they'll be asked to try to respond to classmates' queries and remarks. Of course, you don't want this to deteriorate into a competitive effort by pupils to try to "stump" their classmates.

Special care should be taken when your course covers especially controversial topics such as privacy interests attendant to the termination of pregnancy or end-of-life issues. It's helpful to explicitly acknowledge that many have disparate views, informed by religious principles, moral scruples, or cultural indoctrination. Encourage the class to focus on the reasoning of the judiciary as they adjudicate disputes relating to polemical issues, scrutinizing the efficacy of the courts' analyses.

Eliciting the Test

One way you can stimulate class participation is by trying to elicit the court's analysis, such as a tripartite test a court has constructed, rather than feeding it to your students. You might ask students to articulate the general legal rule; you can then set forth a series of circumstances that seem inappropriate to come within the rule and so would give rise to a list of exceptions or provide the bases for defenses. Or you could see if you can draw out the factors judges consider when they make determinations about the cognizability of a particular claim.

Take a claim grounded in defamation, for example. What are the *prima facie* elements? Instead of simply asking the question directly to see who managed to memorize them in time for the class, you might ask a series of questions. If I say that a convicted killer is a murderer, can I be held liable? Your students will quickly see that truth is a defense. Suppose I say that a murderer is imprisoned in Kansas, but in fact he's incarcerated in Kentucky. Will my mistake subject me to an award of damages? You've now got the class thinking about issues relating to substantial truth and defamatory import.

Suppose that your false statement referred to a woman. Is it defamatory to falsely state that a woman has been a victim of rape? Now you've focused attention on the policies underlying the element of defamatory import.

What if I reasonably relied on a credible source for information I included in my published report, but the information ultimately proved to be erroneous? Should I be held accountable nevertheless? Now you've stimulated thought about standards of fault. Is there a difference between criticism of an elected official and a private figure? Might the former have more access to means for rebutting false charges? Students begin to form notions about the dichotomy between public and private figures.

What if I say that "a man" has been convicted of murder? Now you've stimulated thought about the claim's "of and concerning" requirement. You've provoked discussion by embellishing on factual situations to make a point. The next step is to refine the issue by asking tougher questions. What if you physically and otherwise describe the man who you falsely said had been convicted of murder so that his identity assuredly is one of a dozen possibilities? Or one of a hundred?

You can integrate application of the elements you elicited with questions about the judicial opinions you assigned. What do we understand about the standard of truth when we look at *Philadelphia Newspapers, Inc. v. Hepps*?[88] What ancillary issues emerge about the status of the defendant as a member of the press? In today's content-saturated environment, who in fact is a member of "the press"? How will we make that determination?

Along the way, you can probe for the policy rationales underlying the analyses (*see infra* at 143). Why are these factors relevant? What countervailing interests might overcome them?

This technique can be used to focus on a specific legal principle or the analysis set forth in a single court decision. Or the approach can be used to introduce a topic in order to flesh out the claim's broad criteria, from which the class can embark on more in-depth discussions about each element's gloss of judicial precedent and factual permutations.

Virtually Universally Applicable Questions

There are certain questions you can pose that are applicable to a wide range of subjects and can be used in various contexts. One or more of these can be incorporated into each class session or included in your lecture notes as an optional point to raise in the event you've been able to get through most of your prepared points and still have more time left in the class session (*see supra at* 132).

What test did the court apply and what factors seemed especially influential? Your students may dutifully have read the case excerpt and prepared for class with an outline of the facts, issues, and holding. But what moved the court to rule as it did? What factors seemed especially significant?

Were there "atmospherics" to the factual case pattern to which the judge didn't make explicit reference when he explicated his holding but likely influenced him? Was there a disparity in the parties' status? Was one party a minor and indigent, asserting a claim or defense against a formidable and well-resourced corporation? Would a contrary result have been blatantly unjust?

Probing for such factors demands reflection on the likely overall impact of the claim asserted. This training helps prospective lawyers maintain perspective as to whether their arguments will be received sympathetically even when they may be technically persuasive.

---

88. 475 U.S. 767 (1986).

How did the court's application of precedent affect the ruling? Did the court apply a well-articulated, principled analysis? For example, does a determination of a fundamental right by scrutinizing historical tradition entrench prejudice, misguided trends, or anachronistic practices? Or does resort to such experience mitigate subjective determinations by the judiciary? Consider Justice Scalia's wry dissent in *County of Sacramento v. Lewis*, in which the majority Court reiterated that a due process violation is founded upon a showing of conduct that is "conscience shocking."[89]

> [T]oday's opinion resuscitates the *ne plus ultra*, the Napoleon Brandy, the Mahatma Ghandi, the Celophane of subjectivity, th' ol' "shocks-the-conscience" test.... [R]ather than ask whether the... conduct here at issue shocks my unelected conscience, I would ask whether our Nation has traditionally protected the right the respondents assert.[90]

Was the court faithful to applicable principles of *stare decisis*? Can the decision be reconciled with prior judicial determinations as a matter of evolving law or were *stare decisis* principles circumvented? When the U.S. Supreme Court overruled *Bowers v. Hardwick*[91] in *Lawrence v. Texas*,[92] was its rationale for the reversal well-founded, notwithstanding the clear justification for the ultimate result? Justice Scalia, dissenting in the subsequent case, characterized the majority's decision to overrule *Bowers v. Hardwick* as a departure from a previously-articulated standard as a decision that has "proven 'unworkable.'"[93] "Today's approach to *stare decisis*," Justice Scalia maintained, "invites us to overrule an erroneously decided precedent (including an 'intensely divisive' decision) *if*: (1) its foundations have been 'eroded' by subsequent decisions; (2) it has been subject to 'substantial and continuing' criticism; and (3) it has not induced 'individual or societal reliance' that counsels against overturning."[94] Did the Court revise the standards of *stare decisis* set forth in *Planned Parenthood of Southeastern Pa. v. Casey*, "expos[ing] *Casey*'s extraordinary deference to precedent for the result-oriented expedient that it is," as Justice Scalia suggested?[95] Or, because the doctrine of *stare decisis* is not "an inexorable com-

---

89. 523 U.S. 833, 847 (1998).

90. *Id.* at 861-62 & n.1 (Scalia, J., concurring in the judgment) (attributing the "exemplars of excellence in the text" to Cole Porter's "You're the Top").

91. 478 U.S. 186 (1986).

92. No. 02-102, 2003 U.S. LEXIS 5013 (U.S. June 26, 2003).

93. *Id.* at *52 (Scalia, J., dissenting) (quoting *Planned Parenthood of Southeastern Pa. v. Casey*, 505 U.S. 833, 855 (1992)).

94. *Id.* (citations omitted).

95. *Id.* at 60.

mand," is precedent appropriately disregarded when it has not induced individual or societal reliance, as the majority concluded?[96] Clearly, "*Bowers* was not correct when it was decided, and it is not correct today."[97] Is that alone not adequate reason to deny it status of binding precedent?

Do you agree with the court's holding? Do you agree for the same reasons the court relied on to reach its conclusion? Students often presume that judges, by virtue of their appointment or election and experience, must be right. Novice professionals sometimes bestow on judges a virtually irrebuttable presumption of reason. Encourage your students to respect the judiciary but still scrutinize its rulings. Is the Court's analysis in *Bowers v. Hardwick*[98] premised on constitutional principles or on the views of the justices that comprised the then U.S. Supreme Court's majority as to normative practices of sexuality? Is the ruling reconcilable with the dissenting view in *Lawrence v. Texas*?[99]

Would another result have made sense as well? Emphasize to your class that there rarely is a single "correct" answer or a clear and concise statement about "the law." The practice of law demands analysis, the application of theory and principles to new factual situations. In what ways might the class explain disparate holdings rendered by different courts?

What are the underlying policy rationales for the legal doctrine? When students understand the purpose of a rule, they're more apt to understand the rule, remember it, and anticipate ancillary legal principles. A discussion of legal theory and policy also helps inform the efficacy and utility of the justification for the rule.

Consider the notion of contractual unconscionability, for instance. Does such a rule for exempting an agreement from enforceability suggest appropriate consumer protections or undue paternalism? Does it affect the predictability of agreements' enforceability? Is it an appropriate consideration for a court or the product of judicial activism at the expense of free bargaining?

How did changing social norms, modified circumstances, or nascent technological developments affect the court's determination? As the court interprets law, how malleable are its tenets? Had those who drafted and ratified the Constitution "known the components of liberty in its manifold possibilities, they might have been more specific. They did not presume to have this insight. They knew times can blind us to certain truths and later generations can see that laws once thought necessary and proper in fact serve only to oppress. As

---

96. *Id.* at 35 (majority opinion).

97. *Id.*

98. 478 U.S. 186 (1986).

99. No. 02-102, 2003 U.S. LEXIS 5013 (U.S. June 26, 2003).

the Constitution endures, persons in every generation can invoke its principles in their own search for greater freedom."[100] How can construction of the Constitution and other laws consistent with moral justice ensure appropriate adherence to "traditional democratic action" so that the court eschews "tak[ing] sides in [a] culture war, departing from its role of assuring, as neutral observer, that the democratic rules of engagement are observed"?[101]

What does the court's opinion evince about how the judiciary envisages its role? As you critique the test applied by the court, consider whether it is sufficiently elastic to accommodate new technologies and emerging legal developments. Is it the role of the judiciary to devise malleable doctrines or is such a task within the exclusive purview of the legislature, elected by democratic process?

How did procedural aspects of the case come into play? Was the court likely moved by the requirement that it assume the allegations were true because the argument was asserted in the context of a motion to dismiss? What sort of evidence might each party proffer if the same positions were advanced in a motion for summary judgment?

Building On and Integrating the Holding

Analytical skills can be fostered through an incremental construction of legal doctrine and theory derived from the material students were asked to read. First, elicit the facts, issue, holding, and reasoning of a case you've assigned. Your students probably will be quite comfortable with this; they've been trained (or are being trained) to do this, and they were expecting you to ask. Well, at least the ones who prepared for class are expecting to do so. They'll be delighted to hear a question they can answer. What a relief.

Now build on this. There's a reason that game shows begin with easier questions and build up to more difficult ones. And why the sample question on all those standardized tests (at least the way I remember them) asked whether Chicago is "(a) a planet, (b) a country, (c) a state, or (d) a city." You gained a smidgen of confidence, flush with the success of blackening the correct answer grid with your #2 pencil.

You can use this approach to initiate a discussion and lure students into participating. After you've covered one case, do the same thing with another case. Again, more relief. Ah, but now ask your class to compare the two. Can the holdings be reconciled? Can we glean a doctrinal principle from having read these two judicial opinions in juxtaposition?

---

100. *Id.* at *37.

101. *Id.* at *77, *79 (Scalia, J., dissenting).

Integrate a third case. Has the principle we thought we summarized been refined when we factor in the next decision?

Advocating the Opposing Position

Another option is to ask one or more students to zealously advocate a particular position. Perhaps assign them the task of advancing the arguments of the plaintiff in a particular civil case. Once they've forcefully delimited the position, ask them to assert the adversary's defenses and any applicable counterclaims.

This exercise trains the advocate to think about the merits of his opponent's position in order to prepare rebuttals. Just as significantly, the exercise demands consideration of the flaws and vulnerabilities in the position advanced, leading to ultimate conclusions as to the degree to which the argument originally asserted was morally justifiable and legally meritorious.

You might close the exercise with a discussion about the relative persuasiveness of the positions and the advisability of initiating suit and of defending against it. Should the plaintiff have brought suit in the first place? Should the defendant have endeavored to settle the case? At what stage? If a settlement could not have been achieved because the plaintiff intransigently adhered to his position, should the defendant have conceded liability and tried to narrow the award of damages? The task sensitizes students to the utility of resolving a dispute through means other than litigation, reminds them of the risks inherent in an adversarial process, and mitigates a natural propensity toward entrenching the presumed forcefulness of the position they've been assigned to represent.

Offering Context

One of the challenging aspects of the case method (*see infra* at 154) is that the scope of students' knowledge about the applicable facts and circumstances surrounding the dispute that gave rise to the judicial decision is confined to what has been set out in the decision itself. Typically, court opinions included in casebooks are truncated both because they're presented in excerpted form and because they're appellate rulings that don't comprehensively review all procedural and factual circumstances attendant to the matter.

A broader perspective may be offered by consulting trial transcripts, ancillary published opinions, the pleadings and briefs the parties submitted, and contemporaneous press accounts of the suit. Bar association and continuing legal education programs are another valuable source of historical accounts of the dynamics relating to important legal proceedings, as they frequently sponsor panel discussions with those who participated in the litigation.

As you consider the decision issued in *New York Times Co. v. United States*[102] (the "Pentagon Papers case") in a Media Law or a Communications Law course, for instance, you can help contextualize the dispute by taking a moment to review some of the political unrest that surrounded the American military intervention in Viet Nam. (With respect to a collaborative exercise relating to the Pentagon Papers case, *see infra* at 165.) Consider, too, whether the government's effort in 1971 to enjoin *The New York Times* and *The Washington Post* was designed to prevent continued publication of the Pentagon Papers, which covered events through 1968, or to deter similar or even more revealing publication in the future. What relief did the government reasonably anticipate? What can we infer about a plaintiff's likely strategy in pursuing litigation, as distinguished from his ostensible plea for redress?

Did the Pentagon Papers include military secrets or information about ongoing diplomatic efforts? Why did *The New York Times'* outside counsel, Lord, Day & Lord, advise against publication?[103] How did James Goodale, the newspaper's in-house counsel at the time, analyze the risks differently to conclude that "the law was clear[] that it was damn hard for the government to get an injunction based on[, amongst other cases,] *Near v. Minnesota*"?[104]

Abe Rosenthal, then Managing Editor of *The New York Times,* deemed the question for the newspaper "not how could we print such material, but how could we not?"[105] But former President Richard Nixon was later to characterize the principle at stake in the case as the allocation of the discretion to publish; "it is the role of the government, not the *New York Times,* to judge the impact of a top secret document...If we did not move against the *Times* it would be a signal to every disgruntled bureaucrat in the government that he could leak anything he pleased while the government simply stood by."[106] Were the newspapers, as Whitney North Seymour, then the U.S. Attorney for the Southern District of New York, charged, interested in exclusive publication?[107] Or was the most significant aspect of Nixon's point, as attorney Floyd Abrams

---

102. 403 U.S. 713 (1971).

103. *See* Transcript of the American Bar Association Forum on Communications Law, First Annual Conference, vol. 14, no. 4 (Winter 1997) at 7.

104. *Id.* (quoting James C. Goodale, then General Counsel of *The New York Times*).

105. *Id.* at 6 (quoting A.M. Rosenthal, then Managing Editor of *The New York Times*).

106. Richard Milhous Nixon, *RN: The Memoirs of Richard M. Nixon*, 509 (Touchstone Books 1990).

107. Transcript of the American Bar Association Forum on Communications Law, First Annual Conference, vol. 14, no. 4 (Winter 1997) at 8 (statement of Whitney North Seymour, Jr., then U.S. Attorney for the Southern District of New York).

of Cahill Gordon & Reindel LLP pointed out, that Nixon "doesn't talk about national security at all. He's not complaining here about harm to national security. He's complaining about what he perceives, so he says, to be a harm to a principle about who decides what"?[108] To whom should the constitutional prerogative be allocated?

Shifting the Context

Another approach is to probe the elasticity of the legal doctrine you're discussing by applying it to a different set of circumstances. You could illustrate a legal point by referring to a work of fiction or a poem, for example. During a discussion about the First Amendment and defamatory speech, you could allude to William Shakespeare's statement about reputation:

> Good name in man and woman, dear my lord,
> Is the immediate jewel of their souls:
> Who steals my purse steals trash; 'tis something, nothing;
> 'Twas mine, 'tis his, and has been slave to thousands;
> But he that filches from me my good name
> Robs me of that which not enriches him
> And makes me poor indeed.[109]

Or you might pluck a renowned example from history and posit it in modern day to elicit an analysis of the legal implications attendant to the conduct. What if Raphael had been commissioned in modern times to paint "School of Athens" for the *Stanza della Segnatura*? The painting depicts such philosophers as Aristotle, Plato, and Socrates, but some of the figures are actually portraits of Renaissance artists; Leonardo da Vinci is portrayed as Plato, for example. Would da Vinci have a right of publicity or misappropriation claim against Raphael? Would it matter if Raphael painted the portraits on coffee mugs and offered them for sale? Assuming that there was a clear consensus that Michelangelo was portrayed in the painting by Raphael as "brooding" and "self-absorbed," could he assert a viable false light invasion of privacy claim? Is such a depiction defamatory?

What societal benefits in artistry and speech are imperiled if such claims are sustained? Are the claims' cognizability equally affected if the painting is parodic?

---

108. *Id.* at 10 (quoting Floyd Abrams of Cahill Gordon & Reindel LLP, outside counsel for *The New York Times*).

109. William Shakespeare, *Othello*, act III, scene 3.

As opposed to retrospectively considering an issue in modern times, you might shift the context of a historical discussion prospectively. In today's Internet era, you have ample opportunity to analogize the factual situation to an on-line communication or transaction, for example. How might your class draft a search warrant that would cover law enforcement agents' access to an individual's hard drive?

The Fourth Amendment provides that "the right of the people to be secure in their persons, houses, papers, and effects, against unreasonable searches and seizures, shall not be violated."[110] "At the very core" of the Fourth Amendment "stands the right of a man to retreat into his own home and there be free from unreasonable governmental intrusion."[111] In *Kyllo v. United States*,[112] the U.S. Supreme Court considered whether the use of a thermal-imaging device aimed at a private home from a public street to detect relative amounts of heat within the home constituted a "search" within the meaning of the Fourth Amendment. The majority Court concluded that because the government had used a device that was not in general public use to explore the interior of a home that previously could not have been probed without physical intrusion, the surveillance did constitute a "search" that was presumptively unreasonable without a warrant.[113]

Justice Stevens dissented from the ruling, expressing concern about the durability of the Court's analysis for application to other developing technologies:

> Instead of trying to answer the question whether the use of the thermal imager in this case was even arguably unreasonable, the Court has fashioned a rule that is intended to provide essential guidance for the day when "more sophisticated systems" gain the "ability to 'see' through walls and other opaque barriers." The newly minted rule encompasses "obtaining [1] by sense-enhancing technology [2] any information regarding the interior of the home [3] that could not otherwise have been obtained without physical intrusion into a constitutionally protected area...[4] at least where (as here) the technology in question is not in general public use." In my judgment, the Court's new rule is at once too broad and too narrow, and is not justified by the Court's explanation for its adoption. As I have suggested, I would not erect a constitutional impediment to the use of sense-en-

---

110. U.S. Const. amend. IV.
111. *Silverman* v. *United States*, 365 U.S. 505, 511 (1961).
112. 533 U.S. 27 (2001).
113. *Id.*

hancing technology unless it provides its user with the functional equivalent of actual presence in the area being searched.[114]

Under what circumstances are existing legislative and constitutional precepts adequately malleable to encompass unforeseen applications? Nearly a century ago, the Court declared, "Legislation, both statutory and constitutional, is enacted...from an experience of evils.... [But] its general language should not...be necessarily confined to the form that evil had theretofore taken... [A] principle to be vital must be capable of wider application than the mischief which gave it birth."[115] How do technological devices or normative social practices that are not susceptible to facile contemplation when statutes were drafted by the legislature or earlier disputes were adjudicated by the judiciary affect subsequent determinations? One court observed, "New technologies create interesting challenges to long established legal concepts. Thus, just as when the telephone gained nationwide use and acceptance, when automobiles became the established mode of transportation, and when cellular telephones came into widespread use, now personal computers, hooked up to large networks, are so widely used that the scope of Fourth Amendment core concepts of 'privacy' as applied to them must be reexamined."[116]

During a lecture on First Amendment issues pertaining to obscenity, indecency, and pornography, Joel Kurtzberg of Cahill Gordon & Reindel LLP explained the judiciary's reliance on society's traditional disdain for such material as a basis for its disinclination to accord it the solicitude with which other types of speech are regarded. Kurtzberg then cleverly referred to the *Paris Adult Theatre I v. Slaton* decision, in which the U.S. Supreme Court observed that most of the states that had ratified the Constitution by 1792 punished the related crime of blasphemy or profanity despite the guarantees of free expression in their constitutions.[117] Indeed, in 1712, Massachusetts criminalized the publication of "any filthy, obscene, or profane song, pamphlet, libel or mock sermon" in the imitation or mimicking of religious services.[118] The reference vividly illustrated challenges attendant to legal pronouncements in the face of changing social convention.

---

114. *Id.* at 46-47 (Stevens, J., dissenting).

115. *Weems v. United States,* 217 U.S. 349, 373 (1910).

116. *United States v. Maxwell,* 45 M.J. 406, 410 (C.A.A.F. 1996), *mandamus denied,* Misc. Dkt. No. 97-04, 1997 CCA LEXIS 515 (A.F.C.C.A. Sept. 25, 1997).

117. 413 U.S. 49, 104 (1973) (citing Acts and Laws of Massachusetts Bay Colony (1726), Acts of 1711-1712, c. 1, at 218).

118. *Roth v. United States,* 354 U.S. 476, 482-83 (1957) (quoting Acts and Laws of the Province of Mass. Bay, c. CV, §8 (1712); Mass. Bay Colony Charters & Laws 399 (1814)).

And what of new inventions that were not universally expected to be commonly used? Hornbook authors Harvey Zuckman, Robert Corn-Revere, Robert Frieden, and Charles Kennedy recount that in 1829, Martin Van Buren, then Governor of New York, wrote to President Andrew Jackson to implore him to forestall the development of

> "a new form of transportation" – the railroad.... "As you may well know, Mr. President, 'railroad' carriages are pulled at the enormous speed of 15 miles per hour by 'engines' which, in addition to endangering life and limb of passengers, roar and snort their way through the countryside, setting fire to crops, scaring the livestock, and frightening women and children. The Almighty certainly never intended that people should travel at such breakneck speed."[119]

Judicial opinions are replete with presumptions and factual findings about the state of the world, implicitly predicting the impact that the rulings likely will have on future events. To what extent should a court endeavor to fashion an analytical test that is sufficiently elastic to transcend the particular factual situation with which it is confronted, and try to anticipate possible changes? How do shifts in social conventions affect traditional *stare decisis* precepts and the predictability they afford?[120]

Segregating the Class for Comparative Commentary

Another way you can promote class participation is by dividing the class and assigning different material to various students as a means of encouraging them to share the material they've reviewed. In order to comprehensively cover the subject matter, students will readily infer that their respective contributions are essential. Such an approach also might help reduce pupils' tacit reliance on classmates to have prepared for class.

You might assign different judicial opinions to each student or to groups of students that address the same or a similar theme. Perhaps a split in the federal appellate courts on a particular topic will spur a dialogue about the soundness of each court's reasoning. Each class faction can first be asked to summarize the facts and legal analysis of the decision for which it was re-

---

119. Harvey L. Zuckman, Robert Corn-Revere, Robert Frieden, Charles Kenney, *Modern Communications Law* 159 (West Group 1999) (footnote omitted).

120. *See* Madeleine Schachter, *Informational and Decisional Privacy,* 194–98 (Carolina Academic Press 2003).

sponsible. The professor can then ask them to compare and evaluate the reasoning. Or you could ask some class members to explain the majority court's view and others to delineate the dissent's objections. In addition to implicitly recognizing the need for their involvement in the class discussion in order to inform the rest of the class about the case or opinion they read, students will be sensitized to conflicting viewpoints and may well begin to fashion their own views about the efficacy of the legal doctrines and theories offered by the judges.

Similarly, you might assign individual students responsibility for consideration of issues in different jurisdictions. The class becomes dependent upon the contribution of each in order to contrast the approaches. If you're teaching a Trusts and Estates course, for example, you could ask students to delineate the requirements for a valid will in each of a number of different states.

Such comparisons likely will substantially increase the burdens on you to read more material and spend even more time preparing for class. You might decide to use the technique only sporadically throughout the semester. Perhaps the approach is most efficiently utilized in an early session of the course in order to establish a practice of participation.

Keeping the Class Attentive

In the Spring of 2003, Susan Sontag implored students graduating from Vassar College to "[p]ay attention.... Attention is vitality. It connects you with others. It makes you eager. Stay eager."[121] Students occasionally become distracted, however, and their enthusiasm and interest may vacillate throughout the semester. It's often readily apparent when the class' attention begins to wander. You're the recipient of less eye contact. There are fewer hands going up when you ask questions. Maybe there's even a bit of rustling or chatter. You need to grasp hold of their concentration again. But how can you do this as you try to stay on course with your lesson plan?

You can modify your inflection. Change the pitch of your voice. Ironically, you might well do better to *lower* rather than *raise* your voice. There will be a subtle implication that the students need to quiet themselves in order to be sure they don't miss something.

Adjust your body language. Walk away from the podium and approach your students. Use a visual aid to direct students' focus (*see supra* at 109).

---

121. Susan Sontag (quoted in Sam Dillon, *Reflections on War, Peace, and How to Live Vitally and Act Globally*, N.Y. Times (June 1, 2003) at 41).

Consider incorporating humor. Irma Russell refers to episodes of the television show "Seinfeld" in the Contracts class she teaches. "Visualize Kramer and Newman dancing in a frenzied circle, each with one hand clutching a radar detector and the other hand gripped around a motorcycle helmet. The two agreed to trade the goods (a sale under the [Uniform Commercial] Code), but neither trusted the other enough to deliver first."[122]

If you've been speaking for some time, look for an opportunity to engage the class. It can be quite challenging to remain attentive to a lecture for a sustained period. In my experience, students enjoy participating, especially when it's on their terms so that they retain some autonomy as to when they'll contribute to the discussion as opposed to being called on.

Refer by name to students who have participated already, even when you're not calling on them. "This is related to the point Eric made before because...." "Some years later, the appellate court affirmed the ruling Diana explained but on other grounds...." At the very least, you'll have awakened Eric and Diana. There's some sort of inevitable phenomenon we all experience when we hear our names, even if we've not really been listening. We turn our heads in the direction of the one who uttered our names. And in this case, that would be you.

Of course, there's always the sure-fire reference to "the following will be on the final exam...." If your class has become downright unruly, consider shouting this out. You can always look up after a pause, smile, and say, "I'm just kidding. But now that I finally have your attention...."

Pedagogical Techniques

There are several pedagogical techniques currently available to law professors and innovative exercises are continually formulated by creative faculty. You may find that one of these is particularly effective for the subject you're teaching or you may wish to use them in combination, experimenting to incorporate a diversity of approaches. Integrating multiple techniques can help maintain interest and accommodate different learning styles by presenting material in aural, visual, and participatory ways.

Although legal education includes some lecturing, much of the pedagogy is designed to involve students in the learning process. This sometimes is re-

---

122. Irma S. Russell, *Why I Use "Seinfeld" as Precedent,* Institute for Law School Teaching, The Law Teacher (Fall 2002), *at* <http://law.gonzaga.edu/ilst/Newsletters/Fall02/russell.htm>.

ferred to as "active learning," which "means that the students engage in something more than listening, such as discussion, small-group projects, simulation, interactive computer tutorials, field work, and writing."[123] Many credit active learning with "help[ing] to overcome attention problems."[124]

Certain educational techniques are unique to legal pedagogy. Students must be taught to "brief" a case to divine the decision's issue, rule of law, application, and conclusion (sometimes referred to by its acronym, "IRAC"). It's important to learn to further refine review of caselaw to distinguish between the facts and the law, and within such distinctions between disputed and undisputed facts, between material and tangential facts, and between the rule of law and the court's dicta. "The aim of teaching [is] to develop the [pupil's] own powers and faculties rather than to impart facts; to show not so much what as how to learn. The important thing [is] not the end result but the process of learning...."[125]

Historically, English legal training was through the Inns of Court in London and evolved to an American system of apprenticeship. Educational entities developed as lawyers dedicated to teaching and training apprentices attracted students. By 1784, Judge Tapping Reeve established a law school in Litchfield, Connecticut, which operated until 1833.[126] The Litchfield Law School, like other early educational institutions, relied predominantly on pedagogy through lecture.[127]

Thereafter, the Socratic method emerged; its genesis has been widely attributed to Christopher Columbus Langdell who taught at Harvard Law School in the 1870s. He approached the study of law methodically, premised on a belief that law can be deduced from a logical set of principles gleaned from the rulings and reasoning of appellate courts. In Langdell's view, two fundamental principles animate the teaching of law and its study: "that law is a science and that all the available materials of that science are contained in printed books."[128] This philosophy was embedded initially at Harvard Law

---

123. Gerald F. Hess and Steven Friedland, *Techniques for Teaching Law*, 13-14 (Carolina Academic Press 1999).

124. *Why is Active Learning Important?*, Campus Instructional Counseling, Indiana University, *at* <http://www.iub.edu/~teaching/dear52.html>.

125. Anthony Chase, *The Birth of the Modern Law School*, 23 Am. J. Legal Hist. 329, 343 (1979) (quoting K. Silber, *Pestalozzi: The Man and His Work* 126 (1965), quoted in David D. Garner, *The Continuing Vitality of the Case Method in the Twenty-First Century*, 2000 B.Y.U. Educ. & L.J. 307 n.1 (2000)).

126. *See generally id.* at 311.

127. *Id.*

128. Christopher Columbus Langdell, *Teaching Law as a Science*, 21 Am. L. Rev. 123, 123 (1887).

School, marking a pedagogical shift from the apprentice system that had prevailed through much of the nineteenth century.

The Socratic and Case Methods

The Socratic pedagogy remains a venerable part of law school education. The method is premised upon a layered dialogue carefully designed and deliberately navigated to explore concepts through questioning by the professor to elicit responses from students. Socrates introduced Pythagoras' Theorem not by informing him of the answer but by eliciting it from the student; "the suggestion... is that each of us has within him or herself the resources for answering the question.... The further suggestion is that... no one truly has the answer who has not arrived at it for him or herself."[129] The approach is premised on the presumption that students themselves are capable of reasoning the resolution to a legal problem through guided queries; hence students are required to reason rather than merely recite. The didactic approach is a sustained series of questioning by the professor who posits variations on hypotheses to test the viability of proffered assumptions. The method reasonably may be understood to be the very progenitor of an "interactive" approach.

Some regard the term "Socratic" to be "a misnomer for what would better be termed the "Langdellian" or even "Protagorean" method."[130] Others draw a distinction between the Socratic method and the case method, noting that "[t]he Socratic method is a perfect complement to the case method in that it tends to further the primary objective of the case method by requiring students to examine the bases and implications of a line of reasoning in order to build new knowledge."[131]

Amongst the virtues of the technique is that it brings students into the learning process, as they must actively engage in the dialogue. The method is relied on predominantly to teach students to synthesize legal principles and develop skills in critical thinking and contemporaneous articulation. An ancillary benefit is that it vividly sensitizes students that legal issues are not readily susceptible to facile and definitive resolution.

---

129. James R. Beattie, Jr., *Socratic Ignorance: Once More Into the Cave,* 105 W. Va. L. Rev. 471, 477 (2003).

130. Craig T. Smith, *Practice and Procedure: Synergy and Synthesis: Teaming "Socratic Method" With Computers and Data Projectors to Teach Synthesis to Beginning Law Students,* 7 Berkeley Women's L.J. 113 n.1 (2001).

131. David D. Garner, *The Continuing Vitality of the Case Method in the Twenty-First Century,* 2000 BYU Educ. & L.J. at 311.

Notwithstanding students' extensive involvement in the process, the Socratic method demands extensive preparation and attentive participation by the professor. Effective use of the method requires the professor to be conversant with relevant legal doctrine and theory and to be knowledgeable about the assigned material. But the professor also must be able to listen carefully to students' responses, both in order to guide the discourse cogently and to glean instances of possible confusion or error. "Because student responses can suddenly steer the dialogue onto tangential detours, the method requires patience and intellectual agility of both professors and students."[132]

Reliance on the Socratic method also demands careful consideration of the ways in which students' participation will be elicited. Some professors prefer to use a seating chart, systematically or arbitrarily calling on students to ensure that all members of the class are solicited equally to contribute to the discourse. Students may be assigned specific class meetings in which they're expected to be prepared as a means of mitigating concerns – from faculty and students alike – that class members will not be adequately prepared.

One study concluded that "[t]here was a small negative correlation between the level of teaching experience of the professor and the degree to which a professor uses the Socratic method (correlation coefficient: -12). This means that as the number of years of teaching experience increased, the tendency to use the Socratic method likewise increased."[133] The phenomenon may be due, at least in part, to the tendency of those professors who had been taught through the Socratic method to apply it and a predilection of newer academicians to experiment with alternative pedagogical methods. It's also possible that the "intellectual agility"[134] required by the Socratic method tends to relegate its predominant use to more experienced academicians.

The Socratic and case methods have been widely scrutinized. Criticisms include questions about their utility for addressing practical problems that do not attend litigation. Professor Michael Perlin opined, "Our slavish adherence to the 'case law method' – while doing a fine job in preparing a certain percentage of our students for becoming top-notch appellate litigators – fails mis-

---

132. Craig T. Smith, *Practice and Procedure: Synergy and Synthesis: Teaming "Socratic Method" With Computers and Data Projectors to Teach Synthesis to Beginning Law Students,* 7 Berkeley Women's L.J. 113.

133. *See* Steven I. Friedland, *How We Teach: A Survey of Teaching Techniques in American Law Schools,* 20 Seattle Univ. L. Rev. 1, 39 (1996).

134. Craig T. Smith, *Practice and Procedure: Synergy and Synthesis: Teaming "Socratic Method" With Computers and Data Projectors to Teach Synthesis to Beginning Law Students,* 7 Berkeley Women's L.J. 113.

erably in most other ways."[135] Extra-judicial factors and potential resolutions are minimized during the discussion. Socio-political and cultural factors, for instance, may be largely absent from the discussion, especially if the court decisions omit any reference to them. Skills critical to the practice of law, such as interviewing clients, drafting pleadings, and engaging in legal research, are not emphasized, if indeed they are touched on at all, through the Socratic or case method. Nor is there necessarily adequate emphasis on alternatives to litigation; the case method arguably impliedly trains students to regard litigation as perhaps the only, if not the most efficacious, means to resolve a problem or even to redress a wrong. Focus on legislative possibilities is diminished, contractual resolutions are omitted virtually entirely from discussion, and even prophylactic counseling to avoid the potential of ensuing disputes is rarely discussed. Within the context of litigation, there's seldom probing deliberation as to whether the parties should have earlier considered settlement or perhaps considered foregoing a lawsuit entirely. And yet these tactical considerations comprise an essential aspect of the attorney's role as legal counsel.

Some students complain that they find the Socratic and case methods extraordinarily frustrating insofar as they demand extensive preparation and diligence without commensurate rewards of definitive resolution. Even when successfully implemented, the method may leave the class without a cogent understanding of a legal rule.

Amongst the most ubiquitous criticisms of the Socratic method is that it intimidates students and is unnecessarily combative in approach, inducing students to "analyze and dissect everything that someone says...not so much to find the truth, but just for the sake of arguing and pointing out frailties."[136] The concern, while arguably valid, is ironic in light of the method's tacit presumption that students themselves are capable of reasoning towards resolution, a presumption that in theory should instill a great deal of self-confidence. The nature of the professor's questioning, combined with the adequacy of the student's preparation and the resilience, agility, and poise with which he responds to questions, are critical factors in determining whether the method instills confidence or trepidation and even intimidation. The professor's demeanor can feed this tendency or temper it. As well, the student's perception of the demeanor and process is an important determinant of the range between enlightenment and humiliation.

---

135. Michael L. Perlin, *Creative Problem Solving Conference: Stepping Outside the Box: Viewing Your Client in a Whole New Light,* 37 Cal. W.L. Rev. 65, 68 (2000).

136. Thomas Shaffer and Robert Redmount, *Lawyers, Law Students, and People,* 154 (1977) (quoted in James R. Beattie, Jr., *Socratic Ignorance: Once More Into the Cave,* 105 W. Va. L. Rev. 471, 488 n.57 (2003)).

The Socratic method also laudably places a premium on deliberative, rather than merely intuitive, reaction. John Stuart Mill opined that when an opinion "is strongly rooted in the feelings, it gains rather than loses in stability by having a preponderating weight of argument against it. For if it were accepted as a result of argument, the refutation of the argument might shake the solidity of the conviction; but when it rests solely on feeling, the worse it fares in argumentative contest, the more persuaded its adherents are that their feeling must have some deeper ground, which the arguments do not reach."[137] Former Harvard Law School student Scott Turow recounted:

> In our discussions with the professors, as they questioned us and picked at what we said, we were also being tacitly instructed in the strategies of legal argument, in putting what had been analyzed back together in a way that would make our contentions persuasive to a court. We all quickly saw that that kind of argument was supposed to be reasoned, consistent, progressive in its logic. Nothing was taken for granted; nothing was proven just because it was strongly felt. All of our teachers tried to impress upon us that you do not sway a judge with emotional declarations of faith.[138]

That's not to say that the sentimental reactions attendant to circumstances that implicate legal issues should be ignored or even that the effective advocate should not articulate the emotional costs that will result from an adverse ruling. Rather, the emphasis on analytical reasoning is designed to nurture a discipline of thinking in which prospective attorneys are trained to search for and fashion rational and justifiable bases for their positions. Legitimacy is premised on the soundness and logic of the underlying rationale rather than merely the fervor with which the position is advanced.

Ultimately, the Socratic method likely is destined to remain a venerable part of traditional legal education. The approach sharpens analytical skills and doctrinal reasoning. The degree to which it must predominate in any single particular course is open to considerable discretion. Even in courses in which it plays a significant pedagogical role, skills can be cultivated and developed through the use of complementary techniques.

---

137. John Stuart Mill, *The Subjection of Women* (1869) (quoted in Alasdair Gray, *The Book of Prefaces: A Short History of Literate Thought in Words by Great Writers of Four Nations from the 7th to the 20th Century,* 570 (Bloomsbury Publishing 2002 ed.)).

138. Scott Turow, *One L: The Turbulent True Story of a First Year at Harvard Law School,* 73 (Warner Books 1997 ed.).

Hypotheticals, Case Studies, and Simulations

Presenting factual situations for students' consideration, whether based on actual or fictitious depictions, can facilitate reasoned application of legal principles. Seemingly mere platitudes or generalities become more concrete when considered in context. This may foster a better understanding of such conventional legal guidelines as "reasonableness," "good faith" and "bad faith," and "timeliness." Equitable principles such as "unclean hands" take on a clearer meaning when the parties' specific conduct is compared.

Case studies are often used by business schools and in business-related courses as a means of examining the facts and circumstances surrounding a corporate plan or strategy and its consequences. Hypotheticals are used throughout the law school experience to fashion potential or contrived events as a means of eliciting reasoned analysis. The factual premises underlying hypotheticals are generally fluid, enabling the teacher to embellish, shift, or even contradict prior factual assumptions to challenge students' reasoning and solicit new applications of legal principles.

Susan Hanley Kosse, who teaches at the Louis D. Brandeis School of Law in Louisville, Kentucky, incorporates the book *The Buffalo Creek Disaster* by Gerald Stern in the legal writing course she teaches.[139] The book describes the author's representation of survivors of a tragic coal mining accident in West Virginia in a suit against a coal company, providing grist for consideration of such issues as piercing the corporate veil. Other books, such as *To Kill a Mockingbird* by Harper Lee[140] or *One True Thing: Love What You Have* by Anna Quindlen[141] offer fodder for discussions concerning the impact of views about race and gender on the law. Movies that depict courtroom scenes, such as "Inherit the Wind" or "My Cousin Vinny" can be used to stimulate consideration of evidentiary rules. Even episodes of a television series, such as "Law and Order," can generate discussion in courses on Criminal Procedure or Trial Tactics.

Simulation techniques place students in the position of having to assume particular roles from which the class infers conclusions. Students discuss a hypothetical through a vicarious approach designed to resemble actual situations confronted by practitioners. Professor Paul Ferber describes a simulation as an activity that includes "the performance of a lawyering task," the use of "a

---

139. Susan Hanley Kosse, *Buffalo Creek Prevents Legal Writing Class Disaster,* Institute for Law School Teaching, The Law Teacher (Spring 2003), 13, 14, *at* <http://law.gonzaga.edu/ILST/Newsletters/Spring03/Spring03Newsletter.pdf>.

140. Little, Brown & Company 1988 ed.

141. Dell Books 1995.

hypothetical situation which emulates reality," and "a 'significant' (relative to the task to be performed) period of time to perform the task."[142] Thus, unlike a situation in which the professor sets out a hypothetical problem to the class, students prepare responses and assume roles attendant to the situation. Ferber cites as but one benefit of the technique the students' "depth of learning[;...s]tudents seem more often to recognize the presence of jurisprudential theory in cases they read in other courses. They seem more comfortable in engaging in jurisprudential discussions about issues they previously viewed as solely a question of rules."[143]

Simply because one has been an attentive passenger in a car doesn't automatically mean he's able to drive a car and navigate hazardous road conditions. Simulations help bridge the gap between novice and practitioner by affording an opportunity to rehearse client interviews, trial tactics, oral arguments, and other tasks that law students will be called upon to undertake once they begin their legal careers.

Such practice dramatizations have been utilized, for instance, in the study of legal ethics.[144] A fictitious corporate takeover can be illustrated with press releases, stock price postings, and due diligence request lists. An understanding of American and foreign national legislative processes also may be illustrated through simulation. A Civil Procedure or Evidence class might be divided into groups, each moiety given different information and asked to determine what could be discovered from the other side or admitted into evidence. A Law and Medicine course could encompass discussions amongst class members assigned to assume the roles of a live organ donor and his spouse, a patient in critical need of a transplant, a surgical team engaged in promising but experimental organ transplant research, and a hospital in-house counsel.

Counseling and negotiating techniques are encompassed within law school curricula, sometimes offered as distinct courses themselves. Simulations can be used to train students who have been indoctrinated by the Socratic method to endeavor to forge a consensus to resolve a dispute.

Simulations may even be conducted throughout the semester. For example, a Civil Procedure course might use the technique to contrast various types of motions and probe the ways in which discovery and motion practice can

---

142. Paul S. Ferber, *Adult Learning Theory and Simulations—Designing Simulations to Educate Lawyers,* 9 Clinical L. Rev. 417, 418 (2002).

143. *Id.* at 421.

144. *See, e.g.,* Ben Sheehy, *Sinners, Saints and Lawyers: Exercises for Teaching Ethics,* Institute for Law School Teaching, The Law Teacher (Spring 2003) at 4, *at* <http://law.gonzaga.edu/ilst/Newsletters/Spring03/Spring03Newsletter.pdf>.

be exploited to acquire information and advance the client's cause. The technique may be integrated repeatedly into an Evidence course to consider alternative means by which a factual matter may be substantiated even when one avenue is foreclosed by rules relating to admissibility.

Role-playing also affords an opportunity to consider issues ancillary to the representation of clients. In addition to practice interviews of clients, students may be asked to consider whether it's appropriate to take on the case or to counsel the client to consider alternative dispute resolution or settlement. Fee arrangements and representation of multiple parties also may be discussed.

Mock oral arguments and examinations of witnesses may be conducted, even if the course is not specifically devoted to advocacy issues. Students may be assigned the role of counsel and judges. Or they may be asked to assume the position of clients who are charged with evaluating the efficacy of their representation and the reasonableness of the courts' rulings.

Roles of particular judges may be assigned as well. In a Constitutional Law course, for instance, you might assign a few cases with concurring and dissenting opinions by various justices and ask students to be prepared to anticipate how specific justices likely would rule on a hypothetical or case study. This helps students infer doctrinal approaches by individual justices and begin to distinguish amongst the members of the U.S. Supreme Court.

In what is sometimes referred to as a "reverse moot" situation,[145] a teacher could present an oral argument, designating the class or individual class members to act as appellate judges. Questions could be asked of the advocate-professor, and students could then confer to rule (with or without dissenting opinions). The teacher could even present arguments on behalf of both the plaintiff and the defendant, exposing the class to the utility of zealous advocacy from which students can infer that both sides likely have reasonable aspects to their respective positions.

These techniques may be used alone or in conjunction with one another. An Accounting for Lawyers course, for example, might examine the events that gave rise to a federal investigation of auditing procedures. The case study's real facts need not constrain the discussion, however; they may serve as a mere impetus for the class discussion. (Of course, it's a good idea to cue students when you begin to deviate from actual facts that have been substantiated.)

Hypothetical scenarios can be offered to vary the actual events in order to coax creative thought about how a court might apply extant legal principles

---

145. Jean Koh Peters (quoted in Gerald F. Hess and Steven Friedland, *Techniques for Teaching Law*, 221 (Carolina Academic Press 1999)).

to disputes not previously adjudicated. Throughout, students may be assigned various roles to dramatize the discussion and help them visualize the competing interests. You might, for instance, assign students to represent the plaintiff and defendant in a civil case or the prosecutor and defendant in a criminal case. Students might act as an auditor in an Accounting for Lawyers course, a reporter in a Communications course, or a victim in a Criminal Law course. In addition to appointing a student to act as a judge, you might assign someone to assume the role of an in-house client, a corporate executive, an industry trade group representative, or the defendant's insurer.

Notwithstanding the fluidity of the ensuing discussion and dramatization, preparation is critical. Inspiration for hypotheticals may come readily from relevant judicial opinions that you've not assigned or from disputes that have arisen but have not yet been adjudicated. As you sketch out a brief description of the facts in your notes, pause to reflect about other directions the facts might have taken. Who might have intervened in the action and on what basis? What other facts might have tipped the balance of considerations in favor of the party who ultimately was defeated? For what reasons might an appellate court reverse the ruling? Carefully review your notes so that the hypo's permutations are fresh in your mind before class begins; during the session, you'll find it easier to revert to your plan after you've accommodated meanderings resulting from students' comments and questions.

The Problem Solving Method

Closely related to pedagogical instruments of hypotheticals, case studies, and simulations is the problem solving method. The class is assigned a complex legal matter, often by furnishing a summary of the facts in advance of class. Students must then creatively and analytically contrive a resolution. "The ability to engage in creative thinking is essential to problem solving. Problem solving is the essence of what lawyers do. If we are to train students to become effective lawyers, then we must train them to be creative thinkers."[146]

The first task is to listen to or read the facts carefully and to identify the problem. Students must then reflect about whether the facts furnished are relevant and whether additional information is needed. Can further investigation be accomplished by exploiting applicable discovery rules? Will other means of factual investigation, such as witness interviews or searches of websites and news databases, be necessary?

146. Janet Weinstein and Linda Morton, *Stuck in a Rut: The Role of Creative Thinking in Problem Solving and Legal Education*, 9 Clinical L. Rev. 835, 835-36 (2003).

What legal principles are apposite? Legal research can then be undertaken to facilitate the development of a legal theory and evaluate its cognizability. The student, like the practitioner, essentially is asked to determine whether he can transmute amorphous lamentations into an actionable claim.

Brief exercises in the problem solving method can be incorporated into the course curriculum. If you're teaching a Legal Drafting class, for example, encourage students to bring in examples of legal documents. Are there ambiguities in the agreement relating to their cell phones? Is the release proposed when they inquire about renting roller blades or leasing a horse for equestrian sports clearly stated? Similar illustrations may provide a basis for discussion in a Contracts class. Are such agreements binding and enforceable? What is the consideration for the arrangement?

Students might be asked to draft a contract as well. This task can comprise an interim self-evaluation technique for first-year students whose grades might otherwise be the product of a single year-end cumulative exam.

As students consider the problem presented, they might be asked to delimit the client's likely expectations and objectives. If the client's goal is lawful but unreasonable, should the lawyer counsel the client against pursuing the goal?

The problem solving approach arguably more closely mirrors the functions of a practicing attorney than does the Socratic method. Students must sort through relevant and immaterial facts and law to come up with one or more causes of action that can advance their clients' cause. Potential defenses can be considered even when they were not advanced in a particular action. And the class can consider creative resolutions to the problem presented that do not involve litigation. Students also can be asked to re-visit the utility of their theories as additional facts are presented.

Collaborative Learning Tasks

One way to disrupt the potential monotony of routine lectures is to incorporate collaborative or cooperative learning tasks. Clifford Zimmerman of DePaul University College of Law distinguishes between cooperative learning, which "focuses on individual mastery of the subject via a group process," and collaborative learning, which "focuses on group work toward a unified final product."[147] Both techniques foster critical teamwork and negotiation skills. Once students begin to engage in the practice of law, they'll readily see that

---

147. Clifford S. Zimmerman, *"Thinking Beyond My Own Interpretation": Reflections on Collaborative and Cooperative Learning Theory in the Law School Curriculum*, 31 Ariz. St. L.J. 957, 961 (1999) (footnote omitted).

their daily work lacks an arbiter to orchestrate communication. A conference won't be run by a professor who will determine, as you have been, the sequence of speakers or whether anyone even may speak at all. Collaboration also potentially builds confidence; a forged consensus may inspire a member of the team to articulate the conclusion, secure in the belief that others have vetted its soundness. Collaborative approaches may be particularly suited to inter-disciplinary courses to enable students with disparate backgrounds share perspectives and substantive knowledge and to facilitate problem-solving.[148]

Some also believe that cooperative endeavors mitigate "the fundamental angst" experienced by law students, noting that

> regardless of the pedagogical method or structure, one primary goal of legal education is to challenge students to think critically and develop judgment. While this challenge can take many forms, any pedagogy that reaches this end should be welcomed and realistically considered for use. Ideally then, pedagogies such as cooperative learning and collaborative learning, which develop critical thinking and judgment while minimizing or reducing student anxiety levels, should be readily embraced.[149]

The astute pupil will also learn from situations in which the process was not completely successful. One teacher, Kathryn Plank, recounted her experience as a student assigned to a group charged with building an "eggship" from toothpicks, drinking straws, and chewing gum to protect an egg that was to be dropped. Her teammates enthusiastically constructed an efficacious eggship, but Plank felt excluded from the process, relegated to merely recording the endeavor. Plank attributed the dynamics of the group to gender differences, a lack of confidence and experience, and unfamiliar jargon. Although the group's eggship succeeded in its technical construction, the team did not function as inclusively and collaboratively as it might have. Plank noted that even had the eggship been unsuccessful, the failure could have been explored together, possibly leading the team to "arrive at a solution none of us would

---

148. *See, e.g.*, Paula E. Berg, *Using Distance Learning to Enhance Cross-Listed Interdisciplinary Law School Courses*, 29 Rutgers Computer & Tech. L.J. 33 (2003) (discussing collaborative distance education in a public health course that included both public health and law students).

149. Clifford S. Zimmerman, *"Thinking Beyond My Own Interpretation": Reflections on Collaborative and Cooperative Learning Theory in the Law School Curriculum*, 31 Ariz. St. L.J. at 969-70 (footnotes omitted).

have been capable of independently."[150] Thus the most valuable lesson of the collaboration lies in the *process,* not the *product.*

Which means that when you critique your students, you'll want to focus not only on their ultimate submission, but also on their interaction and demeanor. Did they work diligently to include all members of their team? Did they make efforts to compromise when there were differences of opinion? Were they respectful of each other's views, even when they disagreed or another merely repeated a thought previously expressed? Did the group prize consensus over autocracy?

Try to point out positive aspects of the endeavor. Praise a member's attribution of input to his teammate. Explain that it reflected acknowledgement of the endeavor as a group effort that drew on the strengths of each member.

Some professors assign a collaborative project such as a paper. One even offered students the option of collaborating on an exam.[151] These can be valuable learning devices. They may, however, encumber the grading process to some degree. Unlike a classroom exercise, where you can at least partially observe individual input, you'll receive a finished written project upon completion without opportunity to monitor the process. Students may feel some trepidation as well, troubled that their individual preparation and effort will not be adequately rewarded, especially relative to an inferior or lackadaisical contribution from a teammate who will receive the same grade.

One way to address this issue is to expressly articulate your grading approach. At the outset, indicate that there may be a perceived or even an actual disparity in the students' relative contributions. But the success of the *project,* and the grade value to be assigned, is dependent upon the success of the *process.* Explain that you presume that all students have both strengths and weaknesses that can be effectively and cooperatively assessed and exploited through collaboration.

Another relevant factor may be how the groups are organized. You'll want to consider the size of the groups, likely ranging from pairs to triads to groups of five or six. Each group should be small enough to allow all members to actively participate and allow you at least some opportunity to observe or otherwise assess all members' participation.

The way in which the members of the groups are selected also is a matter deserving of consideration. If you've composed the teams, indicate that you've

---

150. Kathryn M. Plank, *The Process and Product of Collaborative Activities Or Three Men and an Egg,* The Penn State Teacher II: Learning to Teach; Teaching to Learn, *at* <http://www.psu.edu/celt/PST/KMPcollaborative.html>.

151. *See* Douglas R. Haddock, *Collaboration on Exams,* Institute for Law School Teaching, The Law Teacher (Fall 2002), *at* <http://law.gonzaga.edu/ilst/Newsletters/Fall02/haddock.htm>.

carefully reviewed the class composition and worked to match students whose abilities and temperaments offer potential for collaboration as well as for the development of needed skills. If you've arbitrarily formulated the groups, such as through random seating arrangements or the alphabetical order in which students' names appear on your class roster, note that the group to which each student has been assigned has been determined fortuitously. If the students have selected their teammates themselves, you could point out that they have the advantage of having chosen people who they believe will work well together. Try to convey the notion that collaborative and cooperative learning tasks presuppose mutual respect amongst students as the techniques essentially are premised on the belief that all students have the potential for achieving and sharing scholarship. Regardless of how the groups were formed, the task offers an opportunity to achieve through effective cooperation; explain that both the process and the result are best subverted by intimidation, poor communication, and a failure to include all members of the group.

The best way to mitigate a potentially distorted evaluation is by incorporating a collaborative task as but one component of a multi-faceted grade. A student's overall course grade will be less impacted by having been assigned to a putatively "weaker" group and conversely will not receive undue benefit such that deficient performance throughout the semester will be offset entirely. Collaborative exercises that are integrated into class sessions may alleviate many of these concerns, not only because you have at least some opportunity to observe the interactions, but also because the assessment of the assignment can be subsumed within the class participation scores.

Grading issues attendant to collaborative exercises can be greatly diluted by utilizing them as part of students' class participation scores for only one class session. I've used the technique during a Law of Internet Speech course discussion on the First Amendment and publication of matters pertaining to national security. Is government censorship ever warranted? How can we delimit justifications for the extraordinarily rare instances when the government might lawfully secure a prior restraint?

New York Times Co. v. United States[152] is a *per curiam* decision with several separate opinions. During the Viet Nam War, the U.S. government sought to enjoin *The New York Times* and the *Washington Post* from publishing the contents of a classified study entitled "History of U.S. Decision-Making Process on Viet Nam Policy." The case thereafter became widely known as the "Pentagon Papers case."

---

152. 403 U.S. 713 (1971).

The Court succinctly reiterated, "'Any system of prior restraints of expression comes to this Court bearing a heavy presumption against its constitutional validity.'"[153] The government was unable to bear its heavy burden of showing justification for the imposition of such a restraint. But the brevity of the U.S. Supreme Court's *per curiam* opinion belies the significance of the decision in First Amendment jurisprudence. Insight into the justices' rationales for the decision is gleaned primarily from their separate opinions.

At first blush, it's relatively facile to cluster the concurring and dissenting opinions and simply infer two divergent views. In order to distinguish amongst them, I break the class into groups, loosely configured simply by fortuitous seating arrangements that particular day. Each justice's opinion is assigned to a different group. I sometimes also assign one group to represent the family of a soldier stationed in Viet Nam. The groups then have approximately five minutes in which to review their respective positions, formulate a response to the family members, and appoint an initial spokesperson.

The ensuing discussion facilitates an understanding of the bases for the individual justices' opinions. How did Justice Black's understanding of federalism principles inform his view about the ability of the executive branch of government to direct the press to refrain from publishing information about the workings of government? What do we ultimately learn about the role of the press in the context of a democratic system? What responsibilities attend the press' functioning? How did Justice Black rely on the historical underpinnings of the First Amendment when he chided that the executive branch in its quest for injunctive relief "seems to have forgotten the essential purpose and history of the First Amendment"?[154]

As Justice Stewart considered an interplay between principles of federalism and the role of the press in a democratic society, as well as the appropriate evidentiary standards to be applied, what is the rationale for his concurrence in light of the fact that he was "convinced that the Executive is correct with respect to some of the documents involved"?[155] Why did Justice White concur in the decision despite the fact that he "confident[ly]" concluded that revelation of the documents in issue "will do substantial damage to public interests"?[156] How do procedural aspects of the injunctive remedy sought by the

---

153. *Id.* at 714 (quoting *Bantam Books, Inc. v. Sullivan*, 372 U.S. 58 (1963); citing *Near v. Minnesota ex rel. Olson*, 283 U.S. 697 (1931)).

154. *Id.* at 715 (Black, J., concurring).

155. *Id.* at 730 (Stewart, J., concurring).

156. *Id.* at 731 (White, J., concurring).

government influence Justice White?[157] What do these conclusions evince about the nature of the burden imposed on the government to enjoin publication, notwithstanding that "it is elementary that the successful conduct of international diplomacy and the maintenance of an effective national defense require both confidentiality and secrecy"?[158]

Justice Marshall deemed it "beyond cavil that the President has broad powers by virtue of his primary responsibility for the conduct of our foreign affairs and his position as Commander in Chief,"[159] but considered the implications of the separation of powers doctrine. Congress had expressly declined to enact legislation that would have authorized the President to enjoin publication in the instant case and criminalize the newspapers' conduct. The class members who represent Justice Marshall's view explain how his conclusion is informed by his understanding of the Court's incapacity to overrule Congress.[160]

How was Justice Douglas' view animated by his reference to the language of the First Amendment that "'Congress shall make no law...abridging the freedom of speech, or of the press'"?[161] Why does "'[t]he fact that the liberty of the press may be abused by miscreant purveyors of scandal...not make any the less necessary the immunity of the press from previous restraint in dealing with official misconduct,'" even though "'reckless assaults upon public men, and efforts to bring obloquy upon those who are endeavoring faithfully to discharge official duties, exert a baleful influence and deserve the severest condemnation in public opinion....'"?[162] As some students put forth the dissenters' views, those who explain Justice Douglas' position espouse the reasons that secrecy in government is abhorrent to fundamental notions of a democratic government.[163]

Justice Douglas relied, too, on the rationale for adoption of the First Amendment, noting that its "dominant purpose...was to prohibit the widespread practice of governmental suppression of embarrassing information."[164] Is Justice Blackmun's dissenting opinion essentially a rebuke? How does he question the plurality's deference to the First Amendment, which, "after all,

157. *See id.* at 740.

158. *Id.* at 728 (Stewart, J., concurring).

159. *Id.* at 741 (Marshall, J., concurring).

160. *See id.*

161. *Id.* at 720 (Douglas, J., concurring) (quoting U.S. Const. amend. I) (footnotes omitted); *see also id.* at 742.

162. *Id.* at 723 (quoting *Near v. Minnesota ex rel. Olson,* 283 U.S. at 719-20).

163. *See id.* at 723-24.

164. *Id.*

is only one part of an entire Constitution. Article II of the great document vests in the Executive Branch primary power over the conduct of foreign affairs and places in that branch the responsibility for the Nation's safety;" has the Court "subscribe[d] to a doctrine of unlimited absolutism for the First Amendment at the cost of downgrading other provisions"?[165]

Justice Brennan offered guidance about the requisite analytical evidentiary standards to be applied. "The entire thrust of the Government's claim throughout these cases has been that publication of the material sought to be enjoined 'could,' or 'might,' or 'may' prejudice the national interest in various ways. But the First Amendment tolerates absolutely no prior judicial restraints of the press predicated upon surmise or conjecture that untoward consequences may result."[166] The class factions representing these justices must explain whether the caution is a technical point premised on a literal reading of the Constitution or whether it evinces deference to the role of free speech generally.

Thus, in addition to distinguishing amongst the justices' rationales for their opinions, the nature of the standard set forth by the Court is probed. If earlier dicta suggested that the First Amendment's ban on prior restraint may be overridden, albeit only when the nation "is at war,"[167] to allow the government to "prevent actual obstruction to its recruiting service or the publication of the sailing dates of transports or the number and location of troops,"[168] how imminent and proximate a nexus must the government demonstrate between the putative risk and publication? Is the appropriate standard whether publication would directly and immediately jeopardize life or whether publication might result in national embarrassment or potentially disrupt ongoing diplomatic efforts? Would an injunction be countenanced only to prevent disclosures that would imperil the nation as a whole, such as divulging during wartime the means of formulating a nuclear bomb?

The exercise also focuses the class' attention on the case's procedural and pragmatic aspects. Chief Justice Burger and Justice Harlan dissented, lamenting that the dispute reached the Court in "unseemly" and "frenetic" haste,[169] and that the Court had been "almost irresponsibly feverish in dealing with these cases."[170] This was attributed at least in part to the way in which *The New York Times* obtained and reviewed the purloined documents, secretly review-

---

165. *Id.* at 761 (Blackmun, J., dissenting).
166. *Id.* at 725-26 (Brennan, J., concurring).
167. *Schenck v. United States,* 249 U.S. 47, 52 (1919).
168. *Near v. Minnesota ex rel. Olson,* 283 U.S. at 717.
169. 403 U.S. at 748, 749 (Burger, C.J., dissenting).
170. *Id.* at 753 (Harlan, J., dissenting).

ing them for approximately three months prior to publication.[171] Students may be queried as to the journalistic rationales for the newspapers' delay between review and publication of the Pentagon Papers. Might the newspapers have wanted to assess not only whether in fact imminent risk of harm would result from disclosure, but also the degree to which the contents were both newsworthy and authentic?

Whitney North Seymour, then the U.S. Attorney for the Southern District of New York, was vexed that his office basically had a mere week to review the relevant details.[172] Five volunteer law clerks without security clearance assisted the Second Circuit with its interim appellate review.[173] And yet, ironically, Judge James Oakes, dissenting from the Second Circuit's decision, was troubled that the government's claims of top secret classification were overstated in light of their delay in pursuing the restraining order from June 12, 1971 to June 14, 1971.[174]

Thus the class members who represent Chief Justice Burger must explain whether the Court had adequate time to consider the matter or was so "pressured" that "the result is a parody of the judicial function."[175] To what degree were the dissenting justices troubled by the pace with which the appeal proceeded? Might the capabilities of more modern technology, including improved computerized databases of legal research, e-mail, wordprocessing, and facsimile, affect its concerns?

Justice White noted, "Normally, publication will occur and the damage be done before the Government has either opportunity or grounds for suppression."[176] The pedagogical exercise now facilitates a segue to issues pertaining to electronic communications. How might Internet functionality, such as caching and mirroring, pragmatically affect the case were it brought today? In a case in the United Kingdom, a city council objected to postings on the Web by British journalists of a government report. When the council sought an injunction against the journalists (premising the right to such relief on a charge of copyright infringement), the links reportedly were posted to mirror sites so that the substance of the report was available from other sites whose operators previously had downloaded and re-posted the report. One reporter ob-

---

171. *Id.* at 749-50 (Burger, C.J., dissenting).

172. Transcript of the American Bar Association Forum on Communications Law, First Annual Conference, vol. 14, no. 4 (Winter 1997) at 8 (statement of Whitney North Seymour, Jr., then U.S. Attorney for the Southern District of New York).

173. *See id.* at 10 (statement of Judge James Oakes).

174. *See id.* at 11.

175. *New York Times Co. v. United States,* 403 U.S. at 752 (Burger, C.J., dissenting).

176. *Id.* at 733 (White, J., concurring).

served, "By the time the document was removed from British sites, it had already zinged its way around the globe."[177] How does the Internet effectively confound efforts to quell disclosure?

Should the futility of injunctive relief obviate its grant? In one case, the plaintiff alleged that the defendants had misappropriated trade secrets and posted the information on their web-sites.[178] The trial court enjoined the postings by the defendants, but pointed out that it was "mindful of the many enforcement problems. However, a possibility or even a likelihood that an order may be disobeyed or not enforced in other jurisdictions is not a reason to deny the relief sought."[179] In another case, the U.S. District Court for the Southern District of New York posited:

> If a plaintiff seeks to enjoin a defendant from burning a pasture, it is no answer that there is a wild fire burning in its direction. If the defendant itself threatens the plaintiff with irreparable harm, then equity will enjoin the defendant from carrying out the threat even if other threats abound and even if part of the pasture already is burned.[180]

Pragmatic considerations relating to the utility of the type of redress sought are explored as well. Students are reminded to reflect at the outset about the ultimate viability of their objectives in pursuing recourse through litigation.

In the collaborative class exercise relating to the Pentagon Papers case, the family members' group helps personalize the issue for the class, focusing students on claims surrounding the potential impact of publication. And as the discussion evolves, there's an opportunity to elicit the views of class members who were not designated to be their groups' spokespersons. The students' proximate, albeit brief, review of the Pentagon Papers case refreshes their recollection of the facts and holding and the group exercise and subsequent discussion sharpens their focus on a dispute of grave proportions. Not infrequently, someone who has been relatively reserved in class discussions feels a

---

177. Ashley Craddock, *Little Pig, I'll Blow Your Site Down*, Wired News, *at* <http://www.wired.com/news/politics/0,1283,4418,00.html> (June 13, 1997).

178. *See DVD Copy Control Ass'n, Inc. v. McLaughlin*, No. CV 786804, 2000 WL 48512 (Cal. Super. Jan. 21, 2000), *rev'd sub nom. DVD Copy Control Ass'n, Inc. v. Bunner*, 113 Cal. Rptr. 2d 338, 93 Cal. App. 4th 648 (6th Dist. 2001) (reversing grant of preliminary injunction under state trade secrets law, enjoining defendants from posting decryption code in issue), *rev'd and remanded*, No. S102588, 2003 Cal. LEXIS 6295 (Cal. Aug. 25, 2003)(considering question of alleged First Amendment violation).

179. *DVD Copy Control Association, Inc. v. McLaughlin*, No. CV 786804, 2000 WL 48512 at *3.

180. *Universal City Studios, Inc. v. Reimerdes*, 111 F. Supp. 2d 294, 344 (S.D.N.Y. 2000), *aff'd sub nom. Universal City Studios, Inc. v. Corley*, 273 F.3d 429 (2d Cir. 2001).

bit fortified by the support of his teammates when he speaks up to support the opinion of the justice to whom his group has been assigned.

Excursions

The notion of incorporating field trips into an academic curriculum seems relegated to elementary school educational experiences. But there are instances when an excursion can vividly illustrate competing interests or the context for the evolution of a legal principle.

A course covering issues relating to Construction Law or Disability Law might benefit from a trip to a construction site, perhaps in conjunction with a guest appearance by a general contractor or an architect. A Trial Tactics class might gain considerable insight from a trip to the local courthouse to observe a trial, *voir dire* proceedings, or a hearing on a post-trial motion. A Civil Procedure class likewise may find that watching oral arguments on a motion to dismiss and a motion for summary judgment contextualizes the procedural significance of the respective motions. Courtroom observations simultaneously, albeit paradoxically, demystify the proceedings and imbue respect for the process. Students observe that counsel experience delays, witness the impact of inadequate preparation, and learn firsthand the logistical demands of timely witness appearances. More importantly, they see the immediacy with which rulings can sometimes impact the parties, the drama of a highly emotional or especially contentious cross-examination, and the respect accorded to a judge when people rise as he enters and leaves the courtroom.

A trip to a broadcast television or radio station or to a newspaper's newsroom can be highly informative for a Media Law class, viscerally illustrating the impact of deadlines on investigative endeavors, the delicate coordination of reporting within temporal or spatial limitations, and the process of editorial review. A Securities Law class taught in the New York metropolitan area might appreciate a tour of the New York Stock Exchange. A Criminal Law class might learn much from a tour of the FBI.

The professor must make any necessary arrangements for the visit, reviewing the court docket for a trip to a courthouse or requesting permission to tour a newspaper's facilities. If the excursion cannot be fit within the assigned class hours for the course, the professor should make efforts to the extent possible to avoid intruding on other courses' assigned slots, lest students miss another class in order to attend the trip. In the event conflicts are inevitable, it's appropriate to acknowledge the scheduling issues to the class and make the trip optional.

The excursion should be contextualized within the subject matter of the course's curriculum. The Civil Procedure class that will be observing hearings on various motions, for instance, might first review the disparity in standards applicable to motions to dismiss and motions for summary judgment. After the trip, it's helpful to spend some time reviewing what the students observed, explaining how the proceedings relate to the judicial decisions and other readings assigned to the class and offering to answer questions. Student reflection can be formalized by distributing a questionnaire to be completed, requiring assessment of such impressions as the ways in which the judge's pronouncements affected the pacing of the proceeding, the tactics used by each side, and the perceived efficacy of the claims and defenses advanced.

You also might consider trying to arrange for someone affiliated with the facility you'll be visiting to be available to answer students' questions. Perhaps an FBI agent could respond to questions from a Criminal Law class about the training he receives regarding the legal prerequisites for a search warrant or a reporter could discuss with a Media Law class his experience as a defendant in a libel suit.

Games and Gimmicks

An occasional respite from an intensive course may be found in the use of games and gimmicks. These may be used to help students memorize some essential legal terms or as a means of interrupting a bit of lassitude. Decades after I took the bar exam, I still remember a study tip to use the acronym "SPARERIBS" for affirmative defenses (statute of frauds, performance, arbitration or award, *res judicata*, estoppel, release, infancy or incompetency, bankruptcy, and statute of limitations). The moment or two that it takes to explain the acronym briefly entertains, assists with memorization, and scarcely detracts from the overall rigor of the course.

The American Bar Association's Forum on Communications Law occasionally hosts a round of a "Jeopardy"-type game at its Winter Conference. The audience is divided into groups according to their seating arrangements. "Answers" are selected from a poster board that sets them out in ascending order of value and increasing levels of difficulty; these may consist, for example, of questions about media cases. The audience selects an "answer" and tries to formulate the "question." Points are awarded for correct "questions."

Other game formats can be used for similar exercises. A game affords an opportunity to test the participants' knowledge of legal authority and relevant terminology and provides a means to bond in a friendly competition. Or you could fashion a crossword puzzle to help students gain familiarity with relevant legal jargon. The puzzle could be distributed to students to do at their leisure (if they wish to do it at all) so as not to detract from valuable class time.

Cultivating Practitioner and Theoretician

Significant concerns have been raised about the degree to which law school graduates are adequately prepared to embark on legal careers. Concomitantly, pedagogical issues have been debated about the appropriate role of legal education. Ultimately, should the law school experience emphasize academics or training? Should it nurture theoreticians or produce practitioners?

Paul Douglas Callister, Law Reference Librarian and Assistant Professor of Library Administration at the University of Illinois College of Law, pointed out that "[e]tymologically, 'train' and 'educate' have similar root meanings," but the former connotes "condition[ing] to apply, in a specified manner, certain tools and methods to a particular type of problem," while the latter suggests teaching "to thoughtfully analyze the characteristics and nature of the problem at hand in order to develop the most appropriate technique for solving the problem, given one's understanding of the strengths and weaknesses of the various tools and resources at hand."[181]

> In the view of many in the legal academy, law students should and will learn to practice law when they actually enter practice through self-study, advice from other practitioners, a mentor, a law firm training program, or their own failures. To many commentators, however, the academic community's antipractice attitude has spawned an unhealthy dichotomy between theory and practice, a... dissonance or gap between law school and practice [that] significantly contributes to the fact that most law graduates are substantially unprepared to function as lawyers when they enter the profession.[182]

There's some tension between those who deem instruction in practical skills as critical preparation for lawyering and those who regard law school as a "graduate academy." "Proponents of a graduate school model advocate a curriculum concentrating almost exclusively on the theoretical and policy underpinnings of legal doctrines and generally disdain courses intended to develop 'grubby' skills considered useful only in practicing law. A trade school

181. Paul Douglas Callister, *Beyond Training: Law Librarianship's Quest for the Pedagogy of Legal Research Education*, 95 Law. Libr. J. 7, 8 (2003).

182. Rodney J. Uphoff, James J. Clark, and Edward C. Monahan, *Preparing the New Law Graduate to Practice Law: A View From the Trenches*, 65 U. Cin. L. Rev. 381, 381 (1997).

model, on the other hand, presumes that a law school exists to train students principally to practice law."[183]

A significant study by the American Bar Association Section of Legal Education and Admissions to the Bar led to a report, entitled "Legal Education and Professional Development, An Educational Continuum Report of The Task Force on Law Schools and the Profession: Narrowing the Gap," commonly known as the "MacCrate Report." The report encouraged schools to promote the competency of practitioners and concluded that professional development should be central to the mission of legal educational institutions.[184] The MacCrate Report suggested that "there is no 'gap'" between education and practice; "[t]here is only an arduous road of professional development along which all prospective lawyers should travel."[185]

Professor Lucia Ann Silecchia noted, "As legal education in the United States moved from apprenticeship to academy, the need to retain a practical component was clear."[186] There are various pedagogical approaches that can help bridge legal education and the practice of law, whether conceptualized as continuum or fissure. A balance between so-called traditional courses, in which didactic, case method, and hypothetical techniques are utilized, and practical experience such as clinics, externships, and research assistance, can render a law school graduate better poised to begin the profession of practicing law. Systematic integration of legal training and inculcation of legal skills may be undertaken concomitantly with the study of law and the development of professional values through clinical programs and externships and the integration of *pro bono* activities into the legal education experience.

Experiential Training

One way professional training can be inculcated is through experiential learning in clinics, externships, and work experience. Law school clinical programs generally consist of faculty-led seminars in conjunction with supervised student representation of clients. Externships, by contrast, typically consist of field work by students in governmental agencies, with prosecutors, as student

---

183. Harry H. Wellington, *Challenges to Legal Education: The "Two Cultures" Phenomenon*, 37 J. Legal Educ. 327, 329 (1987).

184. *See Selected Excerpts from the MacCrate Report: Legal Education and Professional Development*, "The Gap Between Expectation and Reality" (July 1992), *available at* <http://www.abanet.org/legaled/publications/onlinepubs/maccrate.html>.

185. *Id.*, "The Continuing Process of Professional Development."

186. Lucia Ann Silecchia, *Legal Skills Training in the First Year of Law School: Research? Writing? Analysis? Or More?*, 100 Dick. L. Rev. 245, 246-47 (1996) (footnotes omitted).

clerks, in public defender offices, companies, or law firms. Some schools bifurcate the externship program into general and not-for-profit legal services, and other schools restrict externship participation to not-for-profit entities, student judicial clerkships, or government agencies. Other variations on externship programs include hybrid experiential training, in which students attend a faculty-led seminar and engage in non-legal volunteer work at community-based organizations such as a domestic violence shelter. Or a program might engage the entire class in the representation of a single public service group, taking on the legal needs of the group over the course of the semester.

Students sometimes secure their own employment at the same types of organizations that host externs; while externs generally earn course credit, employees may be compensated monetarily or students may work on a volunteer basis. It's not uncommon for a student to work on a part-time basis at a law firm or other entity where he was employed during a summer (providing such employment doesn't exceed any hourly restrictions placed on matriculating students by the school's regulations).

Clinics and supervised externship programs provide opportunities for experiential learning that enable students to formulate and implement a course of action. In recognition of these benefits, ABA-approved law schools offer "live-client or other real life practice experiences."[187]

Although approaches vary amongst professors and schools, there is ample opportunity for the integration of discussions about professional values; efforts to emulate negotiation, counseling, and advocacy techniques and styles; and the study of legal principles, legislation, and policy. Such practical experience offers an opportunity for students and faculty to engage in a common quest for knowledge and experience. These techniques may be especially critical to bridging the void between the theoretical and the practical educational experiences. One professor noted that the bulk of lawyers' education is derived not from the "scant three years" they spend in law school but in the "thirty or fifty years in practice.... They can be a purblind, blundering, inefficient, hit-or-miss learning experience in the school of hard knocks. Or they can be a reflective, organized, systematic learning experience – *if* the law schools undertake as a part of the curricula to teach students effective techniques or learning from experience."[188]

187. Section of Legal Education and Admissions to the Bar, Am. Bar Ass'n, Standards for Approval of Law Schools, Standard 302(c)(2) (2002), *available at* <http://www.abanet.org/legaled/standards/chapter3.html>.

188. Anthony G. Amsterdam, *Clinical Legal Education: A 21st Century Perspective*, 34 J. Legal Educ. 612, 617 (1984), *available at* <http://www.pili.org/library/cle/clinical_legal_education_as_a_21st_century_experience.htm>.

Experiential programs also may mitigate the stultification that occasionally occurs when students are immersed in reviewing century-old legal precedent or the sometimes tedious review of lengthy statutory provisions, as some courses require. The personalization of legal needs provides ample fulcrum for student motivation.

Students can be encouraged to record initial expectations in a journal and reflect at the end of the semester as to whether such expectations and objectives were fulfilled. As the semester progresses, student participation in a clinic or externship program can be memorialized in the journal by identifying the legal needs of the client to whom the student was rendering service. The journals provide a valuable resource for students to share their experiences with the professor and with one another.

The professor might specifically induce reflection about certain issues by proffering questions each week. For example, it's helpful to try to demarcate the role of the lawyer and other support professionals such as social workers, psychologists, and administrators. This helps remind prospective in-house counsel about the distinction between legal advice and business strategy. Such dichotomies relate not only to the scope of the student's future role, but also to such matters as determining when a communication with an attorney is subject to privilege on the ground that he was rendering or being solicited for legal advice.

Combined with reflection and feedback, "[t]he clinical process is thus a blueprint for professional growth."[189] Clinical education and externships promote learning through experience, mitigating the effects of what some have referred to as the "'banking'" of education that regards "knowledge as a gift bestowed by those who consider themselves knowledgeable upon those who consider themselves to know nothing."[190] Such pedagogy may encompass class sessions, individual student-faculty meetings, collaborative projects, journal records, simulations, and assistance in the rendering of legal services to members of the community. Unlike traditional law school courses, in clinics and externships, "the catalyst for learning is the experience component."[191]

Advocates of clinical education point out that values and skills attendant to the practice of law are encompassed in ways that the academic case method can-

---

189. Kimberly E. O'Leary, *Evaluating Clinical Law Teaching – Suggestions for Law Professors Who Have Never Used the Clinical Teaching Method,* 29 N. KY. L. Rev. 491, 495 (2002).

190. William P. Quigley, *Introduction to Clinical Teaching for the New Clinical Law Professor: A View From the First Floor,* 28 Akron L. Rev. 463, 474 (1995) (footnote omitted).

191. *Id.* at 500.

not achieve alone. Claudio Grossman, Dean of American University Washington College of Law, suggested that the case method has been criticized on the ground that it is "incapable of developing a theoretical understanding of the law, and the historic processes that shape it."[192] V. Pualani Enos and Lois Kanter pointed out that "[t]he importance of building a positive working relationship with each client is lost on most students," noting that for many students, "the relationship with a client is often abstract and minimized."[193] Clinics and externships, in conjunction with academic tutelage, are highy educational. Experiential work fosters good communication and listening skills as well as the opportunity to conduct interviews. Such training necessitates careful consideration in advance as to how students will acquire needed information, perhaps operating within certain time constraints depending upon the availability of a particular client or witness. Important organizational and planning skills relating to the ways in which factual points can be substantiated through admissible proffers and the maintenance of files in the course of investigation are at work. Emotional aspects of the task, such as empathizing with professional detachment regarding a harm suffered, become part of the experience of practicing law, something quite difficult to convey through mere textual review.

Professor Shin Imai of York University in Toronto worked as a staff lawyer at Keewaytinok Native Legal Services, a legal aid clinic. He observed that during law school he "learned important skills: to reconstruct events, to restate the law and to package a new reality.... [He] had, in effect, been trained to become an epistemological imperialist: invading, subjugating and transforming other peoples' realities into forms and concepts that made sense in the world of law."[194] But his community-based experiences demanded complementary skills: collaboration with members of the community and a sense of community perspective about legal problems.[195]

Clinical programs broaden students' perspectives about the community and possibly even the world. Seminars led in conjunction with field experience can feature guest speakers or foreign participants in an on-line chatroom. Signif-

192. Claudio Grossman, *Critical Essay: Building the World Community: Challenges to Legal Education and the WCL Experience*, 17 Am. U. Int'l L. Rev. 815, 819 (2002) (footnote omitted).

193. V. Pualani Enos and Lois H. Kanter, *Problem Solving in Clinical Education: Who's Listening? Introducing Students to Client-Centered, Client-Empowering, and Multidisciplinary Problem-Solving in a Clinical Setting*, 9 Clinical L. Rev. 83, 86 (2002) (footnote omitted).

194. Shin Imai, *Problem Solving in Clinical Education: A Counter-Pedagogy for Social Justice: Core Skills for Community-Based Lawyering*, 9 Clinical L. Rev. 195, 196-197 (2002).

195. *Id.*

icantly, students are exposed to the needs of the community in which the school operates and have a valuable opportunity to interact with lawyers and other professionals who tend to those needs. Ultimately, law school clinics and externship programs benefit the school's broader community by furnishing legal assistance to generally under-represented persons. According to one report, five of eight clinics at Tulane Law School provided more than 65,000 hours of free legal services in 1997, contrasted with fewer than 100,000 hours estimated to have been donated by the entire Louisiana state bar in 1998.[196] Another study estimated that law school clinics account for millions of hours every year of legal services provided by students free of charge.[197]

Another advantage of such programs is their capacity to integrate ethical aspects of the practice of law as students grapple with issues relating to privilege and conflicts of interest. "In addition, the work of student-lawyers and faculty in clinical programs sometimes brings them in contact with ethical issues often faced by lawyers representing poor and unpopular clients – interference in case and client selection and restrictions on the means of representing a client. The interests of politicians and of university alumni and donors add an additional level of outside interest and potential interference in law school clinic activities."[198]

Professionalism, Professional Responsibility, and Pro Bono Activities

Sensitizing law school students to community service can be done through *pro bono* work and even through the pedagogy of legal education itself. Students' eagerness to learn legal rules and memorize case captions must be subordinated to maintaining a sense of moral scrutiny. Legal doctrines frequently embody a determination of the dominant value when multiple interests compete. There are conflicts within society that don't necessarily import predictable or uniform resolution. Even when global legal doctrines can be crafted, the adequacy of their elasticity inevitably is called into question when they're applied to accommodate disparate equities to serve the needs of social justice.

---

196. *See* Robert R. Kuehn, *Access to Justice: The Social Responsibility of Lawyers—Denying Access to Legal Representation: The Attack on the Tulane Environmental Law Clinic*, 4 Wash. U.J.L. & Pol'y 33, 36 n.14 (2000).

197. *See* David Luban, *Taking Out the Adversary: The Assault on Progressive Public Interest Lawyers*, 91 Cal. L. Rev. 209, 236 (2003).

198. Robert R. Kuehn and Peter A. Joy, *An Ethics Critique of Interference in Law School Clinics*, 71 Fordham L. Rev. 1971, 1974 (2003).

Professors also can help instill a sense of professionalism and professional responsibility in the law school setting to sensitize future lawyers about the need for a commitment to undertake *pro bono* work and even to assist students work to advance social justice causes while they are still in school. In so doing, members of the faculty further the interests of under-represented groups, advance their own professional aspirations and responsibilities, and perpetuate a shared commitment to service. In addition to sensitizing students to community needs during classroom discussions, such endeavors may be integrated into clinical programs and externships or incorporated in temporary employment situations.

Such activities may encompass assistance to legal aid and public defender services; participating in the legal activities and policy advocacy of public interest organizations; advising state, national, and even foreign legislative and other governmental officials on legal issues and law reform; participating in bar association activities; and promoting legal education in secondary schools and community-based entities. Clinical and externship programs (*see supra* at 174) often focus on the needs of the not-for-profit community. In addition to programs directed to such issues as domestic violence, criminal defense, and immigration rights, even programs dealing with securities issues can present special opportunities for students to become aware of the plight of under-represented individuals. At the Fordham University School of Law Securities Arbitration Clinic, for example, students represent small investors allegedly disserved by unsuitable investment recommendations, churning, unauthorized trades, material misrepresentations, omissions, and other breaches of industry rules by brokers and brokerage firms. Clinical Associate Professor of Law and Supervisory Attorney of the Securities Arbitration Clinic Marcella Silverman points out, "Bridging the gap between public interest law and private sector practice, the work of the [Clinic] not only advances the rights of consumers of limited means but also sensitizes future lawyers to the importance of adherence by the brokerage industry to rules of fair dealing."[199] The clinical experience not only directly serves those represented by the students, but it also entrenches a perception of the impact improper trading can have on individuals, rendering those who practice on behalf of financial services entities better equipped to recognize the value of professional dealings.

---

199. Interview with Marcella E. Silverman, Professor of Law and Supervisory Attorney of the Securities Arbitration Clinic, Fordham University School of Law (July 1, 2003, July 8, 2003).

According to the Association of American Law Schools, more than a dozen law schools in the United States require students to perform some law-related *pro bono* work as a condition of graduation. The AALS noted that "[m]ost pro bono programs provide desperately needed legal services to people who cannot afford them. That value alone justifies encouraging students to volunteer their time. But law schools are primarily in the business of educating law students, not in the business of providing direct public service, and it is the important educational values of pro bono programs that justify the commitment of substantial law school resources to their support."[200] Incorporating programs into the legal education experience not only sharpens students' skills and provides a means of acquiring practical legal experience, but also it viscerally sensitizes future practitioners to community needs and helps entrench a commitment to support under-represented persons.

There are ancillary benefits as well. Prospective lawyers learn a sense of balance, of coordinating tasks attendant to their educational experience and service to others. As they begin their legal careers, they've seen firsthand that despite other demands, they were able to allocate time to *pro bono* activities.

Furthermore, they begin to develop contacts within community-based and legal organizations. Or, by assisting a local law firm with its *pro bono* work, the student and the firm become familiar with one another and the student gains meaningful insight as to the nature and scope of the firm's commitment. In addition, students may become open to engaging in such legal services work on a more expansive basis. There's a fairly significant disparity between the daily routine of a law student and that of a practicing attorney. By engaging in *pro bono* work as a student, one is able to glimpse the commitment by a practitioner in the field and thereby gain insight into the role of an attorney engaged in rendering legal services to the community.

City, county, and state bar associations may provide fertile ground for information about *pro bono* needs in the community in which your school is based. Your school's clinic and externship programs may have suggestions as well. In addition, the AALS Pro Bono Programs publishes a *Directory of Individual Law School Pro Bono Programs.*[201] The AALS Commission on Pro Bono and Public Service Opportunities has set out specific recommendations about the nature of *pro bono* projects schools should foster and how to develop a viable school plan, including consideration of such factors as whether the pro-

---

200. *A Handbook on Law School Pro Bono Programs*, The AALS Pro Bono Project (June 2001) at 27, *available at* <http://www.aals.org/probono/probono.pdf>.

201. *See id.* at 35.

gram should be mandatory or voluntary, staffing and supervision issues, and ways to secure necessary funding.[202]

A *pro bono* program also can be devised for faculty members to provide critical legal services to under-represented clients. Active participation by faculty not only perpetuates a commitment to render service to the community, it also entrenches the significance of *pro bono* work as a model for emulation by students. As AALS observed, "Law teachers teach as much about professional responsibility by what they do as by what they say."[203]

As a teacher and as a mentor, you'll want to maintain an intellectual curiosity and contribute to the scholarly endeavors of the legal profession. In addition to trying to stay current about legal developments in your area of specialty, you'll want to contribute to the ongoing intellectual discourse by writing articles for publication; engaging in scholarly discourse with your students, colleagues, and others; and attending and participating in conferences and programs. With careful planning and a staunch commitment, this can be achieved even as you stay sensitive to time constraints so that such pursuits do not detract from your commitment to conscientious preparation for your classes.

The Semester's Classes

The First Class

You can expect the first day of class to be just a bit unsettling for both you and your students. First-year students are adjusting to a new school, mindful of the rigorous competition for acceptance and proficiency. Upper-classmen are probably eager to assess their interest in an elective course as it's held during the school's drop/add period when they can continue to modify their course selections. You will have prepared a substantive lesson plan, of course, and may reasonably (although a bit optimistically, perhaps) expect the class to have completed the posted reading assignments for the first session. But the number of administrative tasks to complete and the need to contextualize the course will shape the session and diminish the time you're able to delve into the subject matter.

Begin by introducing yourself and state the name of the course. This, at the very minimum, will alleviate an exodus mid-way through the session if there was a glitch in the room assignments and a group mistakenly thought that a different professor was teaching another class at that time.

---

202. *Id.*, The Commission's Specific Recommendations.

203. *Id.*

You might want to briefly give a bit of background about your career. I don't believe that you need to explain your credentials; students will tend to presume that if the school has entrusted their legal education to you, you're well-qualified. You might say something to the effect of, "it's a pleasure for me to be here. I've been teaching Contracts for a number of years, and I'm looking forward to adding this course on the Uniform Commercial Code."

You might wish to ask students to briefly introduce themselves. In addition to stating their names, you can suggest that they indicate "a bit about themselves," or, with respect to an elective course, why they're interested in the subject matter. I've done this in courses I've taught, but I preface the request for the information with an acknowledgement that it's acceptable to respond, "I needed two credits on a Tuesday in this time slot." If you find it challenging to master names, while it's not a common practice, you could even consider distributing name tags for the first session or two.

Clarify the description of the course (*see supra* at 41). Bear in mind that students may arrive with preconceived ideas, many of which may be misconceptions, about what they think the course will cover based on its title. It may even be appropriate to indicate what you're planning to exclude from the course curriculum.

Course requirements are another item on the agenda for the first class session. This places the students on notice about your expectations. Upperclassmen, who are taking elective courses, appropriately take into account the nature of requirements as they coordinate their schedules. It's quite reasonable for a student to consider whether a courseload that demands four or five in-class final examinations may be a bit too burdensome relative to a combination of papers and final exams. You'll also want to explain the components of the course grades. If you're going to factor class attendance and/or class participation into the grade, advise your class at the outset so that students will understand the ramifications of any deficiencies.

Reiterate the textual materials that are assigned and explain whether they're available in the school bookstore, through Internet access, or on faculty loan at the library. It's important that students acquire the correct edition of a casebook, for example, so that the pages referenced in the syllabus correlate with the text and so that they have access to complete and current reading assignments.

You may want to take a moment to clarify your role for the class, especially if you're an adjunct faculty member engaged in practice or some other legal endeavor. You could state that you regard your role as an intellectual catalyst to inspire deliberation about complex legal concepts and to provoke discussion. So, for example, when you phrase a question along the lines of "but don't you think that the defendant should have been held liable in light of what can be characterized as an admission in his correspondence with the plaintiff?," you're not necessarily offering an opinion but rather working to stimulate a response.

This may be important for two reasons. First, as a general matter, students often approach the study of law fairly literally and assume that there are specific "answers" to legal questions. There's a tendency, therefore, to labor to divine the "answer" from your statements, and even, perhaps, from your inflection or body language. As the expert in the room, your statements are bestowed with an imprimatur of knowledge and respect, and students may believe that acquiescing to what they regard as the position you're advocating will afford them a correct understanding of the law (and even a higher grade). Emphasize that you're looking to challenge them and that you welcome articulation of disparate conclusions, provided that they're premised on efforts to engage in sound legal reasoning.

Second, you may want to remind students that even when you're expressing an opinion, you're doing so in your personal capacity. You're not presuming to represent the views of the academic institution with which you're affiliated or any company, firm, or other entity by whom you are or may have been employed.

During the first class session, try to anticipate logistical questions your students may have. Are you intending to use a seating chart? Do you permit eating in class? What is your policy about recording their attendance if they arrive late or depart early?

Also indicate your general availability. Specify whether you'll be holding office hours or whether students will need to make appointments with you in advance. Will you be available by telephone or e-mail? Particularly if you're an adjunct professor engaged in private practice, you may want to mention that students are welcome to contact you if they need academic assistance during the semester but that you would appreciate it if they would try first to contact a classmate about logistical questions such as an announcement about when you'll be making suggested paper topics available. Some students may believe that mere frequency of contact with their professors suggests scholastic enthusiasm; this may be the case under certain circumstances, but it also seems appropriate for students to be mindful that you may have other academic or professional commitments that occupy much of your time.

Don't be overly concerned if the first class session seems a bit unwieldy. Remember that when you make pancakes, the first batch rarely comes out quite as well as those that follow. But chances are they all taste just fine, and if you're the one who is the cook, you're probably much more critical of the initial group of misshapen flapjacks and burnt edges.

Segues and Transitions

Articulating an introduction for each class session is as helpful as briefly reiterating the themes discussed in the immediately preceding session. This is especially important if your class doesn't meet on consecutive days. When I read "Nancy Drew" books to my daughter in the evenings, I began by re-reading the last page of the chapter we had read the evening before; it was helpful to remember where Bess and George were last seen and what clues Nancy had unearthed. Law students are taking multiple courses and possibly juggling part-time jobs or writing law journal articles. Briefly recapping the prior session's themes eases the class back into the context of the course and helps you establish a segue to the next discussion.

Despite your diligence in allocating course material proportionally amongst the semester's sessions, on at least some occasions you probably won't cover all the reading material or all other aspects of your entire lesson plan. Explain to your students that it's understandable for class sessions to "bleed" into one another a bit. Material that could not be covered on a particular day, even though the reading was to have been completed for that session, can be readily absorbed into the next class.

Over the course of the semester, you may want to build in time every few weeks to "catch up." If it appears unlikely that you'll be able to cover your entire syllabus, pause in the few weeks before the semester ends to consider revising the assigned readings. You may decide to omit some or all of the final session's readings. Or it may make more sense to truncate each of the remaining class assignments.

Faculty Self-De-Briefing

It's helpful to take a few moments promptly after each class concludes to record your impressions for purposes of student evaluation, review of approaches for subsequent semesters, preparation of a final exam, and inclusion of updates of legal developments in the curriculum. You might even use a four-subject notebook or different color pens for this task.

First, if you're factoring in class attendance and class participation into the grading system (*see supra* at 82, 83), promptly assign points or values to those who appeared and meaningfully contributed. The number and nature of students' comments might seem quite memorable, but as the semester progresses it becomes far more difficult to distinguish the degree of participation in one class session from another. Keeping track of participation in an organized fashion not only makes your class participation score more reliable, it also renders it ostensibly more reliable; you're able to account to a student if necessary as to how the score was computed and how he fared relative to the class at large.

Second, note some general impressions about the session. Did students seem distracted by the PowerPoint presentation you incorporated into the lesson? Was the material you had hoped to cover appropriately allocated to a single class session? Did the class address most or all of the reading assignments? Were there particular themes that generated special interest? You can review the notes that you prepared before the session to see whether there are points you want to amplify or omit next time or variations on hypotheticals that you want to pose. You also can read through the notes of your impressions of the sessions as you conduct a self-evaluation at the conclusion of the semester (*see infra* at 222).

Third, try to summarize (or even just underline or highlight your class notes) the few global themes that were emphasized in your class. This can be very helpful when you prepare a final exam; you're able to readily review major points that were covered by the class and that reasonably can be expected to be the subject of students' review and evaluation. It can be especially useful if you've taught the course on more than one occasion so that you can refresh your recollection as to which class emphasized specific points. You can even jot down questions that occur to you for possible inclusion on the exam as the semester progresses.

Finally, note significant legal developments as they occur during the course of the semester. If the U.S. Supreme Court issued a decision in an appellate case that you've assigned, you'll want to incorporate the new ruling in future syllabi and as you supplement or revise your materials.

The Final Class

The final class may well be a hybrid lesson; you'll be covering the themes and reading assignments allocated to that class as well as integrating course themes. This last session offers a special opportunity to help your students synthesize the excerpts of caselaw, legislation, and legal commentary you've reviewed with the topics discussed. Offering a broad outline, akin to the headings of your original syllabus (*see supra* at 43), contextualizes the course content.

This doesn't necessarily mean that you're in effect delivering an oral recitation of a course outline for the class. Students should be working to review the material on their own as they search for patterns and emerging legal trends. But you can suggest some connections between discussions at the outset of the semester and the material you covered in subsequent class sessions. If you're teaching a Torts class, for instance, how might the class begin to delineate disparities between intentional torts and acts of negligence? Are there distinctions amongst the defenses that may be asserted to each type of alleged wrong? What do we glean from the policies underlying different jurisprudential approaches? What can we learn sociologically about the allocation of responsibility for harm from the proofs required for each element of the tort, the nature of the defenses that defeat liability, and the degree to which contributory negligence or the assumption of a risk offsets liability or damages?

The final class also is an appropriate time to review the standards you've established for student evaluations and the instructions for outstanding course requirements. If the students will be taking a final examination, for instance, explain how it will be administered, the date on which it will be given, where students must report, whether they'll be permitted to use laptops or other computer equipment, whether the exam is open-book or closed-book, and any page limitations.

Also review the school's policy on requests for postponement because of exam conflicts, illness, a family emergency, or religious observance. For example, it may be appropriate that students make any such requests of the dean of student affairs rather than of you so that you're not able to identify the requesting student as you engage in blind grading. A school administrator is well-positioned to review with the student whether a doctor's note is required in case of illness or how an exam conflict will be resolved.

The final class also provides an opportunity to offer general guidelines with respect to taking tests. This is especially important if you're teaching a first-year class as the nature of law school exams differs considerably from evaluative techniques administered at the undergraduate level. It's not uncommon for students to feel a bit anxious about their first exams. You can make some suggestions about ways to study and prepare, the utility of taking timed practice exams (*see infra* at 234), the pros and cons of participating in a study group (*see supra* at 100), and appropriate ways to allocate time during the exam itself to reading, analyzing, and writing the exam.

You might even acknowledge that the exam period is challenging and tedious. I've sometimes ended my Law of Internet Speech class by offering a quote as a suggestion for students to consider at the conclusion of the exam period; there's a web-site that posts something along the lines of: "Congratulations. You've reached the very last page of the World Wide Web. Now turn off your computer and go outside and play."

Try to help students regain some perspective about the overall impact of grades on their prospective legal careers; many students erroneously presume that a failure to achieve the highest scores will doom their chances to participate on student journals or even to secure meaningful employment. Remember, too, that admission to law school is increasingly competitive and students likely have been high-achievers during their undergraduate careers. They may approach law school with similar expectations (or have such expectations imposed on them by others, only serving to compound their self-imposed pressures).

You can congratulate your first-year students on finishing a challenging year, or congratulate a class of third-year students on their upcoming graduation. You can also thank your class for their diligence and commitment and let them know that you've enjoyed teaching them.

Selected Resources

Integrating Electronic and Digital Multi-Media Tools:

MhonArc Mail-to-HTML Converter
web-site: <http://www.oac.uci.edu/indiv/ehood/mhonarc.html>

Multi-Purpose Internet Mail Extensions
web-site: <http://www.mhonarc.org/~ehood/MIME/>

Ken Strutin, *PowerPoint Bibliography,* Institute for Law School Teaching, The Law Teacher (Fall 2002), *at* <http://law.gonzaga.edu/ilst/Newsletters/Fall02/strutin.htm>

The TLT Group, Teaching, Learning, and Technology
One Columbia Avenue
Takoma Park, MD 20912
tel.: 301-270-8312
fax: 301-270-8110
web-site: <http://www.tltgroup.org/>

Edward R. Tufte, *The Visual Display of Quantitative Information* (Graphics Press 1992)

Edward R. Tufte, *Visual Explanations: Images and Quantities, Evidence and Narrative* (Graphics Press 1997)

Patrick Wiseman, *Teaching (Virtually) Teaching, at* <http://law.gsu.edu/pwiseman/vtt/virtual.html>

Distance Education:

American Bar Association Network, Comprehensive Guide to Bar Admission Requirements
web-site: <http://www.abanet.org/legaled/publications/compguide2003/compguide2003.html>

Pro Bono Activities:

Access to Justice
Chicago-Kent College of Law
Institute of Technology
565 W. Adams Street
Chicago, IL 60661
tel.: 312-906-5000
fax: 312-906-5280
web-site: <http://www.kentlaw.edu/jwc/access.html>

A Handbook on American Law School Pro Bono Programs, The AALS Pro Bono Project, *available at* <http://www.aals.org/probono/probono.pdf>.

American Bar Association Standing Committee on Pro Bono and Public Service
541 North Fairbanks Court
Chicago, IL 60611
tel.: 312-988-5775
fax: 312-988-5483
web-site: <www./abaprobono.org>

Illinois Technology Center for Law & Public Interest
Chicago-Kent College of Law
Institute of Technology
565 W. Adams Street
Chicago, IL 60661-3691
tel.: 312-906-5000
fax: 312-906-5280
web-site: <http://www.kentlaw.edu/jwc/itc.html>

National Bar Association, Legal Resources, Non-Profit Legal Service Providers
web-site: <http://www.nationalbar.org/resources/index.shtml>

Project Diana, An Online Human Rights Archive
Yale Law School
The Lillian Goldman Law Library
127 Wall Street
New Haven, CT 06520
web-site: <http://www.yale.edu/lawweb/avalon/diana/index.html>

The Public Service Law Network Worldwide National Association for Law Placement
1025 Connecticut Avenue NW
Washington, DC 20036-5413
tel: 202-296-0076
fax: 202-296-7752
web-site: <http://www.pslawnet.org/pslnatnalp.asp>

CHAPTER 4

Class Assessment and Evaluation of Faculty

Evaluation of Students

Evaluation of students' progress and performance is a challenging but necessary component of teaching. Assessment is an integral part of the learning process, promoting an understanding as to how the student can continue to improve, as well as an aspect of the school's administrative requirements in order to distinguish amongst students. Providing constructive feedback to students and satisfying the administrative tasks imposed on you by the school demands that you implement the evaluation process in a fair and impartial fashion. You'll also want to promote a perception of fairness.

One way to do this is to be sure that you have clearly and timely placed your students on notice of your expectations. You've already advised them of the course requirements (such as whether they'll be expected to complete a midterm paper and sit for a final exam) and of the other factors that you'll be assessing when you grade (such as class attendance and participation) (*see supra* at 79). You'll also need to specify criteria along the way.

Let's say you're expecting the students to submit an essay in the form of a paper or exam. It's helpful to hand out or append an instruction sheet, specifying your guidelines, and to go over the instructions in class so that students have an opportunity to ask questions. Often a law student can be quite concerned with the procedural aspects, indicating a fair amount of trepidation that he'll exceed a page limitation because he used too small a font.

Should you reward effort even in the absence of proficiency? On the one hand, there's stiff competition in law school and mere indicia of an investment of time doesn't necessarily qualify one as a seasoned jurist. On the other hand, it's important to recognize a student's diligent commitment to the course. I try to reconcile this tension by factoring in effort in the context of attendance and class participation; if the student has regularly attended class and endeavored to make thoughtful comments that reflect preparation for the class and completion of the reading assignments, I'll note this favorably even if a remark has a logical fallacy or a technical flaw. On the final exam, though, he's expected to have mastered the material and applied the law to the facts with reason and deliberation.

Methods of Evaluation

Written Methods

There are a number of options available for the assessment of students' progress. Written evaluative techniques include examinations and papers (*see* Fig. 3). Pupils' contribution to the class can be measured through attendance and class participation.

Examinations

Written examinations are an essential part of the evaluative process in many law school courses. They typically are conducted after the class concludes at the end of the semester. Sometimes mid-semester examinations or mid-year examinations in full-year courses may be scheduled in accordance with the school's requirements or subject to the discretion of the professor. Required courses may have mandatory final exams.

Final examinations generally are scheduled by the registrar's office, which takes into account room accessibility, predominance of conflicts, and the availability of proctors. The registrar probably will arrange to have a staff member proctor the exam, so that you won't need to attend on the day the exam is administered. One exception to this may be if your exam is not designed to be either completely closed-book or completely open-book; in that event, you may want to attend the administration of the exam to ensure that your restrictions are followed. Thus, for instance, if you permit "a reasonably annotated Code only," you can attend the exam to confirm compliance so that proctors are not charged with the interpretation of your instructions.

Your school likely will determine whether written examinations will be handwritten or, at the students' option, typed on laptops they supply. In this increasingly technological age, schools may make exams available through such software programs as ExamSoft, which allow students to download and electronically submit their exams. In that event, you may need to remind your students to arrange to have the software installed and be adequately trained to use the program prior to the commencement of the final exam period.

Student requests for extensions of time and "incomplete" notations in the class are doubtlessly covered by your school's policies. Typically, for instance, it is the responsibility of the student to timely notify the registrar of exam conflicts, medical incapacity, religious observance, or death or medical emergency of a family member or friend. Students making such requests may be required to consult with or secure approval from the dean of student affairs. This sort of policy precludes the disclosure of the student's identity to a professor who is to engage in blind grading.

It's a good idea to avoid using old exams and even to avoid including particular questions from prior exams, as one or more students may be aware of previous tests. Some schools allow routine access by students to old exams and when the institution has no such policy, professors sometimes post old exams or otherwise make them available in order to ensure parity of access by the entire class.

It's also important that, prior to the end of your last class session, you advise students about the requirements for and any restrictions on a take-home exam. For example, students will need to know applicable deadlines, whether they may consult their text and other materials, whether they are expected to engage in external legal research, and a suggested page guideline or page limitation. Briefly reviewing these requirements during a class session allows an opportunity for students to ask questions about your expectations. Including this information in a cover sheet for your exam is a helpful way to reiterate your requirements. As well, it promotes parity amongst students by ensuring that they are uniformly apprised of criteria for their submissions.

You also should remind students that they are prohibited from discussing the exam with anyone until after the examination period concludes. In addition, it usually is a good idea for you to refrain from taking calls from or meeting with students once they are eligible to retrieve a take-home exam. Questions pertaining to the exam's procedural aspects, such as due dates and page limitations, presumably will have been addressed by you during your last class session and reiterated on your exam cover sheet. You should carefully consider whether efforts to clarify substantive aspects of the course material might imbue the process with a lack of parity amongst class members, by tending, however inadvertently, to emphasize a particular point covered on the exam for one student to the exclusion of others.

Take a moment to reflect on the subject matter of your course so that you can clarify for your class what sorts of issues they might address were they in a practitioner or clerkship setting but can now omit. If you're teaching a substantive area of the law, such as Employment Law, you might want to advise your class to ignore issues in a hypothetical that pertain to whether the dispute arose in the context of a motion to dismiss or a motion for summary judgment. If you're teaching an Evidence course, by contrast, you might want to remind students that they needn't spend time explaining the jurisprudential evolution of the *prima facie* elements of the claim because you're more concerned with the allocation of burdens of proof or the admissibility of relevant testimony.

A sample instruction sheet appended to a final exam might look something like this:

> This final examination is an open-book, take-home exam. Please indicate the sources on which you rely, even if you do not directly quote from them. (You need not adhere to formal "Blue Book" citation form, so long as you refer to the source.) You need not engage in any external research; i.e., research into sources that have not been included within the reading assignments and class discussion.
>
> As a guideline, your exam answer should be approximately 12 pages in length. If your exam includes footnotes, please format them at the bottom of the page(s), rather than as endnotes at the conclusion of the exam (but note that sources should be cited within the text of the paper, rather than as footnotes). Exam answers should be typed, in double-spaced format, and stapled.
>
> You *must* include your student identification number on the exam; you should *not* include your name on the exam.
>
> Please answer the exam within 48 hours of your receipt of this exam, and return your completed exam to the Registrar's Office. (Exam answers must be submitted in this fashion. Exams will *not* be accepted by sending them via e-mail, facsimile, or any other alternative.) Completed exams are due to be submitted by graduating students no later than May 15, 2006. All other students must submit their completed exams no later than May 25, 2006.
>
> Remember that you are not permitted to discuss the exam with *anyone* until the entire exam period has concluded.

Encourage students to consider the question that's being asked of them to help sharpen their focus and develop the skill of being responsive to the task at hand. You'll also help them manage the test or paper within their time constraints and page limitations. You might recommend to students that they pause periodically as they're writing to reflect on *why* they're telling you something. Is the matter directly relevant to their theme?

This also may be a different sort of writing than what students are accustomed to because of their undergraduate career, during previous employment, or even in other law school contexts. Law journal articles, for instance, often have more substantial prefacatory material, summarizing at the outset the themes to be discussed.

Crafting an Exam

What's the most valid assessment technique? There probably isn't one. Ideally, a test should evaluate analytical ability and substantive knowledge, perhaps through the application of law to a complex factual situation. The exam you craft should be susceptible to reliable evaluation so that students are impartially and consistently graded. The exam should be sufficiently rigorous so that gradations in submissions can be established and so that grades are not so uniformly high or low that their value is diluted. Nor should the exam be so difficult that even the most prepared and analytical student could not master many if not most of its aspects.

A multiple-choice or true/false test is inherently more objectively reliable because it is subject to definitive scoring. Essays, however, may more effectively probe analytical cognition and the ability to synthesize. State bar exams incorporate both multiple-choice and essay questions, and such a hybrid test is another option for you.

If you're developing multiple-choice questions, you'll want to take care that the questions are not susceptible to intuitive guessing, as, for example, when the wrong answers suggest outcomes that are so blatantly unfair they would be antithetical to a just legal system. You might want to devise the question and then phrase the correct answer, using it as a base from which to develop wrong answers by incorporating a fallacy in the premise of the question or relying on a case that was reversed on appeal. Wrong answers should be plausible but unambiguous.

As you look over the questions, try to gauge whether they include leading language suggestive of the correct answer. You'll also want to decide whether to penalize students for wrong answers (as opposed to omitting any response to a question) to determine whether guessing should be rewarded. You can weight more difficult questions. Check to be sure that you've randomly assigned the order of correct answers; even though it would speed up the grading process to use a repetitive answer key pattern, students can discern patterns and thereby subvert the evaluative objective of the test.

Short answer questions also may be used as a valid testing technique. Complementing your essay question with queries seeking definitions or brief explanations can be a helpful way to close gaps between the matters raised by a lengthy hypothetical and other aspects of the law you covered in class.

Offering a choice of essays is an option, but consider whether it may jeopardize the reliability of your grading. It's quite challenging to craft multiple questions or hypotheticals that seek to elicit comparable analytical skills. You might devise a few shorter essay questions. Or your exam can be an amalgam of multiple-choice, short answer, and essay questions.

Devising a lengthy and complex hypothetical can be challenging. Such exams, particularly those administered for first-year classes, generally consist of lengthy narratives in which students are asked to identify and discuss numerous legal issues.

Sometimes professors find it helpful to give students the exam question in advance. Or the professor might indicate that the exam will include one of several questions that are distributed before the examination date. Doing so can reduce the anxiety that inevitably accompanies the final exam period and may stimulate more focused review of relevant material. Providing multiple questions from which one will be selected by the professor broadens the scope of the students' review. It's obviously important to advise students as to whether they are permitted to discuss the question(s) with other students or with anyone else.

Some professors administer take-home exams. Depending on your school's policies, you may be able to elect to allow students to do a take-home exam, affording students a maximum of, say, 48 hours to take the exam. If you would like students to complete the exam during a specified period, you'll need to coordinate the scheduling with the registrar. You may instead wish to afford students a "rolling exam period" during which they may choose the period. In the latter case, the professor may allow the student to obtain the exam any time during the final exam period, provided the student takes no more than the prescribed period (typically 24 or 48 hours) to complete the exam.

You might want to read through your class notes and any record you made of your impressions of individual class sessions (*see supra* at 185) for inspiration about what to include in the exam so that your test effectively emphasizes the points on which the class focused. You can review exams administered by other professors who teach in your area, either by accessing the files at your school or by accessing faculty web-sites. Law professors sometimes post sample exam questions on their respective sites and you may wish to peruse these, browse compilations of postings at such sites as the Harvard Law School's examination archives[1] or the University of Pittsburgh Law School's Jurist Legal Intelligence site,[2] or consult teachers' manuals accompanying texts relevant to your course's subject matter for inspiration.

---

1. Examination Book Archives, Harvard Law School, *available at* <http://www.law.harvard.edu/academics/registrar/exams.html>.

2. *See* <http://jurist.law.pitt.edu/lawteaching.htm>.

Another approach is to sketch out a hypothetical. Begin by jotting down a brief list of legal principles and theories you discussed in class and covered in the reading assignments. Are there characters you envisage who engage in a variation of the conduct that led to the disputes adjudicated by the courts? Is there a case that's beginning to work its way through the courts where no decision has yet been issued but that you can modify to create an interesting and comprehensive fact pattern?

You may want to deliberately present the facts in a disorderly fashion, embellishing the scenario with immaterial information. This requires students to separate relevant from irrelevant information and to organize their thoughts and discussion in a linear and logical flow.

Consider whether you're expecting students to apply federal law, the law of one or more states, or general common law. Try to identify issues that you don't want students to spend time discussing or particular claims or defenses that should not be covered in their submissions.

As an illustration, a Law of Internet Speech course covered issues relating to defamation, including efforts to impose liability on Internet service providers arising from the posting by third parties of defamatory content; the policies underlying protections for anonymous speech and efforts to secure the identity of anonymous speakers; issues relating to encryption; issues relating to advocacy of the use of force to incite lawless action; copyright infringement claims and the Digital Millennium Copyright Act; domain names and trademark infringement and dilution claims, and the use of trademarks in metatags; common law privacy torts, on-line profiling, and data-mining privacy issues relating to children; spam and trespass to chattels claims; and conceptualization of the nature of "the press." Such themes were incorporated in a narrative hypothetical describing fictitious people and events:[3]

> Robert Ruffles is the Chief Privacy Officer of Endrun Conglomerates, which is based in New City, New State. "Endrun" is a registered trademark of Endrun Conglomerates ("Endrun"), which manufactures trendy neon colors of eyeblack applied by football players to their faces (under their eyes) to prevent glare. Endrun's web-site, located at <http://www.EndRunCo.com>, boasts:
>
> *Teams that use Endrun's nifty neon eyeblack score 5.2% more touchdowns and 8.3% more field goals than those that use traditional black eyeblack. Use of Endrun's strategically chosen eyeblack*

3. Previously published in Madeleine Schachter, *Law of Internet Speech: Teacher's Manual*, 69 (Carolina Academic Press 2d ed. 2002).

> *increases the team's chances of successfully making an end-run by a staggering 27%.*
>
> *College, high school, and elementary school team members: purchase some today! And elementary school students and preschoolers: order some of this fine product now so you can begin to get used to the application techniques! Even if you don't have a school uniform yet, Endrun can match the eyeblack to your lunchbox colors!*
>
> *Remember: Endrun—it's the BEST in neon eyeblack. And it's available in moisturizing, hypoallergenic, and even insect repellent formulas.*

Teams that wish to purchase Endrun's product must pay the requisite subscription fee in order to gain access to restricted pages of Endrun's web-site and use Endrun's unique computer software, known as "ENE," an acronym for "Endrun neon eyeblack." Access to Endrun's ENE computer program is thus conditioned on subscription to Endrun's web-site. The subscribing team inputs its quarterback's hair and eye color, as well as the team's home and away colors, and Endrun's ENE computer program strategically designs and blends the precise hue of eyeblack that so bewitches the opposing team that its players are distracted from effectively blocking plays by the team using Endrun's product. (Endrun permits only one team per game to use the software.) Endrun's computer program utilizes "PEEP," an acronym for "protect Endrun eyeblack product," which is an encryption technology designed to prevent unauthorized access to and copying of Endrun's ENE computer program.

Ruffles is married and has two children. Isabelle Intern, a student enrolled at New State University, worked as an intern in the Compliance Department of Endrun Conglomerates during the summer of 2001. On August 15, 2001, Isabelle was supposed to conclude her internship, complete an exit interview with Robert, and fly home to Old City, Old State to spend a week's vacation with her family before the school year resumed. Isabelle never appeared for her exit interview, however; nor did she board the flight she had booked. Her family's frantic efforts to make contact with her have been unavailing, and an ensuing police investigation failed to locate her. Robert, Isabelle's ultimate supervisor, was interviewed twice by police. He initially denied any having any personal relationship with Isabelle, but during a subsequent interview, Robert admitted that he and Isabelle had been romantically involved. Police reports continue to list Isabelle as "missing."

Danny Disguntlish, a former Endrun Conglomerates employee, operates a web-site located at <http://www.EndrunCompany SucksABunch.com>, which uses the terms "endrun" and "murder" as metatags embedded in the site's HTML code. The site consists of a critique of Endrun's privacy policy; updates on the police investigation into Isabelle's whereabouts; a detailed account of what Danny ate for breakfast, lunch, and dinner on the day preceding each posting; Danny's views on which NFL players are having "good hair days;" and updates on NFL players' injuries.

Jane Doe, whose identity is not known to Endrun, posted the following statement on the web-site <http://www.EndrunCompany SucksABunch.com>:

> *Poor dead Isabelle Intern. If only she hadn't fallen for Endrun's CPO, Robert Ruffles, she would still be alive today. The last known fact about Isabelle is that she was with Robert. To think that poor Isabelle left this world with the last words she ever heard the high, shrill rant of Robert, warning her to stay away from him, from his family, and from Endrun Conglomerates. Robert has no explanation for his whereabouts the night Isabelle disappeared. Coincidence? Hardly.*
>
> *Don't let Robert get away with this. Robert's e-mail address is Robert@SOL.com; his home address is 555 West Street, New City, New State 55555. Forward all your spam to him! Go by his house and leave your trash on his lawn! And be sure to punch him in the nose when you see him. Really hard.*

On September 1, 2001, Danny forwarded Jane's posting to 11,500 current and former Endrun employees. On September 10, 2001, Danny decrypted the PEEP anti-circumvention measures implemented by Endrun with a program known as "DePEEP." DePEEP is a computer code that can decrypt PEEP, enabling access to Endrun's computer program without registering for and subscribing to Endrun's site. On the afternoon of September 10, 2002, Danny posted the technology for DePEEP on the web-site located at <http://www.Endrun CompanySucksABunch.com>. As Super Bowl 2002 approached, Danny invited both teams to use the software and "level the playing field."

The web-sites operated by Endrun Conglomerates and Danny, as well as all of the postings described herein have been transmitted over Internet service provider States On-Line, commonly known as "SOL."

You are Endrun's General Counsel and have been asked to write a confidential memorandum to its Board of Directors, evaluating the following claims, including the defenses thereto: (1) claims asserted by and against Endrun (except that you need *not* discuss any possible claims asserted against Endrun by Robert, Isabelle, or Jane); (2) claims asserted by SOL against Danny; and (3) claims asserted by Robert against (a) Jane; (b) Danny; and (c) SOL.

Grading the Exam

"Grading law school exams has been declared a 'deadening intimacy with ignorance and mental fog' which saps a professor's pedagogical and scholarly energies."[4] Yet evaluation of your students' performance is a critical component of your teaching duties.

Although it can be quite tedious to read and evaluate a large quantity of examination papers, especially when they discuss the same subject matter, it's essential that you attentively and carefully consider the merits of each individually. You'll want to be cautious about jumping to conclusions as to your students' performance based on your first impressions. This concern arises in two ways. First, when you're reading individual papers. Try to keep an open mind throughout; just as "[a] slipshod, inaccurate, or inarticulate beginning does not mean that the entire exam will be substandard[,...] a brilliant opening exegesis does not necessarily predict trenchant analysis."[5]

Second, if you're engaged in norm-referenced or relative grading (*see infra* at 214), you'll need to have a sense of the class' comparative work product. You may want to read, or at least skim, several exams before you actually start commenting and scoring. This will give you a frame of reference for the level of responses. And it will reveal a possible erroneous inference several students drew, perhaps because a particular lecture was a bit rushed or ambiguous. It also may sensitize you to the potential viability of a novel theory, even if you conclude that the theory is flawed because of reasons you didn't discuss in class.

It's also useful to re-read your instruction sheet before you begin grading. You'll want to remember, for example, that you told your students that they

---

4. Ruthann Robson, *The Zen of Grading,* 36 Akron L. Rev. 303, 303 (2003) (quoting Alfred Z. Reed, *Training for the Public Profession of the Law,* 359-60 (Carnegie Foundation for the Advancement of Teaching, Bulletin No. 15, 1921) (1976) (quoted in Steve Sheppard, *An Informal History of How Law Schools Evaluate Students, With a Predictable Emphasis on Law School Final Exams,* 65 U.M.K.C. L. Rev. 657, 687 n.177 (1997)).

5. *Id.* at 312-13.

needn't comply with citation protocols so that you don't mistakenly unduly reward a student who did so or penalize one who didn't.

As you go through each exam, distinguish between local, or specific, comments on the one hand, and more global or comprehensive ones on the other. Margin notes can help direct the pupil's focus to the specific point you believe needs clarification. While you'll want to include targeted comments, unless you're teaching a Legal Writing seminar, you may want to resist the temptation to stylistically edit the work. It may be preferable to confine your editorial remarks to those that help point out ambiguous statements so that students can work on more precise writing in the future, and of course to indicate why an argument is premised upon an erroneous statement of the law or misapprehends the facts. But re-working the structure, syntax, and diction of the paper may usurp valuable time you might otherwise spend carefully reading the student's work and offering constructive advice.

Try as well to make your comments as instructive as possible. Remember seeing that notation of "awk" in the margin of your English essay in elementary school and even agreeing that the phrasing was problematic but having no idea how to remedy it? You want the student to continue to work to formulate a better response but with some specific direction and guidance, especially in light of the deficiency you've noted after reviewing his initial effort.

With respect to both local and global comments, work to point out aspects of the work that the student did well. It's important psychologically to feel encouraged and not to have one's work filled with criticism. But it's useful to offer supportive comments for another reason: students need feedback from you when they've done something well so they can deliberately replicate their positive work. Even a student who scores an "A" on an exam likely hasn't done everything perfectly and shouldn't infer that he did. As to the student who scores a lower grade, it's particularly important that he not feel that his work was replete with problems.

Some professors prepare a grid as they craft their exams, allocating points to issues and analyses. This helps render the grading more uniform amongst class members and diminishes the tendency to excessively reward a well-developed point when another critical issue was omitted from the discussion entirely. If you have a large class, the grid can serve as a helpful reminder of salient points you expect in every paper; even though you've read repeated references to them moments before in earlier submissions, it can be difficult to track discussions in each paper. If you're considering this approach, remember, though, that it's important to keep an open mind about students' submissions. It's possible that a response doesn't necessarily fit neatly within one of the categories on your grid but nonetheless evinces deliberation, synthesis of the legal doctrines encompassed within the course, and critical thinking. It's reasonable that, just as the discipline of legal study and the practice of law encompasses judgment and discretion, so, too, should evaluation of an endeavor to engage in legal thinking include such factors.

It's also appropriate to expressly acknowledge some measure of subjectivity in essay responses. You'll want to reflect on the degree to which you're rewarding or penalizing the quality of the legal writing if the course deals with a substantive subject, although it's understandable that you'll expect your students to cogently and articulately state their reasoning.

Papers

Written exercises help students develop their discipline of legal thinking. The task of explaining legal concepts and writing about their application to factual situations confirms comprehension in a way that occasionally can be circumvented through fortuitous responses on a multiple-choice exam. Exemplary lawyers rely on skills of organization and clarity of expression that can be developed through written work. Papers also offer an effective means for feedback, both as to the students' performance and as to the efficacy of teaching methods used by the professor.

Written assignments can take various forms. They can incorporate legal research or factual investigation and be undertaken outside the classroom setting. Illustrations of such assignments include papers addressing specified questions; drafting memoranda of law, briefs, or other pleadings; writing correspondence with mock clients explaining legal principles; and preparing judicial opinions. A student might be asked to summarize a case decision and explain it to a fictitious client in the context of extant law. Or an actual or fictitious judicial decision may be distributed with instructions to draft a dissenting opinion.

Students also may be asked to draft correspondence to prospective adversaries, such as demand letters; cease and desist letters; and offers, or responses to offers, of settlement. Did the authors of such correspondence misrepresent the law or distort the facts? What ethical issues are raised by such conduct? What tone did the authors take and was such an approach strategic?

Collaborative variations may be utilized as well. For example, you might ask pairs of students to engage in a mock exchange of correspondence as adversarial counsel. You might fashion a panel of appellate judges with disparate inclinations to adjudicate a matter raised on appeal; can they achieve a consensus for a "unanimous" opinion? Will one or more concur or dissent? Or students also may be asked to critique another's written work, such as a ruling issued by a judge.

A book may be assigned for review by the class. The requirements for the submission can be left abstract or made more formulaic. In the latter event, the class may be asked to set forth the author's qualifications; the likely market for the work; and the author's hypothesis, supporting rationales, and conclusions. In assessing whether the author's conclusions were well-founded, pupils may be asked to consider the author's professional background and whether there was a commercial sponsor for the research who stands to benefit from particular conclusions. Such inquiry helps train students to search for potential biases.

Assignments can be specifically tailored to the substance of the course. A Criminal Law class might be asked to draft a sentencing memorandum and decide whether to consider victims' statements. A Contracts class may be charged with the task of drafting an agreement that carves out or imposes liability for certain contingencies. A Law and Medicine class could be asked to draft guidelines authorizing physician-assisted suicide. A Trial Tactics class might compare litigation and alternative dispute resolution methods. The tenor of a response to a demand for additional documents or interrogatory responses or an offer of settlement can be assigned and critiqued, offering an opportunity to sensitize students to the utility of trying to avoid acrimonious communications.

Papers also may be undertaken within the class setting. Professors conducting first-year classes may want to briefly review note-taking methods or approaches to course outlines to assist students as they transition to law school. Some teachers administer occasional quizzes as a means of having students practice timed writing exercises and to mitigate the anxiety associated with a single year-end exam. Brief summaries of lectures occasionally are requested of students as well to monitor attendance, gather feedback about attentiveness and comprehension, and tutor students in the task of concisely elucidating overall themes.

Assigned papers can take the form of open-ended research papers, in which case students engage in external legal research to investigate and analyze a legal issue. This may be the product of individually-developed topics, in which case you'll want to consider asking the class to propose their topics to you in advance for your approval. You then have an opportunity to assess the viability of the topic. If, for instance, the U.S. Supreme Court has definitively clarified a narrow issue proposed as the thesis, the student's legal research may be a bit more facile than you contemplated. The recent publication of a scholarly article comprehensively canvassing applicable law likewise may displace the requisite complexity of the legal investigation and thus affect the challenge of the project. In those cases, you may want to encourage the student to modify his approach to address a permutation not yet resolved by the courts or to consider the impact of changed circumstances. Consultation with you about the topic also provides an opportunity to suggest particular resources or legal authorities that the student may want to review.

Or you can offer a list of suggested topics from which students can choose. In that event, you'll need to decide whether more than one student can select the same topic, and, if so, whether they may collaborate. If the selection of topics is restricted to individuals, you'll want to consider how you'll award the selection if more than one student wishes to choose it. You might make the determination based on a lottery system or the flip of a coin, or based on who made the first request.

A key determinant in establishing your standards about topic selection is whether you wish to have a number of issues explored or have the entire class uniformly consider a problem. In the latter event, your grading inevitably will be more standardized because you'll be comparing the analytical efficacy and thoroughness of research on the same topic amongst all of the students. Note that because there may be a propensity to share some research and thoughts amongst students outside of class, your policy on the degree to which students may collaborate should be clearly stated in advance.

You also can assign a series of shorter papers rather than a single submission. This affords an opportunity (or multiple opportunities) to offer suggestions for improvement in the subsequent submission(s).

With respect to standards for grading papers, many of the guidelines relating to review of examinations are applicable (*see supra* at 200). Pause for a moment to reflect on your overall objectives for the course. A writing seminar, for example, will focus considerably more on the degree to which the student used proper citational form than might a course devoted to a substantive area of the law. Is your primary concern the student's clarity of expression or legal analysis? Have you asked your class to thoroughly explore resources for research purposes or to confine their sources to those in the assigned readings?

Class Contribution

Attendance

If you've decided to regard attendance as a grade determinant, your students' individual scores are fairly easy to determine. You'll need to look over your record of attendance throughout the semester, adjusting as necessary for excusable absences such as illness or injury, a death in the family, or religious observance. You'll also determine whether instances of material lateness or early departure from class should affect an attendance record.

You can create a grid, listing the class roster on the right-hand side of the page and the date of each class session along the top. This can be done on a Microsoft Excel type program or simply handwritten on graph paper. These calculations are predominantly objective in nature and the impartiality and fairness of the scoring is confirmed by the notification you gave to pupils at the outset of the semester about the impact of their attendance records on their grades (*see supra* at 82).

Occasionally a student will contact you during the course of the semester to explain an absence or advise you that he will be missing an upcoming class. Obviously, you'll want to consider the reason for the absence. If the student has a mere scheduling conflict due to theater tickets or a sports event, you may decide to remind him that your attendance policy excuses only certain types of absences. A more difficult question arises if the student's absence derives from a scheduling conflict imposed by the school, such as a meeting of law journal editors. In that event, you might base your determination on whether the meeting is mandatory.

Another option is to impose a lesser penalty for such absences. By way of illustration, you might award ten points for each class attended, grant zero points for each class a student missed, and grant five points for an understandable but not entirely excusable absence. A student who missed a class because of illness or a religious holiday would receive the full ten points. A student who attended but left well before the class concluded might receive only seven or eight points.

Each student's individual attendance scores then would be added to form a cumulative attendance score. This score in turn would become a component of the student's overall course grade.

Class Participation

As you evaluate each student's class participation score, consider the quality of the comments and questions. It's important, I think, to be wary of unduly rewarding the frequency of participation at the expense of the quality of the participation. A student who spoke only sporadically nonetheless may merit a high grade if he volunteered judiciously, expressing his views when he thought that they would meaningfully contribute to the discourse without merely repeating others' prior comments.

Remember, though, as you're assigning a value to comment, to reward risk. There's probably only a few second interval between the time you pose a question and the student's formulation of a response and decision to volunteer to participate. It's impossible for anyone's every utterance to be demonstrably incisive. But experimentation and effort are part of the learning process. It's important to try for the shot even though you miss the basket. Or, to switch to a baseball metaphor, there's a reason why no one bats 1,000. And why statisticians track singles, doubles, and triples and not just home runs.

Learning is incremental. And derived collaboratively. In basketball, the way the ball is passed is critical; the assist, as well as the shot, is recorded. Even when a pupil fails to articulate a point precisely, he's probably contributed to the dialogue nonetheless and facilitated a foundation for the ensuing discussion. Emphasizing the fallacy of a student's contribution without crediting his risk in making the argument will only deter timorous class members from taking similar risks.

One way to track class participation scores is to add points to the students' attendance scores. By way of illustration, a student might be awarded ten points for attending a class and up to twelve additional points for each comment made during class. Whether the student would receive the maximum twelve points for each comment would depend on the quality of the insight, whether it evinced preparation for the class, and the degree to which it reflected attentiveness during class and respect for contrary views.

Methods and Timing of Conveying Feedback

The timing of student evaluations is another aspect to consider. First-year students, for example, understandably will find it quite daunting to have worked diligently throughout the semester only to have their entire grade depend on their performance on one exam taken over the course of a couple of hours. Some schools have policies that address this expressly. At the City University of New York School of Law, for instance, two evaluative methods are expected; a professor might administer a mid-term exam and a final exam or use some combination of class presentations, research papers, tests, and research advocacy memoranda.[6]

It's not uncommon for law students to receive feedback about their entire performance during the course of a semester in single letter grades. The student who receives a "C" or a "D" is left without specific guidance about ways in which his submission and performance were flawed and the studying, preparation, and analytical techniques he might employ to improve. The student who receives a "C-" might have submitted a mediocre exam relative to his classmates, omitted conclusions about each legal problem discussed, or performed admirably on every aspect of the exam except that he neglected to answer one of five essay questions. The student's deficiency might have been the product of inefficient allocation of time or a mere oversight, and yet he

---

6. *See id.* at 311 n.52.

may leave the class mistakenly convinced that he failed to master most of the material or that he lacks adequate skills to proficiently write an exam.

Nearly as problematic is that the student who received an "A" or a "B" may be more satisfied with his grade but just as unenlightened as to his positive accomplishments. This makes it difficult for the student to recognize and replicate the positive elements of his performance. Also disconcerting is the fact that the student who was awarded a very high grade may erroneously presume that he mastered all of the material and effectively analyzed every aspect of the assignment when in fact his grade reflects superior but not perfect performance.

The timing of rendering feedback also is significant. Evaluations conducted exclusively at the end of the course eviscerate any opportunity for demonstrable improvement within the course. Prompt feedback is especially important for first-year students who may perceive an unsettling incongruity between classroom preparation and discussion on the one hand and evaluative techniques on the other.

If it's feasible under the circumstances, try to give students feedback beyond their simple score or grade. You might prepare comments to be sent via e-mail to each student. Or if there's time, try to hold brief meetings with each member of the class. Your ability to do this may well depend on several factors, including the number of students in your class, the length of the papers they submit, and the timing of the administration of the exam at the conclusion of the semester and the likely scattering of students to other pursuits thereafter.

Written Comments

If you are teaching a very large class or are an adjunct professor balancing teaching and other professional responsibilities, the demands on your time may render feedback beyond the score itself unduly burdensome. In such instances, you might confine more extensive communication with those who would benefit most from additional feedback (a sort of "triage" approach) and those who specifically solicit your insights.

If it's feasible, you can offer written comments to each student. Begin by pointing out the submission's positive attributes. As you critique the paper, work to offer constructive remarks, tactfully setting out how the student might have better developed a point, relied on additional legal authority, or organized his paper in a more logical and cohesive fashion. If you're commenting on overall class performance or your comments otherwise include a critique of students' oral participation, try to recall (perhaps by resorting to notes recorded promptly at the conclusion of each class session, *see supra* at 184) specific contributions or insightful questions that were asked. Was a more reticent student perhaps judicious in his participation, laudably declining to volunteer merely for the sake of participating or to reiterate another's previously stated point? If you sense that a pupil is somewhat reserved, this is an excellent opportunity to encourage him to speak up a bit more. Simply praising thoughtful remarks and general preparedness can spark confidence.

Student Conferences

In a relatively small seminar, you might have adequate time to devote to individual student conferences. Or you can make them optional for those students who wish additional feedback. It's quite useful to set out guidelines at the outset. Are students expected to make appointments with you? How long are such conferences expected to last? You'll want to be relatively explicit about time allotments so that students can plan their schedules accordingly without trepidation that they'll risk offending you by having to excuse themselves to attend another class or some other commitment. And you'll want to have some parameters for the length of the conference, even if they're occasionally breached because a student is confused, distressed, or, more hopefully, enthralled by the discussion and inspired to continue.

Self-Evaluation

You also can encourage students to reflect on their performance. As they review their semester's work, how might they have approached their preparation, note-taking, outlining, and studying techniques to improve? You could distribute a questionnaire to help students focus on their respective self-evaluations. What aspects of the class came most easily to them? Did they allocate adequate time to complete reading assignments and review the material? Was it helpful to use commercial outlines or was it more efficient, even if initially more time-intensive, to prepare one's own review materials?

This self-examination process doesn't necessarily have to be a formal process or even one that they must share with you. But it can help pupils focus on ways they can better allocate their time, refine their study habits, and select electives targeted to improve areas of weakness. You might ask the class to delineate the major themes discussed in each topical cluster of class sessions, the degree to which they diligently and routinely prepared for class, the regularity of their class attendance, and the quality and frequency of their class participation. You might also ask students to complete a questionnaire in order to consider how they might more effectively have contributed to the course and improved their studying techniques:

- Logistical Aspects
  - Did you timely obtain the course syllabus and refer to it regularly throughout the semester?
  - Did you timely obtain the required course text or other materials?
- Course Requirements
  - Did you timely complete the reading assignments?
  - Did you read any optional or recommended materials?
  - Did you timely complete any papers, presentations, or examinations?
  - Did you diligently take notes during class sessions? Did you find it helpful to refer to them later? Did the notes effectively remind you of salient course themes?
  - Did you continue to reflect on class discussions and themes after the session concluded?
- Class Contribution
  - Did you attend all class sessions or have a valid reason for any absences?
  - Did you arrive late or leave class early?
  - Did you have a reasoned and articulate response to questions posed of you?
  - Did you volunteer in class or participate only when the professor called on you?
  - Did you listen attentively to comments made by your classmates?
  - Were you respectful of views with which you disagreed?
  - Were you able to distinguish between insightful and erroneous comments made by your classmates?
- Research Techniques
  - If external research was required or permitted, were you able to effectively and promptly locate relevant materials?
  - Did you access a range of sources?
  - Did you consider any actual or potential biases of the authors or sponsors of sources you reviewed?
  - Did you experience any technological difficulties? If so, did you consult with the school's librarian, IT personnel, or other appropriate persons?
- Study Techniques
  - Did you engage in a study group? If so, did you contribute in comparable fashion as the other members? Did you feel that the collaborative study approach was effective for you?
  - Did you outline the course themes? Did you purchase a prepared outline? If you did both, which was more effective for you?
  - Did you ask questions in class or consult your professor when you were confused?

- Evaluative Instruments
  - Did you find the exam fair and comprehensive?
  - Did the exam cover material that didn't seem to have been included in the readings or class discussions?
  - Did you follow all applicable guidelines relating to the exam or paper?
  - Were you surprised by the grade(s) you received?
- General
  - Would you have benefited from taking other courses as prerequisites to this course?
  - Did you enjoy the course? Did you look forward to attending class sessions?
  - Are you interested in the subject matter of the course? Did the class increase your interest in the subject matter?
  - Would you recommend the course to others?

Peer Evaluation

Some teachers also utilize peer evaluation techniques. Competition or awkwardness that might ensue from such evaluative instruments can be mitigated by restricting the review of peer evaluations to the student who is the subject of the review. A benefit of this approach is that students can work to acquire comments from their colleagues and so develop recognition that insights can come from a variety of sources of disparate experience. As well, law students, like lawyers, must learn to gain the confidence to disregard advice with which they disagree and to reconcile contradictory comments.

Peer evaluation of a paper can be facilitated through a questionnaire to be completed by each student. The reviewer can be required to summarize the main theses, the supporting facts, the legal authority relied upon, and the conclusions reached. Such an effort not only helps the reviewer learn substantively and summarize concisely, but it also confirms that he has diligently and thoroughly read his colleague's paper. The reviewer can then be asked to delimit the strengths of the paper and areas for improvement, focusing on the viability of the legal analysis; the breadth of the legal research; the marshalling of relevant facts; and the paper's organization, style, and citational form. The visceral task of having to complete a prepared form tacitly suggests that the student is expected to delimit strengths and weaknesses, rather than to engage in only a cursory review and merely offer a conclusory overall comment.

Review of Model Answers

Some professors distribute model answers to essay questions as a means of reviewing prototypes of effective and weak responses. Certainly if a submission is to be critiqued in front of the entire class or otherwise made accessible to it, it seems only reasonable to craft a fictitious example lest the student who submitted the deficient paper sit uncomfortably as his work is criticized. Even review of a laudable submission may be deserving of fictionalization so that at the very least it's a composite of submissions; otherwise, a student who is performing well may feel self-conscious, or if his identity is ascertained, be subject to reactions of resentment.

I believe that proffers of model answers are problematic for another reason. Law students, vigorously searching for "correct" and definitive legal rules, may misconstrue a professor's discussion of positive aspects of a model answer. The professor may be deemed to be endorsing the paper's position as comprising the "right" answer in a particular format and style that students may work tirelessly to emulate to the detriment of independent and creative critical thinking endeavors.

Grading Standards

General Guidelines

In certain courses, such as small seminars, the professor may review written submissions from students denoted with their names. In advocacy courses, for example, grades typically are returned by the professor according to students' names because mastery of oral skills is a key component of the evaluation. Other times, in-class and take-home exams and even papers may be graded by the law professor on a "blind" basis, which means that the students indicate their student identification numbers (or examination numbers they've been assigned by the school) on the exams but not their names. This promotes objective and non-biased evaluation of the students' work.

Your school may have guidelines regarding evaluation of student work, particularly with respect to required classes, or the school may defer to you to determine the students' grades for exams and/or papers, and for the course generally. Thus, for example, you may be able to decide the extent to which class participation, a mid-term paper, and the final examination each will count towards the students' overall course grades. Students should be generally apprised at the outset of the semester as to how each component will be weighted.

If you are factoring class attendance and/or class participation into the grade, those components cannot be on a blind basis. When you submit the grades for your class at the conclusion of the semester, you'll need to advise the registrar whether computation and weighting is appropriate. For example, if you have decided that class participation and class attendance comprises 20 percent of the students' grades, and the take-home final examination comprises 80 percent of the students' grades, you should so state in a cover letter to the registrar, specifying the class participation and class attendance scores for each student by name, and the final examination scores for each student by student identification number.

Alternatively, you may wish to score class participation by indicating to the registrar how students' scores should be adjusted for their final grades. For instance, you could submit a list of the students' names with indications as to whether their grades should be raised or lowered and to what degree.

Your school also will have policies regarding what constitutes a passing mark and the minimum weighted average students must maintain to remain in good academic standing. With the exception of pass/fail courses, students probably will receive letter grades for each course; these may be assigned a numerical equivalent for purposes of determining cumulative averages, determining whether a student is entitled to Honors, and determining students' relative standing. A fairly conventional comparison is the following (although some schools do not award scores of "A+"):

Letter Grade	Numerical Equivalent
A+	4.3
A	4.0
A-	3.7
B+	3.3
B	3.0
B–	2.7
C+	2.3
C	2.0
C–	1.7
D+	1.3
D	1.0
F	0.0

Grades for graduating students generally are reported as "Honors," "Good," "Pass," or "Fail." "Honors" represents outstanding performance in the course; "Good" represents above average performance in the course; "Pass" represents performance worthy of credit, and "Fail" represents inferior performance that does not satisfy the minimum standard for course credit.

Grades for L.L.M. candidates may have the following equivalents to J.D. candidates' letter grades:

L.L.M. Grade	J.D. Grade Equivalent
Honors	A+
Honors	A
Honors	A–
Good	B+
Good	B
Pass	B–
Pass	C+
Pass	C
Pass	C–
Fail	D
Fail	F

Different grades may be assigned to brief classroom exercises, quizzes, homework, and the like that account for only part of the student's grade. You might consider a tripartite gradation such as "good," "pass," and "re-submit" or "✓+," "✓," and "✓-."

Grading Methodologies

There are various grading systems, all of which are designed to evaluate performance fairly. Students may be assessed in absolute terms, in which case they are evaluated individually according to specified criteria, or on relative or norm-referenced terms, in which case they're compared with their classmates. In either case, it's critical that the system utilized be implemented accurately and impartially.

Absolute Grading Systems

Absolute grading systems are designed to assess the degree to which students have mastered the relevant material and have effectively performed according to criteria applied commensurately amongst their classmates. Some teachers formulate a grid as they undertake to craft a final examination, assigning points to each aspect of the problem that the student is expected to analyze (*see supra* at 201). A professor might credit the spotting of a particular issue in a complex hypothetical by awarding three points, adding an additional point for each apposite legal authority upon which the student relies. The student's score is calculated by aggregating the number of points and awarding a grade based on the range within which it falls.

By way of illustration, if the total number of possible points the student could achieve was 100, and his aggregate score is 87, he may receive an 87 score or a B+ grade.

The advantage of this method is that it works to standardize the evaluation of all students. Even when a certain number of points is reserved for overall subjective impressions, such as the cogency of the student's writing style or the concision of the submission, there is uniformity in the way in which points are earned. The system also tends to promote assessment based on the material covered throughout the course of the semester, as both the exam and the points allocated in the grading grid are expressly directed to fairly specific issues, legal authority, and analysis.

A disadvantage of the method is that the professor may be predisposed to assume that there is a single "correct" response. While it may not be appropriate to credit tangential discussions that rely on material covered in other courses, especially at the expense of adequate analysis of relevant matters, it's also important not to be unduly dismissive of a creative or novel approach simply because it doesn't neatly fit within a prepared grid.

If several students misapprehend a legal doctrine or theory, it's essential to reflect on whether the matter was covered with adequate depth or clarity during the course of the semester. One professor noted succinctly, "Certainly, each student bears responsibility for his or her learning, but as the teacher I have created the context for that learning."[7] If it appears that the entire class is confused about a particular point, it may be appropriate to discount that aspect of the exam as you grade.

Relative Or Norm-Referenced Grading Systems

Grading Curves

Relative or norm-reference grading approaches presuppose that students should be assessed in comparison to their classmates and that their performance likely will follow a fairly predictable curve. Your school may follow a grading curve that is mandatory for courses required for first-year students and/or upper-classmen, with respect to final course grades (i.e., after adjustments for class attendance and participation are taken into account). For example, ten to 20 percent of the class may receive a grade of "A-" to "A+," with a limitation placed on the percentage of students who receive a grade of "A" or "A+;" the latter may be reserved exclusively for exceptional circumstances. The school might confine grades ranging from "B+" to "A+" to 40 to 50 per-

7. *Id.* at 315.

cent of the class, with no more than 33 to 50 percent receiving a grade of "B-;" three to ten percent may receive a grade of "C+" or below; and no specified standard may be set for the percentage of students who may receive grades of "D" or "F."

The school may use a "bell curve" grading system, as follows:

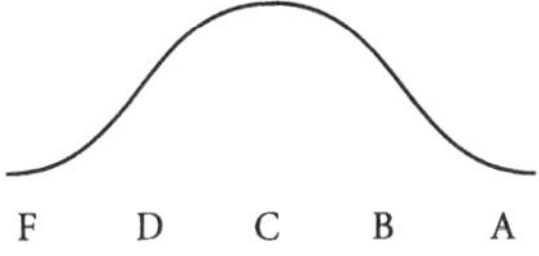

Even when a grading curve is not mandatory for a particular course, the school may recommend that the curve be followed absent an exceptional reason for doing so. Such a policy is intended to promote uniformity and a consistent approach from which prospective employers may draw reasonable inferences about students' relative performance. As well, such an approach discourages students from selecting courses based on the professor's grading tendency and avoids disadvantaging students who either do not select courses based on apparent leniency or who choose courses with more rigorous grading.

The Standard Deviation Method

Student grades may be computed according to the standard deviation method, in which case they are based on their distance from the mean score for the class as opposed to on an arbitrary scale. To calculate the class' standard deviation, the professor would create a frequency distribution of the final scores and identify the mean, or average, score. Software programs and some calculators can be utilized to make the necessary computations.

The formula for standard deviation is as follows:

$$\text{standard deviation} = \sqrt{\frac{N\Sigma X^2 - (\Sigma X)^2}{N(N-1)}}$$

ΣX^2 = sum of all squared scores
$(\Sigma X)^2$ = squared sum of all scores
N = number of scores

The mid-level grade, such as the "C" grade on a scale of "A" through "F" grades, is determined by computing the range from one-half of the standard deviation below the mean to one-half above. Adding one standard deviation to the upper "C" cut-off will yield the results for the "A"–"B" cut-off point, and subtracting one standard deviation from the lower "C" cut-off will yield the "D"–"F" cut-off point. Note however, that use of this method could penalize a student who performed well but competed with other high performers. You therefore may want to use the method only to raise scores, in which event you risk skewing some grades.

T-Scores

A method that's related to the standard deviation method is the T-Score method, which can be used to standardize raw test scores before averaging but then adjust for differences in means and standard deviations. The mathematical integrity of each score is preserved accordingly. A common approach is to use a T-Score of 50 and a standard deviation of ten. As is the case with the standard deviation method, software programs can be used to make the calculations.

The Gap Method

Students' total scores for the course also may be arranged in ascending or descending order; the professor can then scrutinize the range to search for naturally-occurring gaps in the scores' distribution. Although this method may more readily accommodate borderline scores, the gaps may appear arbitrarily and without empirical or direct correlation to student performance.

Submission of Grades

You'll likely submit the grades and scores by creating a list according to student identification numbers or by noting them on a grade roster your receive from the registrar that identifies your class' students by their respective student identification numbers. It's important that you timely submit your grades to the registrar. Meeting the deadlines enables the registrar to verify that graduating students have satisfied their requirements in order to receive their degrees, to determine eligibility for students' receipt of academic honors and prizes, and allows students to timely furnish transcripts to prospective employers. At the conclusion of each semester, the registrar must compute, compile, and record grades for the entire student body, each member of which is taking multiple classes. Timely (or preferably early) submission of grades enables the registrar to complete these tasks.

You may receive an indication in upper-class courses as to which students are graduating so that you can prioritize evaluation of their submissions. Calculation of their cumulative gradepoint average determines whether such pupils are eligible to participate in graduation ceremonies.

Your school will advise you as to how it posts grades, which may be done electronically by the registrar for access by students. If you're permitted to post grades, you'll want to protect the anonymity of the grading system by, for example, blocking out several digits of the student identification numbers so that you reveal only the last four digits with the grade.

There typically also are policies regarding the circumstances under which you may change a grade once it has been submitted to the registrar. For instance, you may be able to correct a computation error or a mistake in recording the grade. Under other circumstances, the dean's approval may be required. Such a policy works to avoid unfairness amongst students. It's another reason you'll want to read papers and exams carefully and deliberate thoughtfully about grades before you submit them.

Absent any procedure imposed on you, it's a good idea to retain exams for a period of one year (especially if the exam has not been returned to the student). This affords ample time for a student to inquire as to whether a computation error was made. It also enables you to review the exam in the event a grade is appealed (*see infra* at 237).

Academic Integrity

When violations of academic integrity occur in law school, they may seem particularly egregious in light of the discipline's overall emphasis on respect for rules, regulations, and ethical conduct. Law schools generally impose upon students an obligation to adhere to a university code of conduct and/or a code of academic responsibility adopted by the faculty. Graduate students may have special additional requirements relating to their theses.

Students suspected of violating applicable codes may be subject to an investigation; if a finding of probable cause is entered, a preliminary hearing usually is conducted by the dean. If the student does not accept the finding of probable cause and proposed sanctions, he may be entitled to a trial on the merits, including a right to counsel.

Faculty occasionally refer cases of cheating. Efforts to deter cheating have long been undertaken by law schools by having proctors monitor exams. Sometimes other prophylactic tactics are used as well; the order in which multiple-choice questions appear are not uniform amongst the exams distributed to the class so that copying answers will be unavailing. Still, there are ways to evade these precautions, perhaps even more so when exams are administered on a take-home basis beyond the scrutiny of proctors. Some go so far as to assign different essay questions to dissuade unauthorized collaboration amongst students. This practice can undermine the parity (or, just as deleterious, the appearance of parity) of the questions' difficulty, however, leading to concerns about the reliability of the assessment of students' relative performance.

Plagiarism is another concern. It basically consists of taking the written work of another, passing it off as one's own without appropriate attribution, and reaping the benefits from its use. The practice may be facilitated by access to the World Wide Web, which houses so voluminous a repository of works that even full-time academicians could not possibly be conversant with the complete range of papers in their respective fields. Some web-sites even offer papers for sale,[8] and the Internet's capacity for caching may impede efforts to remove papers that were posted improperly. E-mail and other on-line communicative devices also ease access to others who are geographically remote or temporally inconvenient to consult who may, knowingly or unwittingly, provide unauthorized guidance to students.

Efforts to deter the sources of written work product for plagiarism purposes have even been undertaken legislatively. Texas criminalizes as a misdemeanor the preparation, sale, offer or advertisement for sale, or delivery to another an academic product if the actor intends to make a profit and knows or reasonably should have known that a person intends to submit or use the academic product to satisfy an academic requirement.[9] But the prosecution of such an offense is questionable (even if the sale were within the state or the exercise of jurisdiction were otherwise appropriate) in light of First Amendment protections relating to speech. As well, the efficacy of such penal sanctions is suspect because some who appear to come within the law's scope may not be subject to prosecution if, at least ostensibly, they conditioned access or sale on a promise not to misrepresent the work as one's own. Such prosecutorial enforcement issues pertain to the purveyor of the content as opposed to its recipient. The student who engages in plagiarism still is subject to disciplinary action by the school. Nor does the statute address plagiarism by resort to published materials that may be even more readily at the student's disposal in this era of global communication.

Sometimes, faced with the pressures attendant to grading and comparative peer performance, it's difficult for students to appreciate that cheating isn't a harmful offense. Although on some level they may understand that their future legal career will require skills and knowledge that they've evaded mastering, the notion seems fairly abstract and remote relative to the immediacy of performance reviews and journal selection. You may want to caution your stu-

---

8. *See, e.g.*, Plagiarism.org (discussing such practices), *at* <http://www.plagiarism.org>; Lisa Hinchliffe, *Cut-and-Paste Plagiarism: Preventing, Detecting and Tracking Online Plagiarism* (May 1998) (listing examples of such sites), *at* <http://alexia.lis.uiuc.edu/~janicke/plagiary.htm>.

9. Tex. Penal Code, Code Ann. §32.50(b) (Vernon 2003).

dents about violations of academic integrity and convey your expectations that they will perform to their highest potential. Cheating and plagiarism indicate disrespect not only for themselves but also for the professor and their classmates. Try to convey enthusiasm for reviewing the students' work product, explaining that you're looking forward to seeing their ideas and the sources upon which they relied to derive their conclusions.

It's also wise to educate students about what constitutes plagiarism. While certainly submitting another's work in wholesale and verbatim fashion as one's own constitutes plagiarism, there are more subtle forms as well. Excerpting large portions of another's work without alteration or attribution also is a matter of concern. Just as failure to attribute a source may be problematic, so, too, is it inappropriate to deliberately suggest that a statement is a verbatim quotation when in fact it's been paraphrased or to intentionally present a statement as an accurate representation of the author's expression when it's been distorted. Pilfering an idea without refinement or attribution may be inappropriate, notwithstanding that it would not infringe a copyright as a matter of law. You also might articulate the consequences, citing the school's academic code as a means of emphasizing the significance both you and the administration place on the conduct.

How might you detect plagiarism if you become suspicious as you review a student's written work? First, reflect on why you feel that the paper is suspect. Simply because a student has been somewhat reserved or even relatively inarticulate in class discussions doesn't necessarily mean that his written work will be comparable. People often find it easier to set out their thoughts in written format, rather than having to speak extemporaneously before a large group. The luxury of time to deliberate about phraseology, diction, and syntax, and to re-read the expression of the thoughts, often leads to superior performance. Nor does mere contact with a more experienced person automatically suggest collaboration. The student hasn't necessarily consulted his older sister who is now practicing in the very field that is the subject matter of the course or an upper-classman with whom the student is close friends who is writing a journal article on a related topic.

Nevertheless, you may suspect that the paper is not the student's work product. Perhaps, for example, the expression reminds you of others' work you've been reading. Or the overall style is not even remotely commensurate with work the student earlier submitted. Maybe the conclusions reached are antithetical to positions taken by the student in class previously. Your suspicions may arise from the fact that the student's submission exclusively utilizes sources within a particular time period, notwithstanding significant subsequent legal developments; this may suggest that the student relied on another's earlier work. Similarly, examination of an issue solely under the law of a specific state when the assignment did not so confine the research may imply use of someone else's work, especially if the state selected is not even where the student resides or is attending school and if highly relevant law has developed in jurisdictions not discussed within the paper. Your suspicions may intensify depending on the egregiousness of any of these factors and whether there's an amalgam of such indications.

As an initial matter, you can consider whether your doubts about the authorship of the paper are well-founded by reflecting on the initial assignment. If there were particular issues or matters that the student was asked to address but omitted, is it possible that he relied on the work of another? Also look for internal inconsistencies in the format of the paper; is the same citational form used throughout, even when it is used incorrectly? Do errors appear to be the product of typographical errors or of erratic format? For example, if a student routinely places the year of the case before the volume number of the reporter, one reasonably may infer that he is not using standard "Blue Book" form. If, however, he sometimes does so but other times uses the correct form, it's possible that he's relying on another's citational form.

You might then briefly review one or more of the sources cited by the student. Perhaps he attributed his use, albeit inadequately. You also can try to assess whether plagiarism has been committed by searching for repeated, extensive, and non-attributed phraseology from another by searching LexisNexis, Westlaw, FindLaw, or other law-based and additional web-sites accessed through conventional search engines. Such computerized databases paradoxically facilitate the commission of plagiarism and its detection.

Some entities, albeit not necessarily directed exclusively to legal scholarship, seek to deter plagiarism generally. Turnitin.com includes an "on-line collaborative learning solution to protect against peer collusion" and resources "for preemptive plagiarism education."[10] Plagiarism.org is "designed to provide the latest information on online plagiarism…offer[ing] detailed information on the technologies behind Turnitin.com, facts about Internet plagiarism, and a report on the growth of 'cheatsites' online."[11] The site utilizes a series of algorithms to create a "digital fingerprint" of a textual document, cross-references it against a local database containing hundreds of thousands of papers, "release[s] automated web crawlers to scour the rest of the Internet for possible matches," and prepares a report for each paper.[12]

---

10. *See* <http://turnitin.com>.
11. *See* <http://www.plagiarism.org>.
12. *See* <http://www.plagiarism.org/technology.html>.

Glatt Plagiarism Services includes a tutorial program that offers computer assisted instruction on what constitutes plagiarism and how to avoid it; a "self-detection program" to avoid inadvertent instances of plagiarism, and a screening program for use by academic institutions and the legal profession to detect infringement of copyright rights.[13] As of mid-2003, Glatt stated that its screening tests have been so accurate that no student had been falsely accused of plagiarism.[14]

Plagiarism and other violations of academic integrity are serious charges and obviously great care should be taken before any accusations are advanced. You'll first want to meet with the student to inquire about the circumstances giving rise to your suspicions, especially when you haven't witnessed an instance of cheating firsthand or an instance of plagiarism hasn't been committed in wholesale fashion. Remember, too, that the use of identical phrases does not automatically impute illicit copying; indeed, even a circumstantial copyright infringement case requires a showing of both substantial similarity and of *access* to the protectible expression. Nor should plagiarism be conclusively presumed based on the mere similarity of ideas expressed even when the prior work was accessed and reviewed; the second author may have absorbed and refined the concept and even unintentionally endorsed it as the product of his own inspiration.

If you find that your suspicions rise to the level of legitimate concern and merit further investigation, you might first meet with the student in a private setting. You could begin by asking him about his paper, working to engage him in a dialogue about the research he undertook and the conclusions he reached. What parts of the legal investigation did he find cumbersome? What aspects of the analysis did he find especially challenging? As you converse, it's quite possible that your suspicions will evaporate. The student may describe his frustration in locating an obscure source in a remote section of the law school library or his gratification in coming upon a helpful web-site with numerous links to other sources. Explicit reference to the contents of particular sources upon which the student relied suggests that he personally consulted them. He may articulate a nuance in his analysis or make repeated references to portions of his paper and thereby confirm his familiarity with the work and the extent of his efforts in preparing it. As well, the student's references to concepts and principles incorporated in the paper during a class discussion tend to negate an inference of complete unfamiliarity with the work.

---

13. *See* <http://www.plagiarism.com/index.htm>.

14. *See* Glatt Plagiarism Screening Program, *An In-Depth Look, at* <http://www.plagiarism.com/screen.id.htm>.

Faculty Assessment

Just as providing feedback to students about their performance during their law school careers is an important part of the educational process, so, too, is faculty assessment an important part of teaching. Feedback can affect decisions relating to promotion and tenure. More significantly, self-assessment, student assessment, and administrative and peer evaluation techniques can help you identify areas of both proficiency and weakness as you continually strive for improvement.

Self-Assessment Techniques

Try to glean constructive insights about your teaching as you assess your students. If most of the class missed a point on the final exam, it's quite possible that the way you covered the material would benefit from another approach.

Reflect on the progress of your experience throughout the semester. Promptly after each class, think about how the class discussion proceeded. Did you feel comfortable with the volume of reading assignments and the number of themes you set out to cover? Was the class active and engaged? Did the students' questions suggest that the discussion was stimulating or that the lecture lacked clarity? You might even keep a "journal" of your thoughts and reactions so that you can review what seemed to work and what seemed less effective (*see supra* at 184). You also can track points of confusion or interest that might generate follow-up to be integrated in future lectures.

At the conclusion of the semester, take some time to consider your overall experience. There are various self-assessment tools available that you can access.[15] Or you can think about your performance and enjoyment in each of the following categories:

- Logistical Aspects
  - Did you arrive timely?
  - Did you repeatedly need to end class before its scheduled conclusion?
  - Did you cancel any classes during the semester? How many? For what reasons?
  - Did you timely post your syllabus?

---

15. *See, e.g.*, Indiana University Bloomington Evaluation Services and Testing, *at* <http://www.indiana.edu/~best/>; Campus Instructional Counseling, Indiana University, *at* <http://www.iub.edu/~teaching/feedback.html>.

   - Did you timely apprise students of course requirements? Did any class members seem surprised during the course of the semester about the course requirements?
   - Did you timely submit your grades?
- Professional Demeanor and Accessibility
   - Did you look forward to each class session?
   - Were you active and engaged during class discussions?
   - Did you stay focused on your planned lessons?
   - Did you listen attentively to student questions and try to be responsive?
   - Did students seem comfortable when they approached you with questions?
   - Did students indicate that they experienced any difficulty in trying to contact you outside of class?
- Class Decorum and Discourse
   - Was the class discourse generally respectful?
   - Did you help foster a civil and intellectual discourse amongst students?
   - Did you tactfully correct mistakes your students made?
   - Were you open and receptive to the discussion of views with which you disagreed?
   - Were students readily able to discern your personal viewpoints in most instances? Did you routinely indicate or elicit countervailing views?
   - Did class members respectfully consider diverse viewpoints?
   - Did you encourage questions from students?
   - Were students actively and attentively engaged in class discussions?
   - Did you cover important themes in every class?
- Course Plan and Preparation
   - As you look over your course description, did you fulfill your objectives?
   - Did your syllabus accurately reflect the material you covered during the semester?
   - Did your syllabus repeatedly require modification? For what reasons?
   - Were any of your lectures rushed? Did any seem to cover an inadequate amount of material?
   - Did students seem to find the reading assignments manageable? Were they generally prepared for class?
   - Were your lessons thoughtfully considered prior to each class session?
   - Did you effectively accommodate deviations from your lesson plan but still adhere to your overall objectives and course themes?
   - Did the hypotheticals, case studies, simulations, or other pedagogical techniques you used bear a logical nexus to the reading assignments you chose?

- Did students frequently ask you questions that required you to do additional research in order to formulate an answer?
- Were multi-media tools you decided to use, if any, effective? Did they enhance the presentation? Did you encounter any technological difficulties?

- Class Assessment
  - Did your evaluative technique appropriately and comprehensively test the material you covered during the semester?
  - Were there some questions or aspects of an exam with which many students grappled extensively?
  - Did you carefully deliberate about the grade for each student?
  - Did you timely apprise students about the components of their grades?
  - Did you receive many challenges to the grades you submitted?

You also might consider auditing other classes, both in the subject matter you're teaching and in others. In fact, attending a session or two of a course in an unfamiliar area of the law may be especially useful because you can focus more on the pedagogical methods than on the scope of the substantive material. What sorts of techniques do other professors use that might be appropriate for your class?

In addition, you can invite a colleague to attend a session or two of the class you're teaching and encourage him to give you feedback. This approach may be very helpful if you have a class with some challenging dynamics, such as several students who are routinely unprepared or others who are excessively vociferous. An experienced academician may be able to offer some suggestions about how to handle a challenging class or provide another perspective about other approaches you might try.

Student Assessment of Faculty

Many schools have protocols for student assessment of faculty members. At the semester's mid-point or sometime thereafter, the school may distribute evaluation forms to students. They'll likely be completed anonymously and made available to you only after you submit your final course grades. This way, your evaluation of students' scholastic performance in the course cannot be compromised, or, perhaps just as detrimental to the process, cannot appear to have been biased. Anonymous submission of student evaluations also promotes impartiality in the event you have an opportunity to teach the student in another course.

Although students' evaluations of faculty may be tempered by their interest in the course's subject matter and even by feedback or grades they received during the semester, such evaluations may provide some insight into the teaching quality. A consensus may emerge, for example, about a problem the professor has been having communicating with the class or thoroughly preparing for each session. While not determinative, such evaluations may inform administrative judgments about promotion, tenure, and even the particular courses to be assigned.

Law schools may make student evaluations of faculty available upon request. Sometimes professors post student evaluations on their faculty websites, even setting out statistical compilations of assessments.[16]

Professor Patrick Wiseman of Georgia State College of Law provided a Web page on which students could continuously and anonymously post evaluations of the course he was teaching.[17] Because there's a natural tendency for students who contact you personally or by otherwise identifying themselves to have more favorable comments, you can encourage your entire class to submit their assessments anonymously. Perhaps your students can complete a form and place it in your faculty mailbox.

If your school has not established a systematic student assessment method, you might ask students to contact you at the conclusion of the semester after the grades have been submitted. Perhaps encourage them to give you feedback before they've been notified of the grade they received as a means of avoiding having their grades influence their evaluation of you. You might simply solicit general comments, prepare a form with specific questions, or consider one of the many student class assessment feedback tools that are available.[18] Much can be learned from such open-ended questions as "what was most/least effectively covered in this class?," "which class sessions did you most enjoy?," "what media did you find most effectively incorporated?," and "how might this class be improved?"

Administrative and Peer Evaluation

Courses also may be evaluated by a faculty committee. If your class is selected for evaluation, you may be given advance notice regarding the process

16. *See* Michael A. Geist, *Where Can You Go Today?: The Computerization of Legal Education from Workbooks to the Web,* 11 Harv. J.L. & Tech. 141 & nn.134, 135 (1997), *available at* <http://jolt.law.Harvard.edu/articles/11hjolt141.html>

17. Patrick Wiseman, *The Virtual Teacher,* Jurist Legal Intelligence, Lessons from the Web, *at* <http://jurist.law.pitt.edu/lessons/lesoct98.htm>.

18. *See id.*

and the date(s) on which faculty will visit your class. These audits may help inform personnel decisions and career advancement.

Because much of the clinical educational experience occurs outside a traditional classroom setting and involves some experiential learning, some contend that law professors who conduct clinics and externships should be subject to different standards of review than other professors. Clinical teachers may be placed on alternative tenure tracking systems. Different roles of both students and faculty in clinical courses, implicating privileged and confidential aspects of their work, suggest the need for different auditing methods, arguably most appropriately utilizing experienced clinicians to conduct peer reviews. One suggested, "Faculty who do not teach in clinics fail to understand some of the extrinsic demands of the clinical teacher. The traditional separation of 'teaching,' 'service,' and 'scholarship' as an evaluation device is often not a helpful construct when evaluating a clinical educator."[19]

If you worked in a collaborative teaching arrangement (*see supra* at 95), seek feedback from those with whom you participated in the course. What were the impressions of your guest lecturer? How did your co-teacher feel about the progress of the class and your teaching style? What feedback can you solicit from a teaching assistant?

Selected Resources

Evaluation of Students:

Peter L. Fitzgerald, *A Brief Comparison of "Courseware" for Exams or Self-Assessment Exercises on the Web*, Jurist Legal Intelligence, Lessons From the Web, *at* <http://jurist.law.pitt.edu/lessons/lesdec99.htm>

Academic Integrity Issues:

Heyward Ehrlich, *Plagiarism and Anti-Plagiarism* (March 2000 ed.), *at* <http://newark.rutgers.edu/~ehrlich/plagiarism598.html>

Glatt Plagiarism Services, Inc.
web-site: <http://www.plagiarism.com/index.htm>

---

19. Kimberly E. O'Leary, *Evaluating Clinical Law Teaching – Suggestions for Law Professors Who Have Never Used the Clinical Teaching Method*, 29 N. KY. L. Rev. 491, 510 (2002).

Lisa Hinchliffe, *Cut-and-Paste Plagiarism: Preventing, Detecting and Tracking Online Plagiarism* (1998), *at* <http://alexia.lis.uiuc.edu/~janicke/plagiary.htm>

Plagiarism.org
web-site: <http://www.plagiarism.org/technology.html>

TurnItIn.com
web-site: <http://turnitin.com>

Evaluation of Faculty:

Suggestions for Teaching with Excellence, A Berkeley Compendium
Student Description of Teaching (Appendix A)
web-site: <http://teaching.berkeley.edu/compendium/appendixa.html>

CHAPTER 5

Interacting with Students

Relating as a Professor to Students

The relationships you develop with your students can be extraordinary, leading to scholarly exchanges and profound bonds. Your respective learning experiences are significant catalysts for moments of shared reflection and insight.

As your pupils' professor, you need to maintain an appropriate professional demeanor. You must guide the class, shape the dialogue, and evaluate students' performance. It's possible that you'll need to engage in some disciplinary measures as well, ranging from penalizing a student for failing to timely complete an assignment to excusing a disruptive student from class.

Thus the relationship between you and the class is an inspiring, albeit delicate, one. You may have occasion to socialize with your students, perhaps by joining in their banter during a break at a study group or chatting at a school-sponsored tea. Informality, particularly outside the classroom, isn't inappropriate, but it's important to negotiate a balance between being approachable and becoming too intimate.

One way you can do this is by being mindful of the extent of your involvement in your students' personal lives. It's certainly appropriate to openly discuss scholastic-related issues; you'll want to know, for example, if a student is struggling a bit as he tries to grasp a concept. Personal problems, by contrast, may be better left to commiseration with the student's peers, or, depending on their nature and the degree to which the student seems affected, with a professional counselor (*see infra* at 245). A personal issue, such as a medical illness or a relationship break-up, nonetheless may be relevant to such matters as a student's request for an extension on a deadline to turn in a paper. It may be sensible to express your concern, address the request, and then inquire as to whether the student might wish to discuss the problem with a counselor or other professional. You also can follow up with the student shortly thereafter to ask how things are going.

Your school may have specific sexual harassment policies regarding dating between faculty and students. Professors are placed in a superior hierarchical position and it's inappropriate to exploit the relative hierarchy for such purposes (*see supra* at 77). It's wise in any event to be circumspect as to situations that can lead to misunderstandings or be susceptible to misinterpretation, both by the student in question and even by others. Repeatedly meeting with one student behind closed doors when others seek the professor's attention may be misunderstood by the student and raise questions in the minds of others, leading to an uncomfortable situation for all. It's possible that you may even need to affirmatively distance yourself a bit from a student, perhaps by offering to address academic concerns in a group setting.

Of course, you'll want to treat all students courteously and respectfully regardless of their gender, race, ethnicity, age, sexual orientation, or religion. Nor should their political views or personal attributes factor into consideration. Obviously you'll avoid making jokes at the expense of others. As well, the stereotypical ruthless law school professor who ridicules a student who is unprepared or misinformed should be relegated to a myth. There are still some, I suppose, who believe that such an approach "toughens" a student and thus prepares him for situations in which he may be questioned aggressively by a judge or bullied by an adversary. This may well be the rationale behind the military's continued use of boot camp and drill sergeants to ready soldiers for battle. There may be some logic lurking there because it likely can be empowering to recall that one has already experienced a difficult situation and survived; skills acquired to "tough out" the situation probably help keep the individual calm and focused. In my mind, however, there doesn't seem to be much point to rehearsing situations that make people miserable. Your students likely will gain confidence by recognizing that they've managed to field increasingly more complex and challenging questions and so will approach new and difficult obstacles secure in the belief that they, too, can be surmounted.

Accessibility to Students

Amongst the "Seven Principles for Good Practice in Undergraduate Education" published by the American Association for Higher Education is the notion that good practice encourages contact between students and faculty.[1] Frequent contact can play a significant role in motivating students, gaining insight into possible areas of confusion amongst class members, and providing feedback about the progression of the course. Personal communication with your students can present important opportunities to reassure an individual that he's "on track," clarify whether a specific topic will be covered later in the class, and respond to logistical requests such as deadline extensions.

Your accessibility to students is probably, paradoxically, simultaneously enhanced and encumbered by the availability and utilization of electronic communicative methods. On the one hand, e-mail access and participation in a discussion board renders you more available. Your students can reach you even when you're not conducting class or holding office hours. They can ask you a question to which you can respond remotely while you're away for the weekend or traveling to another state to participate in a symposium. Temporal constraints are minimized; the student needn't be concerned about waking you when he transmits his e-mail message at 3:00 a.m. And you won't have nearly as much logistical difficulty coordinating your schedule with that of a student who needs your individual attention.

Voicemail also is a useful way to keep in touch with students, especially if they have access to a voicemail system that won't disturb them if messages are left at odd hours. If you're traveling for a few days and don't have ready access to e-mail, checking into voicemail may present a viable alternative.

A student who is a bit reserved about approaching you may feel more comfortable contacting you electronically. It may be easier for him to be able to re-read his query before sending it and to know that he'll have time to digest your response without having the social pressure of contemporaneously continuing a conversation.

On the other hand, electronic communication arguably diminishes the quality of a personal exchange. E-mail messages aren't necessarily devoid of humor. And you still may be able to sense that the student's confusion, which generated the contact in the first place, has been alleviated. But it's simply not equivalent to a face-to-face conversation. When you're laboring to determine whether your student is still confused, your electronic exchange deprives you of visual cues like furrowed brows, shifts in body language suggesting continuing discomfort, and fluctuations in voice inflection. And worst of all, you'll

1. Arthur W. Chickering and Zelda F. Gamson, *Seven Principles for Good Practice in Undergraduate Education,* 39 American Association for Higher Education Bulletin, 3–7 (1987).

miss personally sharing the student's memorable and exhilarating moment of enlightenment.

It seems to me that these advantages and disadvantages are best reconciled by exploiting both methods in combination. If you're a full-time professor, try to hold regular office hours to promote face-to-face contact. If it's possible for you within the confines of your class schedule, and you can hold more than one session of hours, try to schedule them at different times rather than at the same time on two different days if you think that doing so will present fewer conflicts for students enrolled in other classes. Consider arriving a bit early for class, even if it means standing about in the hallway. Try not to rush off after the class concludes if you don't have to. If you give students a brief break during a lengthy class session, try to stay in the classroom to answer individual questions; this may present an especially helpful opportunity if you teach an early or late class that makes it more difficult for commuting students (or for you) to arrive before class or stay after the session concludes. Doing so offers opportunities for causal conversation with students. There's a chance for the student to approach you informally without feeling that he's probably interrupting some more important scholarly pursuit. And these moments of availability mean that a student doesn't have to go through the formal process of scheduling an appointment with you; he perhaps may be concerned that doing so will suggest to you (or maybe suggest to himself) that he is having academic difficulty.

You might also ask your students whether they'd like you to join a study group for a session or two. Encourage them to think beforehand about any specific questions they have. Emphasize that they're not expected to contrive a question if they don't have a particular matter they'd like you to review; they'll likely benefit in any case from listening to the exchange amongst the group.

You might occasionally announce that you'll be having lunch in the school's cafeteria or some other convenient location in case students would like to join you. This informal setting provides a chance for students to socialize with you and one another, ask specific questions about the material covered in class, explore current developments in the field of study, or inquire about career opportunities.

These offers may be especially appreciated if you're an adjunct faculty member. Unlike full-time faculty, adjunct professors generally are not expected to hold specified office hours for student consultations. Schools usually recognize that many, if not most, adjunct professors are engaged in other pursuits and have limited time. It can be very helpful, to the extent you can feasibly arrange to meet with students outside of class, to review material about which they have questions. As with full-time professors, you might try to arrive for class a bit early or wait a bit before leaving at the conclusion of class sessions in order to afford some informal time for students to ask a few questions.

If, however, you find yourself regularly deluged with e-mail messages seeking clarification about various legal and administrative matters or an inordinate number of requests for appointments with individual students, you might try to consolidate the requests. As you peruse the e-mail queries or reflect on the questions asked when you met with students, are there particular questions that recur? Does it seem that several students are confused about the same points? In that event, you might incorporate some review during an upcoming class session. Or you might post a statement or a suggested reading on your faculty web-site. You could draft a composite of the most common queries and post a set of frequently asked questions ("FAQs") or distribute them in hard copy during class.

If you've been burdened with a number of administrative questions, you can use similar approaches. If the questions seem repetitive of items you've already reviewed, such as requests for additional copies of the course syllabus, it's not unreasonable to remind your students that the materials are otherwise available from the registrar's office, your faculty web-site, or even their fellow class members.

Special Student Needs

Student Difficulties

From time to time, students may experience academic or personal challenges. As their professor, you'll want to work to assist them adjust to and enjoy the law school experience. You'll also want to be mindful of resources to which you may refer them for additional support.

Academic Challenges

Substantive Challenges

Although a student may experience academic difficulties at any point during his legal career, law school can present unique challenges to first-year students. There are considerable differences between law school and undergraduate or even other graduate studies. Outstanding scholastic performance in the liberal arts, engineering, or even business disciplines is somewhat akin to having a vast quantity of American currency in a foreign country; it's of significant value in its own context but of little use in a different environ. Moreover, currently, many who enter law school are not coming directly from college or another graduate program and so there has been a lapse of time in their academic career. As a result, even becoming accustomed once again to the rigors and routines of school can be a significant adjustment.

Bear in mind that as acceptance to law school becomes increasingly competitive, students have been chosen primarily from a pool of extremely high-qualified applicants who have demonstrated proficiency in their prior academic careers. They're now participating in a concentrated environment of top-level students, which may serve to heighten the competitive atmosphere, or at least the perception of such competition.

Stress also can be experienced because the nature of conventional legal education through the Socratic and case study methods, hypotheticals, and simulations isn't necessarily replicated through final examinations. Students are trained in the rigors of legal analysis and a discipline of legal thinking, but many lament that what is tested is not necessarily what has been taught. This can be quite frustrating for a student who is accustomed to accolades after a diligent investment of time.

You can try to relieve some of the feelings of anxiety that seem virtually inevitable for first-year students and upper-classmen. A student who seems especially stressed by exams may benefit from consultation with peers in a study group or an individualized meeting with you. If it appears that the student is well-informed and has been diligently preparing for class throughout the semester, it may be helpful to suggest that he take a few practice exams. Repetitively simulating the exam setting may mitigate anxiety on the day of the exam itself; there is, at least to some degree, a feeling of having completed an exam already. Practice also improves students' pacing so that they effectively apportion their time amongst the tasks of reading the question, considering a response, and writing the exam. If you have time to meet with them, the students will benefit from reviewing their practice tests with you. You also can suggest that they discuss their approaches with their classmates.

You might offer some guidance to the class as exam dates approach. In addition to encouraging students generally, you can review your expectations about performance. Are there particular factors that you find tend to improve the quality of an answer or paper? Is it important to you that students cite particular cases or do you tend to look more for a conceptual understanding of rules of law? Explaining the format and related standards you've imposed may help students spend less time focusing on directions set out in the exam that relate to page length, citational form, and the like.

Remind your class that it's valuable to prepare outlines or review their notes by using their own phrasing. While law students regularly purchase prepared outlines, knowledge is demonstrably substantiated by the ability to state the rule on one's own. Concise and accurate paraphrasing also suggests that the student has begun to absorb key concepts. Similarly, it's probably inappropriate to spend excessive amounts of time trying to memorize case names, dates, or other details. Seminal cases likely will be readily recognized by students because they've been emphasized during the course. Other cases should be studied so that they can be integrated into the student's analysis on which to premise a resolution to a legal problem.

Technological and Legal Research Challenges

In today's legal and scholarly environment, it's critical that students have a working knowledge of certain basic technology. In addition to locating and retrieving legal documents and information, students must learn to become "a 'fact sleuth,' someone who specializes in finding facts, in understanding why some facts cannot be found, and in figuring out whether any of the found facts are dependable."[2]

Many students will be quite technologically savvy by the time they enter law school, especially because undergraduate institutions, secondary schools, and even primary schools increasingly are requiring completion of computer classes, mastery of typing skills, and exploration of research techniques. Your school likely offers resources for informational technology difficulties students encounter. A student can be encouraged to seek out some brief advanced wordprocessing, Internet search, or other computer classes for intensive or targeted training. Another resource, depending on the nature of the problem to be rectified, is the company from which your student purchased his computer; there's generally access to a live individual via telephone or e-mail to help troubleshoot.

Law schools also typically cultivate essential computer training by incorporating legal research skills into a first-year required seminar on Legal Writing or Legal Methods. Acquiring such skills is essential for several reasons. Most obviously, legal research skills enable the individual to investigate legal and factual matters to acquire information. In addition, such skills facilitate scrutiny and evaluation of the information acquired; the researcher is not dependent upon a single source but rather is able to assess its credibility and reliability by comparing it with other sources of information. Further, legal research endeavors essentially require the transformation of an amorphous problem into a structured inquisition; the student must refine the issue sufficiently so that he can devise the subsidiary inquiries that will lead to the resolution.

---

2. Josh Blackman, Joshua D. Blackman, David Jank, Joshua Blackman, *The Internet Fact Finder for Lawyers: How to Find Anything on the Net* (American Bar Association 1998) at 13.

Students most assuredly will be trained in the use of LexisNexis and Westlaw. It's important as well to emphasize the accessibility of Internet-based searches. Many web-sites are available, quickly posting recent court decisions, statutes, proposed legislation, regulations, and commentary. Certain information, notably relating to foreign countries' laws, may be expeditiously available on openly accessible web-sites. Some information, such as catalogs, certain publications, and song lyrics, may not even be available through traditional law library software.

Moreover, there are numerous informative web-sites that are accessible without charge, and these likely will increase as court administration systems expand electronic postings. Beginning search inquiries with such sources trains students to be mindful of costs that might otherwise be borne by a client in a practice setting.

Some of these helpful web-sites are hosted by government entities. The U.S. House of Representatives Internet Law Library[3] and the Library of Congress[4] include extensive information about the law. The Library of Congress includes U.S. Congressional Documents and Debates, a substantial collection of records beginning with the Continental Congress of 1774.[5] The Law Library of the Library of Congress originally was established in 1800 as a reference library for Congress; by the end of the nineteenth century, the public could freely consult the library's collections.[6] In the early 1900s, the Law Library worked to become an authoritative reference center for laws of the United States and many foreign nations.[7] The Library includes a multi-national legal database and reference area, on-line law reviews, treaties, and information relating to the United Nations.[8] Other helpful sites include those sponsored by various law schools, notably Washburn University School of Law,[9] Cornell University School of Law,[10] Indiana University School of Law,[11] Emory Uni-

---

3. *See* <http://www.house.gov>.

4. *See* <http://lcweb.loc.gov>.

5. Library of Congress, *A Century of Lawmaking for a New Nation, available at* <http://memory.loc.gov/ammem/amlaw/index.html>.

6. Library of Congress, Law Library of Congress, *About the Law Library, available at* <http://www.loc.gov/law/public/law-about.html>.

7. *Id.; see also* Library of Congress, Law Library of Congress, *Nations of the World (Nations and Associated Jurisdictions), available at* <http://www.loc.gov/law/guide/nations.html>.

8. Library of Congress, Law Library of Congress, *International, available at* <http://www.loc.gov/law/guide/multi.html>.

9. *See* <http://washburnlaw.edu/library>.

10. *See* <http://www.law.cornell.edu>.

11. *See* <http://www.law.indiana.edu/lib/index.html>.

versity School of Law,[12] and the University of Chicago Law School.[13] Factual information, news, and commentary is readily accessible through the use of search engines, such as Google,[14] Lycos,[15] Yahoo,[16] and Alta Vista.[17] Exploration of discussions regarding particular topics can be sought through Liszt,[18] Tile Net,[19] and DejaNews.[20]

You may feel that your entire class or a particular student may benefit from some specialized research instruction. Your school may have a librarian dedicated to technology training who is able to coordinate seminars in a variety of formats. These can range from a visit to the classroom to sessions in the school's computer training room to review of Internet and other electronic resources, in addition to regularly scheduled LexisNexis and Westlaw training classes at basic and advanced levels.

In addition, you may want to review with your class approaches to scrutinizing data that's been retrieved. What is the source of the material? Has the author's research been sponsored by a commercial entity that would benefit from a favorable review of a product or service? It's especially important to remind students to consider sourcing issues when they're engaged in Internet-based research, in which hyperlinking can readily take the visitor to another site with different authorship and sponsorship. Some have noted that "[t]he Net puts the means of instantaneous worldwide publication at everyone's fingertips, from established commercial publishers to schoolchildren. Therefore, until its accuracy has been verified, data retrieved from the Internet must be viewed with skepticism—as must all information from any source."[21]

Addressing Challenges to Grades

If you've been teaching for awhile, chances are you'll encounter a situation in which a student challenges the grade you've assigned. The circumstances under which you may even be authorized to modify a grade may be governed

---

12. *See* <http://www.law.emory.edu>;

13. *See* <http://www.law.uchicago.edu/library/index.html>.

14. *See* <http://www.google.com>.

15. *See* <http://www.lycos.com>.

16. *See* <http://www.yahoo.com>.

17. *See* <http://www.altavista.digital.com>.

18. *See* <http://www.liszt.com>.

19. *See* <http://www.tile.net>.

20. *See* <http://www.dejanews.com>.

21. Josh Blackman, Joshua D. Blackman, David Jank, Joshua Blackman, *The Internet Fact Finder for Lawyers: How to Find Anything on the Net* (American Bar Association 1998) at 16.

by your school's policies, which also may address the means by which the student can appeal your decision. In any event, you'll want to give some thought as to how you'll respond to the student and the basis on which you'll make a determination as to whether a grade change may be warranted. No matter how justified the grade you assigned may be, it's reasonable for a student to get an explanation from you as to how it was calculated.

Your first task, of course, is to listen carefully to the student's complaint. What is the source of his disappointment and what is his objective in raising the issue with you? Is he merely venting? Is he perhaps seeking guidance from you about the potential impact of the grade on his overall legal career? It's quite possible that your conversation with the student will resolve the matter; he may benefit from having had an opportunity to express his concerns and gain perspective about the likely perception of his performance in a single course.

The individual also may be seeking clarification of substantive aspects of the material that gave rise to his confusion. Your meeting with the student may result in a significant learning experience for him.

It's possible, too, that the student may need some general guidance about taking tests, particularly because the format used in many law school courses differs from those used in the undergraduate context. Tips on time management, for instance, may be important in order to allocate time to read the exam, reflect on the issues and analysis, organize thoughts, and write the answer. In addition to your suggestions, you may want to refer the student to various resources about approaches to test-taking techniques.[22]

You can assure a disappointed student that you deliberated carefully about the entire process, endeavoring to balance the scope of the material covered, judiciously apportion the reading assignments throughout the semester, and fairly devise an exam or paper requirement. Explain that you then read through the work product submitted, working to understand the points the student made and assessing the submission on a parity with rest of the class. You may want to expressly acknowledge that you understand that grades are significant in hiring and other career determinations and that, like your students, you take grading seriously. Unless the course grade was based exclusively on objectively verifiable scoring of a multiple-choice test, indicate, perhaps, that you recognize that there is a subjective element but that you labored to minimize its disparate impact. In fact, the subjectivity may have worked to

22. *See, e.g.*, Rogelio Lasso, *The Process to Law School Success*, Washburn Law School (2002), *at* <http://classes.washburnlaw.edu/lass/process.html>.

the student's advantage if you tended to extend the benefit of the doubt on an ambiguous point or if you curved borderline scores upwards.

Affirmatively and deliberately articulate positive aspects of the student's performance, setting out specific examples whenever possible. You might say something to the effect of, "you clearly demonstrated diligent preparation throughout the semester. It was apparent to me that you regularly completed the reading assignments. And your class participation was quite strong. I remember that you made some insightful comments when the class was engaged in a group project." (It may help to refer to your notes about class participation, *see supra* at 184, for reminders about the specific comments the student made.) It's obviously important for the student to understand that, despite his disappointment with his grade, he contributed to the class in some fashion. Citing commendable aspects of his performance also helpfully avoids having your discussion with your student mired in negative comments and criticism. As well, it emphasizes to the student at the outset that you focused on his overall experience in the course and confirms that you accorded some weight to those tasks he performed well.

Just as significantly, you'll be educating the student about the proficient aspects of his performance. It's as important for him to try to replicate what he did correctly as it is for him to try to avoid repeating the mistakes he made.

You also can review the applicable grading standards. If your school has imposed a mandatory grading curve system, take a moment to explain that you're obliged to comply and that the class presented stiff competition. If you've decided to implement a relative-norm grading approach (*see supra* at 214), indicate the basis for your decision and the values you've assigned to the various components of the grade. If you've used an absolutist approach (*see supra* at 213), you might indicate that you worked to mirror the emphasis of the class as you crafted the exam.

You also can review the specific criteria of the grade, alluding to instances in class announcements, references in the syllabus, or indications on your faculty web-site where the student was placed on notice of the relevant factors. This will help mitigate a possible misperception that grades were rendered capriciously. If class attendance was taken into account, did the student attend regularly? If class participation was a factor, explain that the frequency of participation is not the only criterion; the quality of class members' comments is highly relevant. There's a vast difference between a student's question that solicits from you the ruling by a court when the case decision was assigned but not read, and a remark that reflects diligent preparation and reasoned consideration of the material covered.

Of course, you'll want to confirm that the grade was accurately computed and submitted. A student's transcript shouldn't suffer because you made an arithmetic error or transposed numbers when you recorded a score (e.g., by recording a "97" as a "79"). But take care to avoid allowing the student to lobby for a new grade by insisting that you modify your standards for his benefit or excuse some deficiency for which others were penalized. Capitulating to such requests undermines the grading process and sends a message to students that their evaluation can be determined by the force of their advocacy rather than by the quality of their scholastic performance. One of your primary objectives as you assign grades is to engage in the process fairly; an ancillary objective is to promote the appearance of an equitable process lest students lose confidence in the system.

Challenges Relating to Student Temperaments

Individual students may exhibit a variety of temperaments that impact pedagogical challenges. It might be tempting to set forth bullet points or a chart here, describing inattentive, disruptive, reserved, and troubled students and offering a matrix of suggestions as to ways you might deal with each. But such facile taxonomy is inappropriate. Student issues are complex composites of numerous characteristics and labels likely only entrench the behavior you've found problematic or solidify a perception that such conduct will continue. Individuals may manifest certain behavior during particular times, and it's important to recognize that you'll be addressing an amalgam of qualities and conduct that may be merely transitory.

Each student is to be treated with dignity, respect, and courtesy, as well as with due reflection about his particular needs and concerns. Even if approaches to various issues could be standardized—a rather dismal proposition—such consistency could never be applied effectively. Students are a diverse group of individuals with unique personalities and attributes, approaching the study of law from different backgrounds informed by a panoply of life experiences. In addition, students interact with one another within classes to influence the vigor and scope of dialogue, through synergy, mutual support, intimidation, and any number of other phenomena.

Sometimes, too, external circumstances can give rise to student concerns that affect virtually your entire class. I was scheduled to teach a Law of Internet Speech class at Fordham University School of Law in New York City on September 11, 2001. The terrorist attacks necessitated the school's closing, of course. The following week, my class resumed. Students and faculty alike took their places, filled with shock and sadness. The school's setting in New York City vividly added to the intensity of feelings and the daily reminders of the attacks—a peculiar odor from the collapse of buildings and fires at Ground Zero, haphazard mass transit service, loud and frequent sirens of rescue and law enforcement vehicles, the unusual ubiquitous appearance of military personnel on city streets. And, most significantly, loss. For so many, incomprehensible, tragic loss from which there could be no real solace.

There was no manual to guide faculty about how to resume the study of law amidst such unfathomable circumstances. At the beginning of the class, I spoke candidly for a few moments, expressing my sympathy, my concern for my students, and my relief that they were all safe. I explained that while I'd earlier advised the class that attendance and participation were to be factored into grades, I obviously would understand if commitments to family, friends, and the community or efforts to cope precluded satisfaction of these requirements. I reminded students that counseling services and chaplains were available through the school.

My students came to class. They read the assignments. The level of participation did not seem to decline. A few individuals spoke with me outside of class; some indicated that they were having difficulties but were making an effort to continue to come to class. I told them that their efforts were quite admirable but that they should see how they felt before each session and shouldn't hesitate to skip a class or leave during a session if it felt more comfortable to do so.

To reiterate, there really isn't a "guide" to teaching. And there certainly isn't a "guide" to forming a relationship with students. There are merely some thoughts you might consider as you forge your unique bond with your class and endeavor to address some special concerns or problematic conduct.

Inattention

I've been fortunate to have had classes comprised of dedicated, attentive, and respectful individuals. (I recognize that I don't teach required courses; while a student may be looking for a certain number of credits in the particular time slot to which my class has been assigned, generally there's been an affirmative decision to enroll in the course because of an interest in the subject matter. This in turn promotes attentiveness.) If a particular pupil were audibly conversing with his neighbor or otherwise making noise that distracted the class, you could call on the student. Teachers have different styles and some might see this as an opportunity to focus attention on the student, catch him off guard, and ask him a complex substantive question relevant to the lecture at hand. This approach isn't wrong. The student, implicitly chastened, likely would be motivated to pay more attention in the future.

My practice is generally not to call on students in this fashion, though. Why augment any attention they might already have diverted? And in trying to promote a comfortable and respectful atmosphere, I'm loathe to send a message, however subtle, to other students that a brief lapse will subject them to such consequences. If the noise were audible but fairly minimal, I'd presume that the student might be laudably trying to clarify a point he missed during the discussion. If the chatting persisted or was interfering with the progression of the class session, I might turn to the student and say something along the lines of, "Was there something you wanted to add, John?" The ostensible rationale for the query, reflected in a polite and inquisitive tone, would be a concern that John wanted to contribute to the class dialogue and I'd missed an opportunity to call on him earlier.

Disruptions

Of course, if the problem escalates to a point where the student engages in this behavior throughout much of the class session or engages in the conduct on multiple occasions, a more direct approach is called for. During the class session itself, you might just make a polite but firm request that the student refrain from making noise. "Excuse me, Mary, but I think some folks are having difficulty hearing. I need to ask you to just save your conversation until the class finishes."

If the behavior recurs, arrange to speak to Mary privately. Ask her to call you, drop by your office, or arrive a bit early for the next class. Again, a presumption that there has been no intentional disruption generally is appropriate. You might begin by asking whether the student is having any difficulty. "Have you been enjoying the class, Mary? I've been a bit concerned because it seems that sometimes you're distracted." Unless the conduct has been particularly egregious, extend the benefit of the doubt to Mary by at the very least indicating that she's engaged in the behavior sporadically and thus you presume it's aberrational. Then listen carefully to Mary's response.

She might take the opportunity to confide that she's been confused by the material and has been trying to get assistance from another. In that event, you can acknowledge that you appreciate her interest in the course and recognize that reviewing material with a peer can be beneficial. Of course, it's best to do that outside of class so it doesn't cause any disruption. Encourage Mary to ask questions if she's confused. Explain that it can be helpful to other students as well, as they may have similar queries or may likewise be perplexed. And it gives you virtually contemporaneous feedback as to where you might not have been clear or areas that should be reviewed. Additionally, you can reiterate your availability to go over material, citing your office hours and confirming that Mary has your telephone number and e-mail address.

Mary may respond instead to your overtures by indicating that she's been under stress or having some sort of personal difficulty. In that case, you can consider the approaches discussed with respect to students experiencing personal difficulties (*see infra* at 245)

It may well be that the conversation you had with Mary will spur a behavioral change. It's conceivable that Mary may initially react a bit defensively or neglect to apologize. She may not have realized the degree to which her behavior was noticed or may have been unaware that it was disruptive to the class. Having some time to reflect on your comments, and mindful of the faculty-student relationship and the dynamics of grading assessments, Mary probably will make a greater effort.

In the rare instance where the problem does not abate, such as when a student denies any inappropriate conduct and becomes belligerent, try to curtail the conversation. You don't want to engage the pupil so that the reaction deteriorates into an argument. Try to remain composed. If necessary, you can enlist the support of the school's administration. In the meantime, explain to the student that you'd like him to take some time and reflect on your comments, cautioning him that if the problematic behavior persists, you'll have no choice but to take the matter further.

If the conduct doesn't improve, consider consulting with a school dean. Chances are the dean of student affairs has dealt with similar issues before and will have some helpful suggestions for you, including specific references you can make to the school's disciplinary policies when you next speak with the student. During an initial discussion with the dean, you may not even need to identify the student if you prefer not to do so at that point.

If, however, you do name Mary when you speak with the dean, you may learn that other professors expressed similar concerns. This may suggest that it's appropriate at this time for the dean to intervene and schedule a meeting with Mary.

Of course, more urgent action should be taken with respect to any student who has made a threat of physical harm—either to himself or others. Under those circumstances, you may need to engage the assistance of security personnel, counselors, and administrative personnel.

Public Speaking Concerns

Just as many faculty members find it somewhat daunting to speak before large groups or even smaller audiences, so, too, do many students experience trepidation and nervousness when called upon to speak publicly. Classroom discussion may generate feelings of anxiety, particularly insofar as students are asked to extemporize through Socratic questioning. Even gentle probing can be intimidating when the pupil is required to simultaneously recall information from the reading assignments, synthesize principles discussed in class, and respond in front of his classmates to skillful and nuanced questioning by the professor.

As a result, it's not surprising that a considerable number of students decline to volunteer to participate, preferring instead to observe others. It falls to you to draw out the more reserved individual. One obvious method is to call on the student and in effect require that he respond. A similar approach is to preface your question by addressing the student directly. Rather than catching someone off guard who must struggle to re-play your question in his mind while assembling his thoughts, you might simply begin by saying, "Carlos, I wanted to get your thoughts about the next case that was assigned. As we look at the holding in *Smith v. Jones,*...." or "Alex, let's turn to you next as we consider the defenses to the claim...." The student is then poised to listen to the question.

If you have several reserved students, you might utilize the discussion leader approach (*see supra* at 84). This can lessen some feelings of nervousness simply because the date on which they will be called on is assigned in advance and thus the students have more time to prepare.

You can also encourage participation and help diminish trepidation by offering feedback when students do speak up. Positively reinforce contributions to the class dialogue with simple and concise remarks such as "good point," or "well said." Refer to the student later in the discourse, even when an extraordinary insight wasn't offered, by acknowledging the point. "As Leslie indicated, the plaintiff initiated suit shortly after he received the response from the defendant's attorney." There's a subtle but significant message in the acknowledgement that Leslie's statement was correct and worthy of repeated mention.

As well, you can try to motivate students to speak up in class by encouraging them individually. When a student refers to a point during a consultation with you in your office, you can mention that the entire class would benefit from sharing it. You can even praise an astute question, indicating that others may be grappling with the same issue and therefore it would be helpful if the student asked questions from time to time during class.

Some students speak unreservedly and frequently. Typically this is the product of enviable enthusiasm for the course and the law school experience, although occasionally it appears to be the product of an awareness that class participation is a factor in computing students' grades. But a student who volunteers infrequently is not necessarily shy or unprepared. The individual who deliberates about whether to volunteer, first reflecting on the value of his contribution and whether his point will be a mere reiteration of an earlier remark, is to be commended. Sagacious and sensible decisions about whether to participate can be nearly as significant as the content and quality of the comment itself.

Personal or Stress-Related Difficulties

Through the course of your regular contact with your students, you may observe a change in behavior that signals that an individual is experiencing acute stress. Or a student may approach you to discuss a personal problem. Perhaps he is looking to confide in someone or is seeking your guidance about whether to consult a professional. The student's issue may come to your attention in the context of an excuse for having missed a class or a request for an extension on the deadline to submit a paper or postponement of an exam. Indeed, if you receive such a request or you notice that a pupil has missed classes, you may want to inquire as to whether he's been experiencing any difficulty. You may sense that a student might benefit from some additional support. From time to time, students may even explicitly inquire about available counseling services on campus.

Schools generally make counseling and psychological services available to students on a free and confidential basis. You should feel free to refer students who inquire about counseling to your school's counseling services. Services may be staffed by licensed clinical psychologists, a consulting psychiatrist, and/or doctoral candidates in clinical and counseling psychology, and offer both individual and group counseling. Day and evening appointments probably are available. Sometimes small group workshops covering a wide range of topics are offered, including programs designed to improve study skills, reduce stress, improve interpersonal skills, or assist with time management. Campus ministry or chaplain offices also may be available to serve the school community. It's important to encourage the student to explore options that are available for psychological assistance; professional counselors are best suited to the task and you can focus your efforts on supporting the student's scholastic needs.

If you feel that a particular student needs some special support, it may be advisable to speak with the student, to contact the schools' dean of student affairs, and/or to suggest that the student consult with the dean. Administrative faculty can assist not only by helping to refer the student for appropriate psychological support, but also by coordinating a plan to defer the submission of required papers, to postpone exams, or even to arrange approval for a leave of absence from the school.

There are a number of ways to approach the matter with the student. You could point out that law school is a stressful experience for many people, particularly if they're coping with other issues as well. Explain that there are things everyone can do to work through difficult times and that it's often quite helpful to talk with someone to sort out what might work best for him. Try to validate consultation with a counselor by indicating that many students seek out such support and find it beneficial. Refer to options within the community, such as the availability of the school's free and confidential counseling services. Point out that other options exist as well; some people feel more comfortable discussing personal problems with a chaplain or clergyman, for example.

Career Advice and Student Employment

Offering Employment to Students

Many of the law school's professors have been practitioners or have current or recent ties to the practitioner community. Adjunct faculty may be practicing contemporaneously with their teaching duties. You therefore may be in a position to offer or suggest employment to one or more students.

You may have occasion to seek the assistance of a student to engage in legal research. Faculty may have resources to compensate research assistants, but many students are willing to volunteer even when remuneration is not available. Such research assistants can help you investigate a legal issue related to your teaching duties or engage in citational review of scholarly writing on which you're working.

These are valuable opportunities for students to engage in the investigation and analysis of a complex, novel question under your tutelage and supervision. It's also a way for the student to test his interest through a more intensive intellectual experience in the field of study. From the professor's standpoint, a student can furnish extensive assistance, searching for additional resources, pursuing a possible analogy to illuminate a thesis, or confirming the accuracy of citational references. As an expert immersed in your specialty, it can be easy to inadvertently minimize foundational support or state a point a bit ambiguously. As a novice in the field, the student offers another perspective, providing important insights into the potential receptivity by your ultimate audience.

If you become aware of employment opportunities or are yourself in a position to offer employment to a law student, it's helpful to contact the career planning center. The center can assist you by posting information about the position, thereby alerting prospective candidates of the opening. As well, information about the position is of enormous benefit to students seeking employment.

It's possible that students enrolled in your class may seek you out during the course of the semester to apply for employment opportunities in the field in which you teach, to inquire about your impressions of prior clerkships or other positions, or to elicit general career advice about various options. If you consult with students, particularly to the extent you are in a position to guide or recommend for employment only certain members of your class, consider whether it may be appropriate to wait until the semester concludes and grades for the class have been submitted so as to ensure parity amongst all students.

Some schools restrict matriculating students to a specified numbers of hours per week that they may be employed. Before offering employment to or arranging employment of a student, check your school's policies or ask the student to comfirm the policies.

Serving as a Reference

You'll probably get requests from time to time to serve as a reference or write a recommendation for a student seeking employment, graduate studies, fellowships, or other endeavors. Recognize that if you're in a position to heartily endorse the student, such recommendations can be very important in the hiring process and so you'll want to try to make time to do so. Carefully consider the student's demonstrated proficiency and talents and indicate why the student would be a beneficial addition to the prospective employer. If your time is limited, rather than declining to write a reference, you might invite the student to ask the prospective employer to call you directly. In either event, you'll want to carefully tailor your comments about the individual student so that you highlight his attributes and accomplishments. Reciting identical accolades in every recommendation could dilute the value of your endorsement.

If you're not able to positively endorse the student's application, you should decline to serve as a reference. You might simply indicate to the student who requests your recommendation that you're pressed to complete several other matters and can't take on this additional task, or, more directly, indicate to the student that you're not in a position to endorse his candidacy but wish him well with his search.

Advising Students About Career Decisions

It's not uncommon for students to solicit your advice about the direction and course of a legal career. Students frequently benefit from discussions with professors about career options. This is one of the many ways in which the school's faculty serves a valuable function to the student body.

Some pupils canvass several faculty members as well as others in order to gather multiple viewpoints. Others may seek you out specifically because of their interest in the particular field in which you specialize or because they feel comfortable approaching you and respect your judgment.

Ultimately, of course, the decision rests with the student and it's prudent to remind him that he will need to make the choice. It's advisable, absent exigent or unusual circumstances, to refrain from dissuading a student from accepting a reasonable offer or convincing a student to accept an offer; it's the student who must look back on his choice with conviction.

I was once asked to speak on a panel with other in-house counsel, answering questions from law students about conventional paths to employment. A student asked for advice about choosing between an offer from a small "boutique" law firm and a large, nationally-known firm as a prerequisite to an in-house position he wished ultimately to secure. Others on the panel unequivocally counseled him to pursue the large, nationally-known firm, noting its value as a credential for subsequent career opportunities.

I dissented. I suggested that the student consider at which of the two firms he preferred to work. Both were regarded as reputable, although the smaller firm had less of a national reputation. Where did he think he would get more experience? Which firm offered the substantive legal practice he preferred to pursue? Most significantly, at which firm did he feel more respect for his prospective colleagues and those who would be charged with mentoring him?

Planning to spend a few years toiling at a firm that one doesn't expect to enjoy simply because it might establish a credential for subsequent employment seems a fairly hefty sacrifice. The firm preferred by the student might be so enjoyable that he might decide to abandon his long-term plan for a different position. It's a bit daunting for a student to anticipate where he would prefer to practice law when he's merely completing a legal education that offers glimpses, at most, of experiential practice.

Selected Resources

Academic Support:

Barger on Legal Writing: Law School Web Sites for Legal Writing, *at* <http://www.ualr.edu/~cmbarger/otherpeople.html>

Rod Borlase, *Electronic Legal Research for Beginners, at* <http://www.law.uh.edu/guides/elec_leg_res.html>

Jurist Legal Intelligence, Student Life/Law School Exams web-site: <http://jurist.law.pitt.edu/exams.htm>

Rogelio Lasso, *The Process to Law School Success* (2002), *at* <http://classes.washburnlaw.edu/lass/process.html>

Legal Writing Institute web-site: <http://www.lwionline.org>

Library of Congress, The Learning Page: Citing Electronic Sources
web-site: <http://lcweb2.loc.gov/ammem/ndlpedu/resources/cite/>

Villanova School of Law
Office of Academic Support
web-site: <http://vls.law.vill.edu/academics/support/supportabout.htm>

Westlaw
Class Help, First Year Center
web-site: <http://lawschool.westlaw.com/studentcenter/firstyear.asp>

Career Advice:

FindLaw Career Center
web-site: <http://careers.findlaw.com/>

Conclusion

Studying law is a rite of passage, a necessary prerequisite to the practice of law. The bonds forged with fellow classmates, whether the product of friendship, shared inspiration, or simply mutual commiseration, can be profound and long-lasting. The skills inculcated during law school—analyzing, synthesizing, challenging assumptions, extemporizing with articulation and substantiation—help form proficient and able counsel.

Law school education has been the subject of extensive criticism. The Socratic method can be intimidating and highly incongruous with the daily practice of law. Classes, especially first-year classes, can be too large, impeding meaningful access to and interaction with faculty. A common plaint amongst law students, in fact, is that professors are relatively remote. Notwithstanding the proliferation of clinical and externship programs, many continue to harbor concerns that law school education prepares students more to engage in the study of law than in the practice of law.

But whatever the deficiencies of legal education, its rigorous intellectualism and quest for justice through scholarship is extraordinary, inspiring ardent advocacy and a commitment to the service of others. Scott Turow commented:

> The law is a tough business, full of striving souls, and our hungers and ambitions will ever drive us. But law school remains the great common ground of the profession; before we begin a life of sparring with one another, this much is shared. What can and should be commonly instilled is a sense of mutual enterprise, a vision of the worthy, if complicated, ambitions of the profession, and the freedom to take pride in this difficult and venerable calling.[1]

Lawyers have nobly dedicated themselves to furthering the interests of others within a respected framework of justice, continuously refined through a laudable quest to promote fairness.

---

1. Scott Turow, *One L: The Turbulent True Story of a First Year at Harvard Law School*, 287 (Warner Books 1997 ed.).

Legal education can be improved, of course. As a professor, you can work to facilitate better communication with students; incorporate varied pedagogical techniques; utilize available digital, aural, and visual media as appropriate to stimulate interest; endeavor to administer fair evaluative exercises; and assess students' performance fairly, impartially, and consistently. Seven principles have been articulated for good practice in legal education: the encouragement of contact between students and faculty, the promotion of cooperation amongst pupils, the fostering of active learning, offers of prompt feedback, efficient time-management skills, communication of high expectations, and respect for diverse talent and disparate ways of learning.[2] Your zest for the task of teaching, your substantive expertise, and your commitment to your work will increase students' access to effective and meaningful instruction. You can provoke critical thinking, intellectualism, and creative reflection through deliberation, diligent preparation, experimentation in pedagogical methodology, and continuous reflection about the utility of your methods and their efficacy. And by staying true to your individual style, rejecting the methods discussed in this *Handbook* that seem incongruous with the approaches you find most comfortable or are ill-suited to your subject matter and your class.

Graduation from law school is both prelude and culmination. As an avatar of inspiration, you prepare your students to engage in rigorous intellectualism and creative thinking to serve the ends of justice. "Liberty finds no refuge in a jurisprudence of doubt."[3] While one U.S. Supreme Court justice derisively characterized the comment in the context in which it was proclaimed as a "sententious response,"[4] the formidable but laudable task that lies before you and your students is to apply reasoned principle to promote just and lawful results. Charged with the audacious task of cultivating conviction, the educator must help his students integrate principles and a sound moral structure with complex facts to create an intricate filigree of scholarly conclusions. You have unique opportunities to glimpse moments of clarity and comprehension, complicit with your students in efforts to defeat ignorance and dedicated to achieving resolution from discord.

Even with variations in intellect, commitment, and innate affinity for the logic of the course's subject matter, your students inevitably will leave the se-

---

2. *Seven Principles for Good Practice in Legal Education,* Institute for Law School Teaching, *at* <http://law.gonzaga.edu/ilst/7psintro.htm>.

3. *Planned Parenthood of Southeastern Pa. v. Casey,* 505 U.S. 833, 844 (1992) (discussing abortion rights).

4. *Lawrence v. Texas,* No. 02–102, 2003 U.S. LEXIS 5013 at *49 (U.S. June 26, 2003) (Scalia, J., dissenting).

mester better informed than when they arrived. Learning is an incremental process, rewarding you with ample opportunities to witness enlightenment and the sharing of ideas in a continual quest for wisdom and knowledge.

In service of scholarship, the law professor is uniquely positioned to consider and to induce consideration by others of a just and moral legal system. The teacher embarks on and perseveres in this enterprise in collaboration with colleagues and with students, forming extraordinary bonds through shared reflection, diligent commitment, and intellectual debate. Teaching facilitates experience of the power of learning, both in one's students and in oneself. The professor enables fissions of clarity, transforms ignorance to knowledge, shapes amorphous and intuitive reaction into rational analysis, and channels indignation at injustice to reasoned principle.

You are, paradoxically, at once astonishingly and deservedly credited as a catalyst for transmuting confusion to comprehension.

Through teaching, you reach out to another just as your professors reached out to you. You can inspire, educate, and help others become custodians, if not champions, of justice. And maybe, just maybe, you'll even inspire one of your students to teach someday; to reach out to another as you reached out to him.

Selected Resources: General

Legal Research Resources:

American Law Sources On-Line
web-site: <www.lawsource.com/also>

Cornell Legal Information Institute
web-site: <http://www.law.cornell.edu/blocks/collect.htm>

Global Legal Information Network
web-site: <http://www.loc.gov/law/glin/>

HierosGamos
web-site: <http://www.hg.org/>

Jurist Legal Intelligence, Legal Research
web-site: <http://jurist.law.pitt.edu/legalresearch.htm>
web-site: <http://jurist.law.pitt.edu/subj_gd.htm>
web-site: <http://jurist.law.pitt.edu/ref_desk.htm>

Law and Politics Internet Guide
web-site: <http://www.lpig.org>

Law.com
web-site: <www.law.com>

The Law Engine
web-site: <www.TheLawEngine.com>

LawGuru.com Multi Resource
web-site: <lawguru.com/>

LexisNexis, Reference Literature
web-site: <http://www.lexisnexis.com/lawschool/reference/>

LexisOne
web-site: <www.lexisone.com>

Library of Congress, Law Library
James Madison Building
101 Independence Avenue, SE
Washington, DC 20540
web-site: <http://www.loc.gov/law/public/law-about.html>

LLRX.com
web-site: <www.llrx.com>

University Law Review Project
web-site: <www.lawreview.org>

Web Accessibility Initiative
web-site: <http://www.w3.org/WAI/>

Webgator
web-site: <http://www.webgator.org>

Historical Documents:

Avalon Project, Yale Law School
web-site: <www.yale.edu/lawweb/avalon/avalon.htm>

A Century of Lawmaking for a New Nation: United States Congressional Documents and Debates, 1774-1873
web-site: <http://lcweb2.loc.gov/ammem/amlaw/lawhome.html>

Famous Cases
web-site: <www.courttv.com/trial/famous>

Federal Rulemaking
web-site: <www.uscourts.gov/rules/>

History of the Federal Judiciary
web-site: <http://airfjc.gov/history/index_bdy.html>

National Conference of Commissioners on Uniform State Laws
web-site: <www.law.upenn.edu/bll/ulc/ulc_frame.htm>

Project Diana, An Online Human Rights Archive
Yale Law School
The Lillian Goldman Law Library
127 Wall Street
New Haven, CT 06520
web-site: <http://www.yale.edu/lawweb/avalon/diana/index.html>

General Reference for Background and Factual Information:

Acronym Finder
web-site: <www.acronymfinder.com>

Robert J. Ambrogi, *The Essential Guide to the Best (and Worst) Legal Sites on the Web* (ALM Publishing New York 2001)

American Bar Association Law-on-the-Internet Booklist
web-site: <http://www.abanet.org/lpm/magazine/booklist.html>

American FactFinder
web-site: <http://factfinder.census.gov> (includes public records)

Bartleby.com
web-site: <www.bartleby.com> (includes reference, fiction, and non-fiction materials)

Joshua D. Blackman, *The Internet Fact Finder for Lawyers: How to Find Anything on the Net* (American Bar Association 1998)

CIA World Factbook
web-site: <www.odci.gov/cia/publications/factbook>

Freedom of Information Center
web-site: <http://www.misouri.edu/~foiwww/>

Law in Pop Culture
web-site: <http://tarlton.law.utexas.edu/lpop/lpop.htm>

Meta-Index for United States Legal Research
web-site: <http://gsulaw.gsu.edu/metaindex>

Research-It!
web-site: <www.iTools.com/>

The Smoking Gun
web-site: <www.thesmokinggun.com>

Television News Archive
web-site: <http://tvnews.vanderbilt.edu>

United States Census Bureau's State and Metropolitan Area Data Book
web-site: <www.census.gov/statab/www/smadb.html>

The Virtual Chase
web-site: <www.virtualchase.com>

Vital Records Information
web-site: <www.vitalrec.com>

Writers Free Reference
web-site: <www.writers-free-reference.com>

Checklist of Administrative Tasks

prior to the beginning of the semester:

- ☐ prepare course description
  - ☐ title of the course
  - ☐ professor's name
  - ☐ brief description of the course's subject matter
  - ☐ number of available credits
  - ☐ course requirements
  - ☐ prerequisites, if any
  - ☐ enrollment limitations, if any
- ☐ submit biographical sketch
  - ☐ educational background
  - ☐ professional experience
  - ☐ publications and works in progress
- ☐ complete course schedule request form
- ☐ select or develop text/materials
  - ☐ place order for text with school bookstore
- ☐ prepare syllabus
  - ☐ first class reading assignments
  - ☐ syllabus
    - ☐ title of the course
    - ☐ professor's name
    - ☐ text and/or other materials assigned
    - ☐ reading assignments for each class session
    - ☐ classroom location
    - ☐ day(s) and time the class is scheduled to meet

- ☐ optional:
    - ☐ contact information for the professor (telephone number, facsimile number, e-mail address, office address)
    - ☐ office hours
    - ☐ course requirements
    - ☐ recommended readings
    - ☐ the academic calendar
- ☐ establish course requirements
- ☐ collaborative teaching or guest lectures
    - ☐ obtain biographical sketch for introduction of guest lecturer
    - ☐ coordinate reading assignments and placement of the lecture in the syllabus
    - ☐ confirm professor's participation in the class session
    - ☐ inquire about and arrange any special computer or other equipment

during the semester:

during the first class:

- ☐ advise students of course requirements and components of course grade
- ☐ distribute syllabus to class
- ☐ confirm accuracy of class roster
- ☐ arrange seating chart, if desired

throughout the semester:

- ☐ monitor accessibility of links to assigned material and confirm that material has not been de-posted
- ☐ integrate multi-media to be used
    - ☐ confirm budget allotments
    - ☐ confirm equipment operability
- ☐ integrate and contextualize any guest lectures in the course

preparation for the final examination:

- ☐ furnish a copy of your final exam, if any, to the registrar
- ☐ coordinate with the registrar to obtain completed exams and papers that are not to be handed in to you directly

during the final class:

- ☐ review standards and instructions for final exam
- ☐ integrate course themes

at the conclusion of the semester:

- ☐ evaluate students' performance
- ☐ submit students' grades
- ☐ meet with students
    - ☐ who have substantive queries
    - ☐ who have questions about the grades they received

Acknowledgements

I very much appreciate the dedication of my students at the Fordham University School of Law, from whom I always learn a great deal. Dean William M. Treanor, former Dean John D. Feerick, Kenneth Pokrowski, and Susan Santangelo of Fordham Law School have graciously made me feel a part of the faculty. I very much enjoyed working on the Fordham Law School Handbook for Adjunct Faculty with Associate Dean for Academic Affairs Matthew Diller and Director of Adjuncts Daniel J. Capra. I was fortunate to have co-taught with David A. Schulz and Nicholas J. Jollymore, both of whom are knowledgeable, dedicated, and inspiring professors. I learned a great deal about teaching from Martha Chapman, in whose custody I remain a student of ballet and who helps "keep me on my toes" in a context other than legal developments.

I was very fortunate to have had the opportunity to work again with Carolina Academic Press and to have been so enthusiastically supported by Keith Sipe, Linda Lacy, Bob Conrow, Tim Colton, and Reuben Ayres. Joel Kurtzberg of Cahill Gordon & Reindel LLP and a former teacher graciously reviewed the book and gave me enormously helpful editorial insights. Shira Perlmutter lent her considerable expertise in Intellectual Property Law to review excerpts. AnnMarie DiNenno, a student at the Touro Law Center, cheerfully and enthusiastically provided valuable cite-checking assistance.

Most of all, I am, as ever, grateful for the love and support of my families, most especially my husband, David Stagliano, and our children, Mark and Emily.

About the Author

Madeleine Schachter is Deputy General Counsel at Time Warner Book Group, where she specializes in Media Law. She is an Adjunct Professor at the Fordham University School of Law, where she has taught a dozen courses on Law of Internet Speech, Informational and Decisional Privacy in the Internet Era, and Mass Media Law.

She is the author of the books entitled *Law of Internet Speech* (2d ed. 2002, Supplement 2003), and *Informational and Decisional Privacy* (2003), and she assisted Fordham Law School with the preparation of its Handbook for Adjunct Faculty.

Ms. Schachter chaired the New York State Bar Association Special Committee on Cyberspace Law and the Committee on Media Law and co-chaired the American Corporate Counsel Association (New York) Electronic Media and Intellectual Property Committee. She is a member of the Association of the Bar of the City of New York's Pro Bono and Legal Services Committee as well as the Project on the Homeless. She serves on the Dean's Strategic Council of the New York University School of Law.

Ms. Schachter received her JD degree from the New York University School of Law, where she was a Root-Tilden Scholar. She is a *Phi Beta Kappa*, *Summa Cum Laude* graduate of the University of Pennsylvania, where she designed a major program in Medical Ethics and also majored in Political Science.

She is a tutorial student in classical ballet under the direction of Martha Chapman, who has performed with the Anglo American Company.

INDEX